New Revised Edition

# ENCYCLOPEDIA
## of
# HOME DESIGNS

## 450 House Plans

Design T52615 (See Page 265.)

# Contents

Published by Home Planners, Inc., 23761 Research Drive, Farmington Hills, Michigan 48024. All designs and illustrative material Copyright © MCMLXXXIV by Home Planners, Inc. All rights reserved. Reproduction in any manner or form not permitted. Printed in the United States of America. International Standard Book Number (ISBN): 0-918894-38-7.

# Index to Designs

# How To Read Floor Plans and Blueprints

Selecting the most suitable house plan for your family is a matter of matching your needs, tastes, and life-style against the many designs we offer. When you study the floor plans in this issue, and the blueprints that you may subsequently order, remember that they are simply a two-dimensional representation of what will eventually be a three-dimensional reality.

Floor plans are easy to read. Rooms are clearly labeled, with dimensions given in feet and inches. Most symbols are logical and self-explanatory: The location of bathroom fixtures, planters, fireplaces, tile floors, cabinets and counters, sinks, appliances, closets, sloped or beamed ceilings will be obvious.

A blueprint, although much more detailed, is also easy to read; all it demands is concentration. The blueprints that we offer come in many large sheets, each one of which contains a different kind of information. One sheet contains foundation and excavation drawings, another has a precise plot plan. An elevations sheet deals with the exterior walls of the house; section drawings show precise dimensions, fittings, doors, windows, and roof structures. Our detailed floor plans give the construction information needed by your contractor. And each set of blueprints contains a lengthy materials list with size and quantities of all necessary components. Using this list, a contractor and suppliers can make a start at calculating costs for you.

When you first study a floor plan or blueprint, imagine that you are walking through the house. By mentally visualizing each room in three dimensions, you can transform the technical data and symbols into something more real.

Start at the front door. It's preferable to have a foyer or entrance hall in which to receive guests. A closet here is desirable; a powder room is a plus.

Look for good traffic circulation as you study the floor plan. You should not have to pass all the way through one main room to reach another. From the entrance area you should have direct access to the three principal areas of a house—the living, work, and sleeping zones. For example, a foyer might provide separate entrances to the living room, kitchen, patio, and a hallway or staircase leading to the bedrooms.

Study the layout of each zone. Most people expect the living room to be protected from cross traffic. The kitchen, on the other hand, should connect with the dining room—and perhaps also the utility room, basement, garage, patio or deck, or a secondary entrance. A homemaker whose workday centers in the kitchen may have special requirements: a window that faces the backyard; a clear view of the family room where children play; a garage or driveway entrance that allows for a short trip with groceries; laundry facilities close at hand. Check for efficient placement of kitchen cabinets, counters, and appliances. Is there enough room in the kitchen for additional appliances, for eating in? Is there a dining nook?

Perhaps this part of the house contains a family room or a den/bedroom/office. It's advantageous to have a bathroom or powder room in this section.

As you study the plan, you may encounter a staircase, indicated by a group of parallel lines, the number of lines equaling the number of steps. Arrows labeled "up" mean that the staircase leads to a higher level, and those pointing down mean it leads to a lower one. Staircases in a split-level will have both up and down arrows on one staircase because two levels are depicted in one drawing and an extra level in another.

Notice the location of the stairways. Is too much floor space lost to them? Will you find yourself making too many trips?

Study the sleeping quarters. Are the bedrooms situated as you like? You may want the master bedroom near the kids, or you may want it as far away as possible. Is there at least one closet per person in each bedroom or a double one for a couple? Bathrooms should be convenient to each bedroom—if not adjoining, then with hallway access and on the same floor.

Once you are familiar with the relative positions of the rooms, look for such structural details as:

• Sufficient uninterrupted wall space for furniture arrangement.

• Adequate room dimensions.

• Potential heating or cooling problems—i.e., a room over a garage or next to the laundry.

• Window and door placement for good ventilation and natural light.

• Location of doorways—avoid having a basement staircase or a bathroom in view of the dining room.

• Adequate auxiliary space—closets, storage, bathrooms, countertops.

• Separation of activity areas. (Will noise from the recreation room disturb sleeping children or a parent at work?)

As you complete your mental walk through the house, bear in mind your family's long-range needs. A good house plan will allow for some adjustments now and additions in the future.

Each member of your family may find the listing of his, or her, favorite features a most helpful exercise. Why not try it?

# How To Choose a Contractor

A contractor is part craftsman, part businessman, and part magician. As the person who will transform your dreams and drawings into a finished house, he will be responsible for the final cost of the structure, for the quality of the workmanship, and for the solving of all problems that occur quite naturally in the course of construction. Choose him as carefully as you would a business partner, because for the next several months that will be his role in your life.

As soon as you have a building site and house plans, start looking for a contractor, even if you do not plan to break ground for several months. Finding one suitable to build your house can take time, and once you have found him, you will have to be worked into his schedule. Those who are good are in demand and, where the season is short, they are often scheduling work up to a year in advance.

There are two types of residential contractors: the construction company and the carpenter-builder, often called a general contractor. Each of these has its advantages and disadvantages.

The carpenter-builder works directly on the job as the field foreman. Because his background is that of a craftsman, his workmanship is probably good—but his paperwork may be slow or sloppy. His overhead—which you pay for—is less than that of a large construction company. However, if the job drags on for any reason, his interest may flag because your project is overlapping his next job and eroding his profits.

Construction companies handle several projects concurrently. They have an office staff to keep the paperwork moving and an army of subcontractors they know they can count on. Though you can be confident that they will meet deadlines, they may sacrifice workmanship in order to do so. Because they emphasize efficiency, they are less personal to work with than a general contractor. Many will not work with an individual unless he is represented by an architect. The company and the architect speak the same language; it requires far more time to deal directly with a homeowner.

To find a reliable contractor, start by asking friends who have built homes for recommendations. Check with local lumber yards and building supply outlets for names of possible candidates.

Once you have several names in hand, ask the Chamber of Commerce, Better Business Bureau, or local department of consumer affairs for any information they might have on each of them. Keep in mind that these watchdog organizations can give only the number of complaints filed; they cannot tell you what percent of those claims were valid. Remember, too, that a large-volume operation is logically going to have more complaints against it than will an independent contractor.

Set up an interview with each of the potential candidates. Find out what his specialty is—custom houses, development houses, remodeling, or office buildings. Ask each to take you into—not just to the site of—houses he has built. Ask to see projects that are complete as well as work in progress, emphasizing that you are interested in projects comparable to yours. A $300,000 dentist's office will give you little insight into a contractor's craftsmanship.

Ask each contractor for bank references from both his commercial bank and any other lender he has worked with. If he is in good financial standing, he should have no qualms about giving you this information. Also ask if he offers a warranty on his work. Most will give you a one-year warranty on the structure; some offer as much as a ten-year warranty.

Ask for references, even though no contractor will give you the name of a dissatisfied customer. While previous clients may be pleased with a contractor's work overall, they may, for example, have had to wait three months after they moved in before they had any closet doors. Ask about his follow-through. Did he clean up the building site, or did the owner have to dispose of the refuse? Ask about his business organization. Did the paperwork go smoothly, or was there a delay in hooking up the sewer because he forgot to apply for a permit?

Talk to each of the candidates about fees. Most work on a "cost plus" basis; that is, the basic cost of the project—materials, subcontractors' services, wages of those working directly on the project, but not office help—plus his fee. Some have a fixed fee; others work on a percentage of the basic cost. A fixed fee is usually better for you if you can get one. If a contractor works on a percentage, ask for a cost breakdown of his best estimate and keep very careful track as the work progresses. A crafty contractor can always use a cost overrun to his advantage when working on a percentage.

Do not be overly suspicious of a contractor who won't work on a fixed fee. One who is very good and in great demand may not be willing to do so. He may also refuse to submit a competitive bid.

If the top two or three candidates are willing to submit competitive bids, give each a copy of the plans and your specifications for materials. If they are not each working from the same guidelines, the competitive bids will be of little value. Give each the same deadline for turning in a bid; two or three weeks is a reasonable period of time. If you are willing to go with the lowest bid, make an appointment with all of them and open the envelopes in front of them.

If one bid is remarkably low, the contractor may have made an honest error in his estimate. Do not try to hold him to it if he wants to withdraw his bid. Forcing him to build at too low a price could be disastrous for both you and him.

Though the above method sounds very fair and orderly, it is not always the best approach, especially if you are inexperienced. You may want to review the bids with your architect, if you have one, or with your lender to discuss which to accept. They may not recommend the lowest. A low bid does not necessarily mean that you will get quality with economy.

If the bids are relatively close, the most important consideration may not be money at all. How easily you can talk with a contractor and whether or not he inspires confidence are very important considerations. Any sign of a personality conflict between you and a contractor should be weighed when making a decision.

Once you have financing, you can sign a contract with the builder. Most have their own contract forms, but it is advisable to have a lawyer draw one up or, at the very least, review the standard contract. This usually costs a small flat fee.

A good contract should include the following:

• Plans and sketches of the work to be done, subject to your approval.

• A list of materials, including quantity, brand names, style or serial numbers. (Do not permit any "or equal" clause that will allow the contractor to make substitutions.)

• The terms—who (you or the lender) pays whom and when.

• A production schedule.

• The contractor's certification of insurance for workmen's compensation, damage, and liability.

• A rider stating that all changes, whether or not they increase the cost, must be submitted and approved in writing.

Of course, this list represents the least a contract should include. Once you have signed it, your plans are on the way to becoming a home.

A frequently asked question is: "Should I become my own general contractor?" Unless you have knowledge of construction, material purchasing, and experience supervising subcontractors, we do not recommend this route.

# How To Shop For Mortgage Money

Most people who are in the market for a new home spend months searching for the right house plan and building site. Ironically, these same people often invest very little time shopping for the money to finance their new home, though the majority will have to live with the terms of their mortgage for as long as they live in the home.

The fact is that not all lending institutions are alike, nor are the loans that they offer.

- Lending practices vary from one city and state to another. If you are a first-time builder or are new to an area, it is wise to hire a real estate (not divorce or general practice) attorney to help you unravel the maze of your specific area's laws, ordinances and customs.
- Before talking with a lender, write down all of your questions. Take notes during the conversation so that you can make accurate comparisons.
- Do not be intimidated by financial officers. Do not hesitate to reveal what other institutions are offering; they may be challenged to meet or better the terms.

## A GUIDE TO LENDERS

Where can you turn for home financing? Here is a list of sources for you to contact:

Savings and Loan Associations
Savings Banks/Mutual Savings Banks
Commercial Banks
Mortgage Banking Companies
Some Credit Unions

Each of the above institutions generally offers a variety of loan types, interest rates and fees. It is recommended that you survey each type of institution in your area to determine exactly what type of financing is available so that you make an informed decision.

## A GUIDE TO LOAN TYPES

The types of loans available are far more various than most potential home buyers realize. They fall into two categories – Conventional Loans and Government Loans.

**Conventional Loans**

These types of loans usually require a minimum down payment of 5% of the lower of the purchase price or appraised value of the property. However, in many cases, this down payment requirement has been increased to 10% depending on the type of loan and the requirements of the lending institution. Often, the minimum down payment requirement is applied to owner-occupied residences and is usually increased if the property is purchased as a vacation home or as an investment.

The most common type of conventional loan is the **fixed-rate loan** which has a fixed interest rate and fixed monthly payments. The term of the loan may vary, but such loans generally are available in fifteen- and thirty-year terms. The obvious advantage of a fifteen-year term is an earlier loan payoff as well as reduced interest charges.

Let's assume that you apply for a $70,000 loan at an 11% interest rate. Your monthly principal and interest payment on a thirty-year term would be $666.63 versus $795.62 on a fifteen-year term. The amount of interest that you would pay over the life of the loan on the thirty-year term would be $169,985.50 and $73,211.21 on a fifteen-year term.

Other types of conventional loans are called **Adjustable Rate Mortgages (ARM's).** This type of loan usually has a lower initial interest rate than the fixed-rate loan, but the interest rate of payment may change depending on the loan terms and economic conditions. The frequency of these interest/payment adjustments depends on the individual loan, but usually occurs every twelve months.

Some key terms to understanding ARM loans are listed below:

**Adjustment Period** – The period between one rate change and the next. Therefore, a loan with an adjustment period of one year is known as a One Year ARM.

**Index** – The interest rate change is tied to an index rate. These indexes usually go up and down with the general movement of interest rates. If the index rate moves up, so does your monthly payment. If the index rate goes down, your monthly payment may also go down. There are a variety of indexes. Among the most common is the weekly average yield on United States Treasury securities adjusted to a constant maturity of one, three or five years.

**Margin** – To determine the interest rate on an ARM, lenders add a few percentage points to the index rate. These percentage points are called the margin. The amount of the margin can differ from one lender to the next, but is usually constant through the life of the loan.

**Caps** – Most ARM loans limit the amount that the interest rate can increase. There are periodic caps which limit the increase from one adjustment period to the next and overall caps which limit the interest rate increase over the life of the loan.

**Negative Amortization** – Several ARM loans contain negative amortization which means that your mortgage balance can increase even though you are making regular monthly payments. This happens when the interest rate of the loan increases while your monthly payment remains the same.

**Convertibility or Conversion Option** – This is a clause in your agreement that allows you to convert the ARM to a fixed-rate mortgage at designated times. Not all ARM loans contain this option.

All of the above terms should be analyzed and compared when "shopping" for an ARM loan.

There are other types of less-common conventional loans which are offered by many institutions: Graduated Payment Mortgages, Reverse Annuity Mortgages and Bi-Weekly Mortgages. Consult with a financial officer of a lending institution for details on these other loan types.

**Government Loans**

Many people think that the government actually grants a loan to the borrower. This is not true. The Federal Housing Administration (FHA) actually insures these loans against default in order to encourage lenders to write loans for first-time buyers and people with limited incomes.

FHA loans have substantially lower down payments than conventional loans; however, there are maximum allowable loan amounts for these loans depending on the location of the property.

Another type of government loan is through the Veteran's Administration (VA). Like the FHA, the VA guarantees loans for eligible veterans and the spouses of those veterans who died while in the service. Down payment requirements are also extremely low on these types of loans.

There are a variety of loan types available under these government programs including fixed rate, ARM's and graduated payment mortgages. The financial officer of the lending institution will be able to explain these various loan types and the qualification standards.

## GUIDE TO COSTS

There are many costs associated with obtaining a mortgage. Some are standard to the lending industry and others are established by the individual institutions. Below is a list of several fees that tend to differ depending on the lending institution. It is recommended that you become familiar with these costs and fees in order to make an intelligent comparison of lending institutions.

| | |
|---|---|
| Origination Fee | Discount Points |
| Commitment Fee | Application Fee |
| Underwriting Fee | Closing Fee |
| Document Preparation Fee | Tax Service Fee |

## GUIDE TO QUALIFICATION

You should be aware that each lender has certain qualifying guidelines that relate to your employment, assets and credit and to the property you plan to purchase. These are established in order to be certain that you can afford the loan and that it is a good risk to the lending institution.

These qualifying guidelines differ somewhat from one institution to the next and each potential lender should be consulted for individual requirements or variances.

# TREND HOUSES . . . . .

*Increasing land and construction costs, growing awareness of solar orientation and improved housing technology are among factors leading to changing patterns of living. The result is an almost endless variety of new housing configurations. Here is a collection of designs whose floor plans offer a break from past conventions. Their facades may be contemporary or traditional. Inside, an abundance of "extras" are featured - high ceilings, glass expanses, great rooms, etc. The manner in which these trend houses deal with, and satisfy, differing living patterns and requirements is, indeed, innovative.*

## Design T12827 1,618 Sq. Ft. - Upper Level
1,458 Sq. Ft. - Lower Level; 41,370 Cu. Ft.

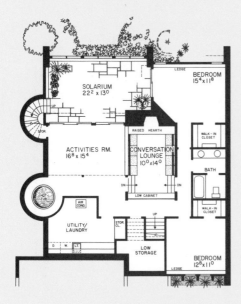

● The two-story solarium with skylights above is the key to energy savings in this bi-level design. Study the efficiency of this floor plan. The conversation lounge on the lower level is a unique focal point.

**Design T12821**
1,363 Sq. Ft. - First Floor
357 Sq. Ft. - Second Floor
37,145 Cu. Ft.

**Mansard Roof
Adaptation**

# A Trend House . . .

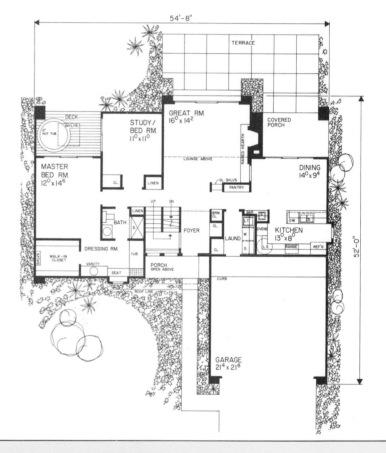

● Here is a truly unique house whose interior was designed with the current decade's economies, lifestyles and demographics in mind. While functioning as a one-story home, the second floor provides an extra measure of livability when required. In addition, this two-story section adds to the dramatic appeal of both the exterior and the interior. Within only 1,363 square feet, this contemporary delivers refreshing and outstanding living patterns for those who are buying their first home, those who have raised their family and are looking for a smaller home and those in search of a retirement home. The center entrance routes traffic effectively to each area. The great room with its raised hearth fireplace, two-story arching and delightful glass areas is most distinctive. The kitchen is efficient and but a step from the dining room. The covered porch will provide an ideal spot for warm-weather, outdoor dining. The separate laundry room is strategically located. The sleeping area may consist of one bedroom and a study, or two bedrooms. Each room functions with the sheltered wood deck - a perfect location for a hot tub.

**Design T12822**
1,363 Sq. Ft. - First Floor
351 Sq. Ft. - Second Floor
36,704 Cu. Ft.

**Gable Roof
Version**

UPPER GREAT RM.

RAILING

CL.

LOUNGE / HOBBIES
16⁰x9²

SKYLITE

CL.

CL.

DN

RAILING

UPPER FOYER

STOR./ BATH

RAILING

BALCONY

LOUNGE / GUEST RM. / GRANDCHILDREN'S RM.
16⁰ x 19²

CL.

CL.

DN

RAILING

UPPER FOYER

BATH

RAILING

ALTERNATE SECOND FLOOR

## ... For the 80's and Decades to Come

● The full bath is planned to have easy access to the master bedroom and living areas. Note the stall shower, tub, seat and vanity. The second floor offers two optional layouts. It may serve as a lounge, studio or hobby area overlooking the great room. Or, it may be built to function as a complete private guest room. It would be a great place for the visiting grandchildren. Don't miss the outdoor balcony. Additional livability and storage facilities may be developed in the basement. Then, of course, there are two exteriors to choose from. Design T12821, with its horizontal frame siding and deep, attractive cornice detail, is an eye-catcher. For those with a preference for a contemporary fashioned gable roof and vertical siding, there is Design T12822. With the living areas facing the south, these designs will enjoy benefits of passive solar exposure. The overhanging roofs will help provide relief from the high summer sun. This is surely a modest-sized floor plan which will deliver new dimensions in small-family livability.

# Design T12878
**1,521 Sq. Ft.; 34,760 Cu. Ft.**

● There is a great deal of livability in this one-story design. The efficient floor plan makes optimum use of limited floor space. Ideally located, the gathering room is warmed by a fireplace. Its sloped-ceiling gives it a spacious appeal. Adjacent is the dining room which opens up to the rear terrace via sliding glass doors for dining alfresco. Ready to serve the breakfast room and dining room, there is the interior kitchen. The laundry, basement stairs and garage door are nearby. Two with an optional third bedroom are tucked away from the more active areas of the house. The master bedroom has sliding glass doors to the terrace for outdoor enjoyment. Study this cozy, clapboard cottage and imagine it as your next home.

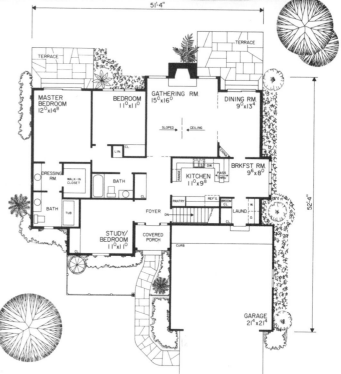

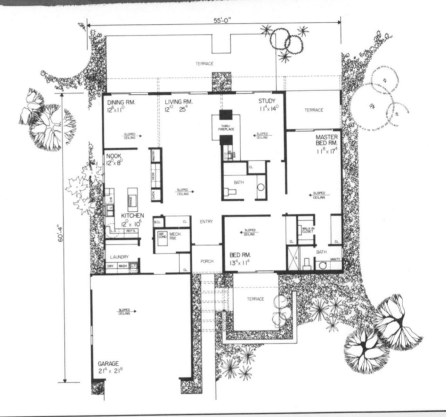

## Design T12754
**1,844 Sq. Ft.; 26,615 Cu. Ft.**

● This really is a most dramatic and refreshing contemporary home. The slope of its wide overhanging roofs is carried right indoors to provide an extra measure of spaciousness. The U-shaped privacy wall of the front entrance area provides an appealing outdoor living spot accessible from the front bedroom. The rectangular floor plan will be economical to build. Notice the efficient use of space and how it all makes its contribution to outstanding livability. The small family will find its living patterns delightful, indeed. Two bedrooms and two full baths comprise the sleeping zone. The open planning of the L-shaped living and dining rooms is most desirable. The thru-fireplace is just a great room divider. The kitchen and breakfast nook function together. Laundry and mechanical room are nearby.

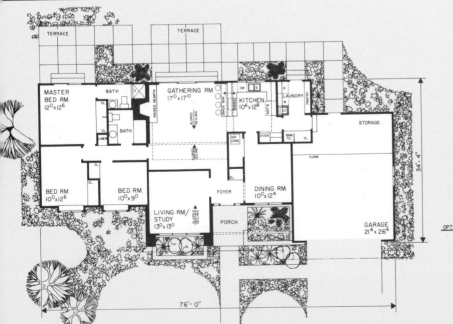

## Design T12818
**1,566 Sq. Ft.; 20,030 Cu. Ft.**

● This is most certainly an outstanding contemporary design. The vertical lines are carried from the siding to the paned windows to the garage door. The floor plan is just as outstanding. The rear gathering room has a sloped ceiling, raised hearth fireplace and a snack bar with pass-thru to the kitchen. In addition to the gathering room, there is the living room/study. Three bedrooms and two closely located baths are in the sleeping wing.

## Design T12823
**1,370 Sq. Ft. - First Floor**
**927 Sq. Ft. - Second Floor**
**34,860 Cu. Ft.**

● The street view of this contemporary design features a small courtyard entrance as well as a private terrace off the study. Inside the livability will be outstanding. This design features spacious first floor activity areas that flow smoothly into each other. In the gathering room a raised hearth fireplace creates a dramatic focal point. An adjacent covered terrace, featuring a skylight, is ideal for outdoor dining and could be screened in later for an additional room.

## Design T12826
### 1,112 Sq. Ft. - First Floor
### 881 Sq. Ft. - Second Floor; 32,770 Cu. Ft.

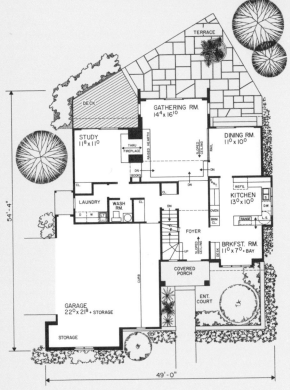

ALTERNATE KITCHEN / DINING RM./
BREAKFAST RM. FLOOR PLAN

● This is an outstanding example of the type of informal, traditional-style architecture that has captured the modern imagination. The interior plan houses all the features that people want most - a spacious gathering room, formal and informal dining areas, efficient, U-shaped kitchen, master bedroom, two children's bedrooms, second-floor lounge, entrance court and rear terrace and deck. Study all areas of this plan carefully.

13

## Design T12883 1,919 Sq. Ft. - First Floor
895 Sq. Ft. - Second Floor; 46,489 Cu. Ft.

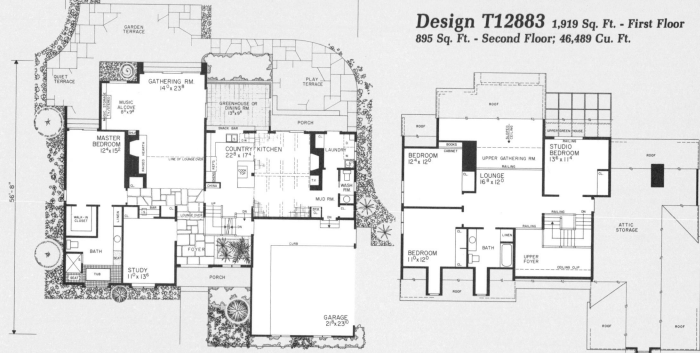

● A country-style home is part of America's fascination with the rural past. This home's emphasis of the traditional home is in its gambrel roof, dormers and fanlight windows. Having a traditional exterior from the street view, this home has window walls and a greenhouse, which opens the house to the outdoors in a thoroughly contemporary manner. The interior meets the requirements of today's active family. Like the country houses of the past, it has a gathering room for family get-togethers or entertaining. The adjacent two-story greenhouse doubles as the dining room. There is a pass-thru snack bar to the country kitchen here. This country kitchen just might be the heart of the house with its two areas - work zone and sitting room. There are four bedrooms on the two floors - the master bedroom suite on the first floor; three more on the second floor. A lounge, overlooking the gathering room and front foyer, is also on the second floor.

## Design T12824
**1,550 Sq. Ft.; 34,560 Cu. Ft.**

● Low-maintenance and economy in building are the outstanding exterior features of this sharp one-story design. It is sheathed in long-lasting cedar siding and trimmed with stone for an eye-appealing facade. Entrance to this home takes you through a charming garden courtyard then a covered walk to the front porch. The garage extending from the front of the house serves two purposes; to reduce lot size and to buffer the interior of the house from street noise. Sliding glass doors are featured in each of the main rooms for easy access to the outdoors. A sun porch is tucked between the study and gathering rooms. Optional non-basement details are included with the purchase of this design. For an equally appealing exterior, an English Tudor version of this design is available. Order blueprints for Design T12825.

OPTIONAL NON-BASEMENT

**TWO COUPLES/SINGLES RESIDENCE**

**CONVERTIBLE ONE-FAMILY RESIDENCE**

# Design T12828 First Floor: 817 Sq. Ft. - Living Area; 261 Sq. Ft. - Foyer & Laundr
**Second Floor: 852 Sq. Ft. - Living Area; 214 Sq. Ft. - Foyer & Storage; 34,690 Cu. Ft.**

● This contemporary home has been designed as a two-couples/singles residence. A home of this type could be bought jointly by two couples or one couple could buy the entire home and rent out one of the units. Complete livability is offered on each floor of this two-story. Each floor has a living room, dining room, interior kitchen, bedroom and bath. At a later date this home could be converted into a one-family residence. The second floor unit would now be a bedroom area.

# Shared Expense –
# Shared Livability

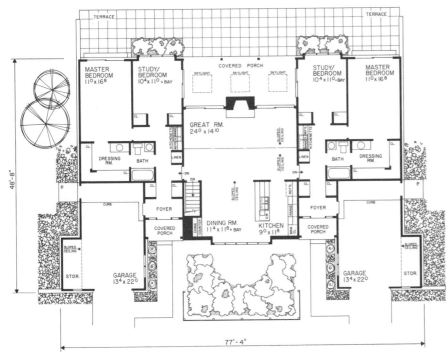

## Design T12869
*1,986 Sq. Ft.; 48,455 Cu. Ft.*

● Like the bi-level on the opposite page, this traditional one-story design offers the economical benefits of shared living space without sacrificing privacy. The common area of this design is centrally located between the two private, sleeping wings. The common area, 680 square feet, is made up of the great room, dining room and kitchen. Sloping the ceiling in this area creates an open feeling as will the sliding glass doors on each side of the fireplace. These doors lead to a large covered porch with skylights above. Separate outdoor entrances lead to each of the sleeping wings. Two bedrooms, dressing area, full bath and space for an optional kitchenette occupy 653 square feet in each wing. Additional space will be found in the basement which is the full size of the common area. Don't miss the covered porch and garage with additional storage space.

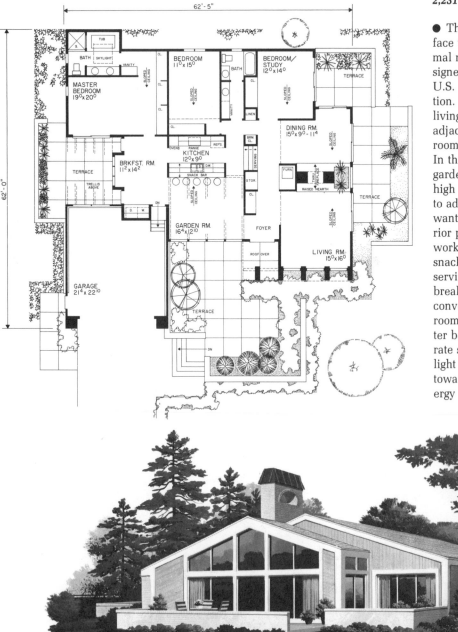

## Design T12858
### 2,231 Sq. Ft.; 28,150 Cu. Ft.

● This sun oriented design was created to face the south. By doing so, it has minimal northern exposure. It has been designed primarily for the more temperate U.S. latitudes using 2 x 6 wall construction. The morning sun will brighten the living and dining rooms along with the adjacent terrace. Sun enters the garden room by way of the glass roof and walls. In the winter, the solar heat gain from the garden room should provide relief from high energy bills. Solar shades allow you to adjust the amount of light that you want to enter in the warmer months. Interior planning deserves mention, too. The work center is efficient. The kitchen has a snack bar on the garden room side and a serving counter to the dining room. The breakfast room with laundry area is also convenient to the kitchen. Three bedrooms are on the northern wall. The master bedroom has a large tub and a separate shower with a four foot square skylight above. When this design is oriented toward the sun, it should prove to be energy efficient and a joy to live in.

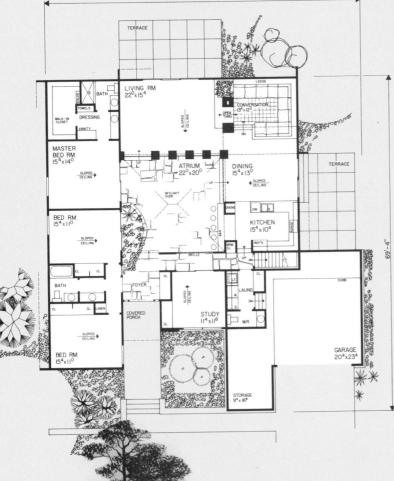

## Design T12832
### 2,805 Sq. Ft. - Excluding Atrium; 52,235 Cu. Ft.

● The advantage of passive solar heating is a significant highlight of this contemporary design. The huge skylight over the atrium provides shelter during inclement weather, while permitting the enjoyment of plenty of natural light to the atrium below and surrounding areas. Whether open to the sky, or sheltered by a glass or translucent covering, the atrium becomes a cheerful spot and provides an abundance of natural light to its adjacent rooms. The stone floor will absorb an abundance of heat from the sun during the day and permit circulation of warm air to other areas at night. During the summer, shades afford protection from the sun without sacrificing the abundance of natural light and the feeling of spaciousness. Sloping ceilings highlight each of the major rooms, three bedrooms, formal living and dining and study. The conversation area between the two formal areas will really be something to talk about. The broad expanses of roof can accommodate solar panels should an active system be desired to supplement the passive features of this design.

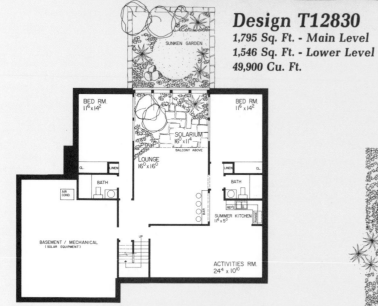

## Design T12830
**1,795 Sq. Ft. - Main Level**
**1,546 Sq. Ft. - Lower Level**
**49,900 Cu. Ft.**

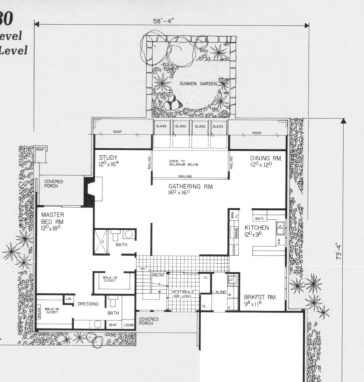

● Outstanding contemporary design! This home has been created with the advantages of passive solar heating in mind. For optimum energy savings, this delightful design combines passive solar devices, the solarium, with optional active collectors. Included with the purchase of this design are four plot plans to assure that the solar collectors will face the south. The garage in each plan acts as a buffer against cold northern winds. Along with being energy-efficient, this design has excellent living patterns.

## Design T12831
**1,758 Sq. Ft. - First Floor**
**1,247 Sq. Ft. - Second Floor**
**44,265 Cu. Ft.**

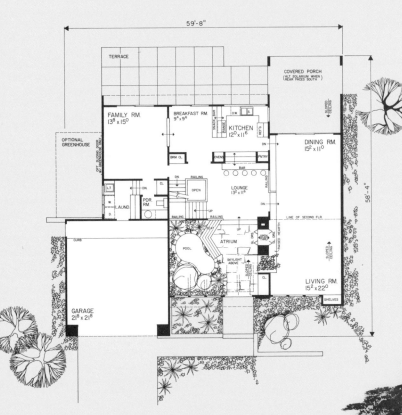

● You can incorporate energy-saving features into the elevation of this passive solar design to enable you to receive the most sunlight on your particular site. Multiple plot plans (included with the blueprints) illustrate which elevations should be solarized for different sites and which extra features can be incorporated. The features can include a greenhouse added to the family room, the back porch turned into a solarium or skylights installed over the entry.

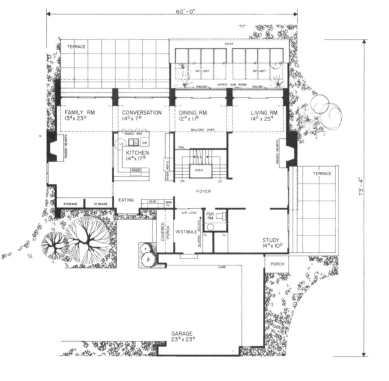

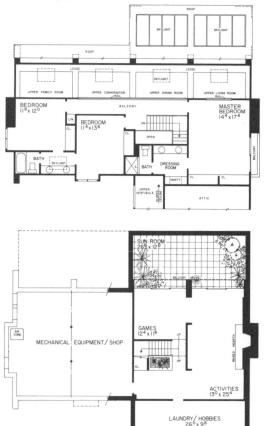

# Design T12834
**1,775 Sq. Ft. - Main Level; 1,041 Sq. Ft. - Upper Level**
**1,128 Sq. Ft. - Lower Level; 55,690 Cu. Ft.**

● This passive solar design offers 4,200 square feet of livability situated on three levels. The primary passive element will be the lower level sun room which admits sunlight for direct-gain heating. The solar warmth collected in the sun room will radiate into the rest of the house after it passes the sliding glass doors. During the warm summer months, shades are put over the skylight to protect it from direct sunlight. This design has the option of incorporating active solar heating panels to the roof. The collectors would be installed on the south-facing portion of the roof. They would absorb the sun's warmth for both domestic water and supplementary space heating. An attic fan exhausts any hot air out of the house in the summer and circulates air in the winter. With or without the active solar panels, this is a marvelous two-story contemporary.

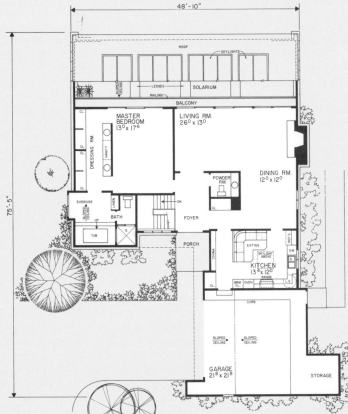

## Design T12835 1,626 Sq. Ft. - Main Level
### 2,038 Sq. Ft. - Lower Level; 50,926 Cu. Ft.

● Passive solar techniques with the help of an active solar component - they can work together or the active solar component can act as a back-up system - heat and cool this striking contemporary design. The lower level solarium is the primary passive element. It admits sunlight during the day for direct-gain heating. The warmth, which was absorbed into the thermal floor, is then radiated into the structure at night. The earth berms on the three sides of the lower level help keep out the winter cold and summer heat. The active system uses collector panels to gather the sun's heat. The heat is transferred via a water pipe system to the lower level storage tank where it is circulated throughout the house by a heat exchanger. Note that were active solar collectors are a design OPTION, which they are in all of our active/passive designs, they must be contracted locally. The collector area must be tailored to the climate and sun angles that characterize your building location.

## Design T12884 1,814 Sq. Ft. - First Floor
### 837 Sq. Ft. - Second Floor; 51,305 Cu. Ft.

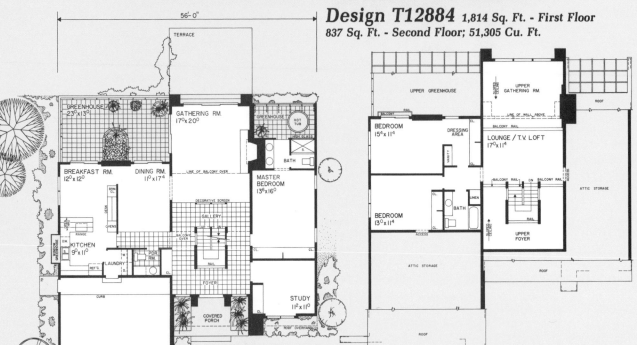

● The greenhouse in this design enhances its energy-efficiency and allows for spacious and interesting living patterns. Being a one-and-a-half story design, the second floor could be developed at a later date when the space is needed. The greenhouses add an additional 418 sq. ft. and 8,793 cu. ft. to the above quoted figures.

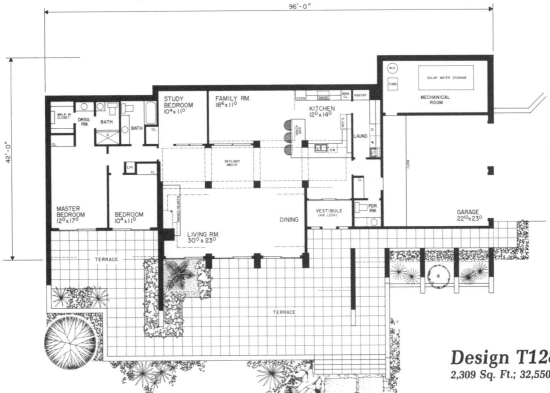

96'-0"

42'-0"

WALK-IN CLOSET · DRSG. RM. · BATH · BATH · CL

STUDY BEDROOM 10⁴ x 11⁰

FAMILY RM. 18⁶ x 11⁰

OVEN · RANGE · BRM. CL · PANTRY

KITCHEN 12⁰ x 14⁰

SOLAR WATER STORAGE

W.H. · FURN

MECHANICAL ROOM

LIN · CL

SKYLIGHT ABOVE

SNACK BAR · REF'G · DW

LAUND. · D.W.

MASTER BEDROOM 12⁰ x 17⁰

BEDROOM 10⁴ x 11⁰

LIVING RM. 30⁰ x 23⁰

DINING

VESTIBULE (AIR LOCK)

PDR. RM. · CL

GARAGE 22¹⁰ x 23⁰

TERRACE

TERRACE

## Design T12838
2,309 Sq. Ft.; 32,550 Cu. Ft.

● Here is another dramatic earth sheltered home which will function with the sun like Design T12860. The spaciousness of the living area in this design is enhanced by the central location of the dramatic skylight. In addition to the passive solar heating gain for the living and bedroom areas, the impressively designed "mansard" roof effect lends itself to the installation of active solar heating panels. The illustration above shows panels only on the garage wing. Consultation with local solar heating experts will determine the effectiveness in your area of additional panels. A special room adjacent to the garage will accommodate mechanical equipment.

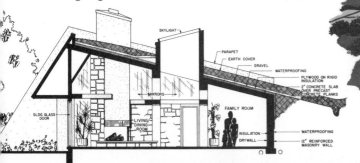

SKYLIGHT · PARAPET · EARTH COVER · GRAVEL · WATERPROOFING · PLYWOOD ON RIGID INSULATION · 2" CONCRETE SLAB OVER PRECAST CONCRETE PLANKS

MIRRORS

SLDG. GLASS DOOR · LIVING DINING ROOM · FAMILY ROOM · INSULATION · WATERPROOFING · DRYWALL · 12" REINFORCED MASONRY WALL

## Design T12861
### 2,499 Sq. Ft.; 29,100 Cu. Ft.

● Berming the earth against the walls of a structure prove to be very energy efficient. The earth protects the interior from the cold of the winter and the heat of the summer. Interior lighting will come from the large skylight over the garden room. Every room will benefit from this exposed area. The garden room will function as a multi-purpose area for the entire family. The living/dining room will receive light from two areas, the garden room and the wall of sliding glass doors to the outside. Family living will be served by the efficient floor plan. Three bedrooms and two full baths are clustered together. The kitchen is adjacent to the airlocked vestibule where the laundry and utility rooms are housed. The section is cut through the dining, garden and master bedroom facing the kitchen.

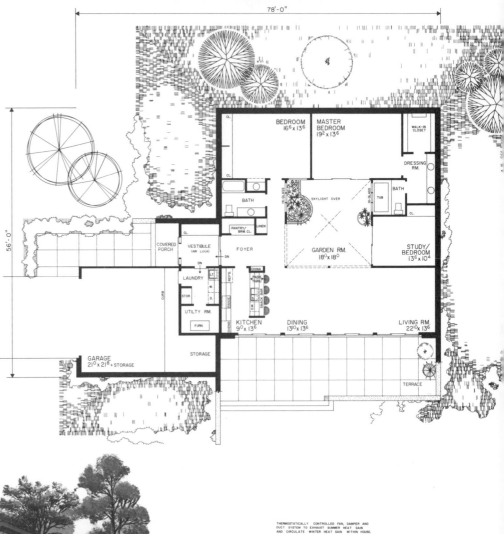

● Earth berms are banked against all four exterior walls of this design to effectively reduce heating and cooling demands. The berming is cost-efficient during both hot and cold seasons. In the winter, berming reduces heat loss through the exterior walls and shields the structure from cold winds. It helps keep warm air out during the summer. The two most dramatic interior highlights are the atrium and thru-fireplace. Topped with a large skylight, the atrium floods the interior with natural light. Shades are used to cover the atrium in the summer to prevent solar heat gain. Three bedrooms are featured in this plan and they each open via sliding glass doors to the atrium. This would eliminate any feeling of being closed in. An island with range and oven is featured in the kitchen. Informal dining will be enjoyed at the snack bar. The family/dining room can house those more formal dining occasions. The section at the right is cut through the study, atrium and rear bedroom looking toward master bedroom.

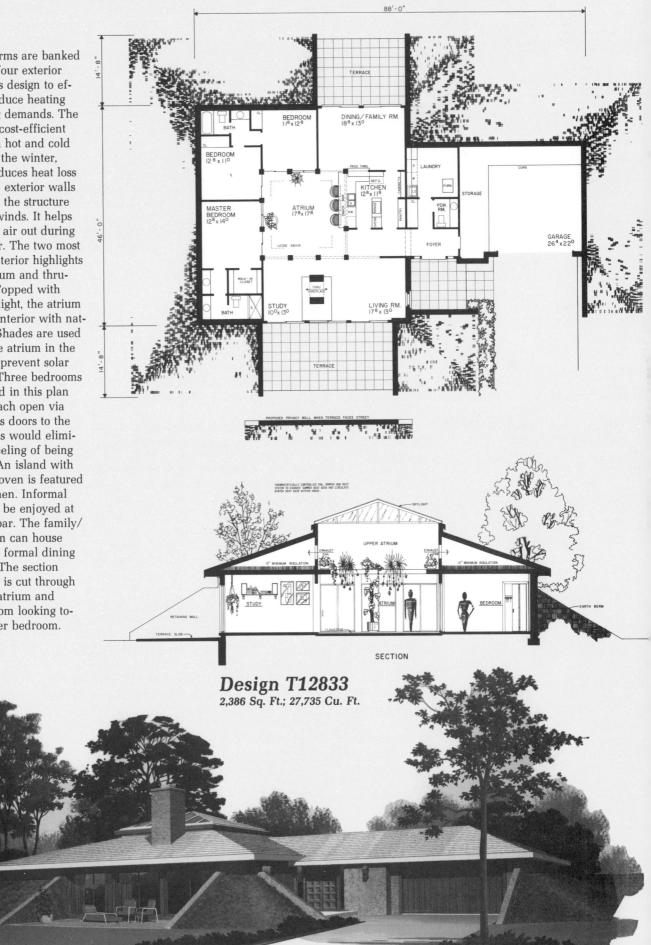

# Design T12833
2,386 Sq. Ft.; 27,735 Cu. Ft.

## Design T12839 1,565 Sq. Ft. - First Floor; 1,120 Sq. Ft. - Second Floor; 58,925 Cu. Ft.

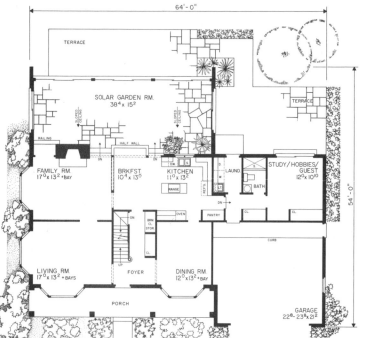

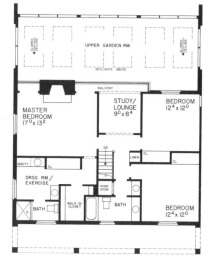

● Bay windows highlight the front and side exteriors of this three-bedroom Colonial. For energy efficiency, this design has an enclosed garden room that collects free solar energy. This area opens to the family room, breakfast room and second floor master suite. The solar garden room incudes 576 sq. ft. and 10,828 cu. ft. These figures are not included in the above total.

# Design T12840 1,529 Sq. Ft. - First Floor; 1,344 Sq. Ft. - Second Floor; 44,504 Cu. Ft.

● This traditional two-story design will keep you warm because it is super-insulated to shut out the cold. It is designed for cold climates and is so well insulated that it can be built facing any direction - even north. The key behind its energy efficiency is its double exterior walls separated by R-33 insulation and a raised roof truss that insures ceiling insulation will extend to the outer wall. Front and rear air locks and triple-glazed, underscaled (24" wide) windows also contribute to the energy savings. The interior floor planning has a great deal to recommend it, too. Formal and informal living areas, plus a study! The interior kitchen area will be hard to beat. It has pass-thrus to the formal dining room and the family room. All of the sleeping facilities, four bedrooms and two baths, are on the second floor. The section at right describes the technical characteristics of this super-insulated house.

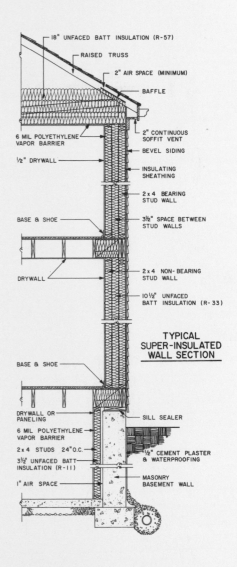

TYPICAL
SUPER-INSULATED
WALL SECTION

# Clutter Room, Media Room To The Fore

● Something new? Something new, indeed!! Here is the introduction of two rooms which will make a wonderful contribution to family living. The clutter room is strategically placed between the kitchen and garage. It is the nerve center of the work area. It houses the laundry, provides space for sewing, has a large sorting table, and even plenty of space for the family's tool bench. A handy potting area is next to the laundry tray. Adjacent to the clutter room, and a significant part of the planning of this whole zone, are the pantry and freezer with their nearby counter space. These facilities surely will expedite the unloading of groceries from the car and their convenient storing. Wardrobe and broom closets, plus washroom complete the outstanding utility of this area. The location of the clutter room with all its fine cabinet and counter space means that the often numerous family projects can be on-going. This room is ideally isolated from the family's daily living patterns. The media room may be thought of as the family's entertainment center. While this is the room for the large or small TV, the home movies, the stereo and VCR equipment, it will serve as the library or study. It would be ideal as the family's home office with its computer equipment. Your family will decide just how it will utilize this outstanding area.

## Design T12915 2,758 Sq. Ft.; 60,850 Cu Ft.

● The features of this appealing contemporary design go far beyond the clutter and media rooms. The country kitchen is spacious and caters to the family's informal living and dining activities. While it overlooks the rear yard it is just a step from the delightful greenhouse. Many happy hours will be spent here enjoying to the fullest the outdoors from within. The size of the greenhouse is 8'x18' and contains 149 sq. ft. not included in the square footage quoted above. The formal living and dining areas feature spacious open planning. Sloping ceiling in the living room, plus the sliding glass doors to the outdoor terrace enhance the cheerfulness of this area. The foyer is large and routes traffic efficiently to all areas. Guest coat closets and a powder room are handy. The sleeping zone is well-planned. Two children's bedrooms have fine wall space, good wardrobe facilities and a full bath.

The master bedroom is exceptional. It is large enough to accommodate a sitting area and has access to the terrace. Two walk-in closets, a vanity area with lavatory and a compartmented bath are noteworthy features. Observe the stall shower in addition to the dramatic whirlpool installation. The floor plan below is identical with that on the opposite page and shows one of many possible ways to arrange furniture.

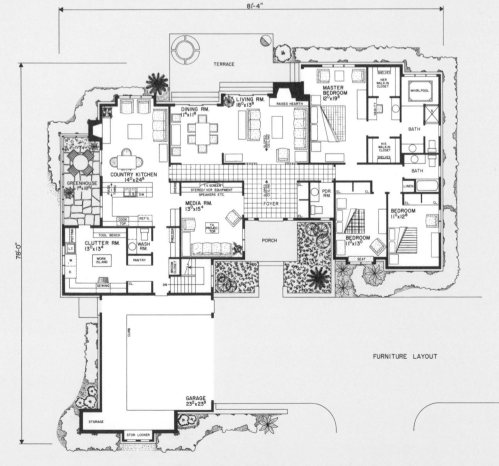

FURNITURE LAYOUT

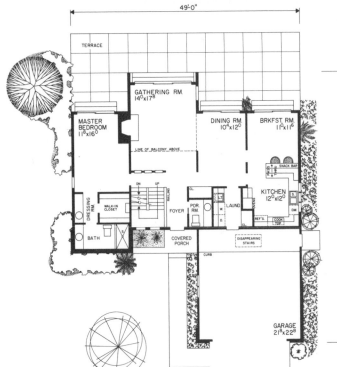

## Design T12905
**1,342 Sq. Ft. - First Floor**
**619 Sq. Ft. - Second Floor; 33,655 Cu. Ft.**

● All of the livability in this plan is in the back! Each first floor room, except the kitchen, has access to the rear terrace via sliding glass doors. A great way to capture an excellent view. This plan is also ideal for a narrow lot seeing that its width is less than 50 feet. Two bedrooms and a lounge, overlooking the gathering room, are on the second floor.

# HERITAGE HOUSES . . . .

*The beauty and charm of early America is wonderfully captured by the picturesque houses built by our forefathers. For generations, Salt Box, Gambrel, Garrison, Cape Cod, Georgian, Federal and Greek Revival houses and their variations have enhanced our countryside. Today, our architectural history is being reclaimed by families building up-to-date adaptations of these favorite heritage houses of yesteryear. The following pages feature a selection of these famous styles with thoroughly modern floor plans which assure the best in present-day family livability.*

● Deriving its design from the traditional Cape Cod style, this facade features clap board siding, small-paned windows and a transom-lit entrance flanked by carriage lamps. A central chimney services two fireplaces, one in the country-kitchen and the other in the formal living room which is removed from the disturbing flow of traffic. The master suite is located to the left of the upstairs landing. A full bathroom services two additional bedrooms.

## Design T12657 1,217 Sq. Ft. - First Floor
**868 Sq. Ft. - Second Floor; 33,260 Cu. Ft.**

## Design T12101  1,338 Sq. Ft. - First Floor
### 1,114 Sq. Ft. - Second Floor; 39,617 Cu. Ft.

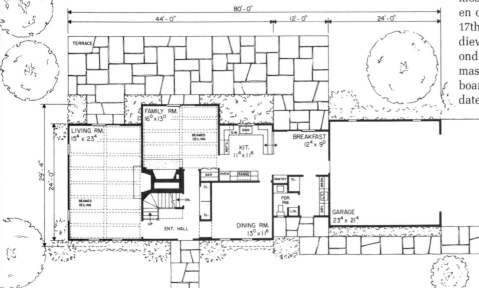

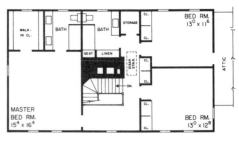

● This is a modified version of one of America's most famous Colonial dwellings, the Parson Capen of Topsfield, Mass. Dating back to the 17th-Century, the English colonists built this medieval adaptation reproducing its bracketed second floor overhang, pendant drops at the corners, massive pilastered chimney and narrow clapboards. The floor plan, of course, has been updated to cater to today's living requirements.

## Design T12191

**1,553 Sq. Ft. - First Floor**
**1,197 Sq. Ft. - Second Floor**
**47,906 Cu. Ft.**

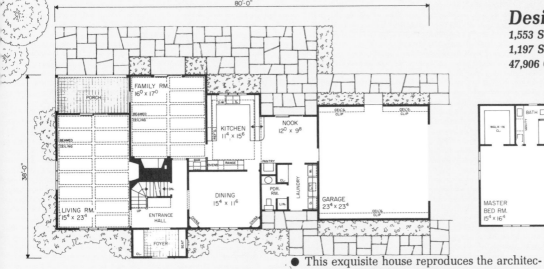

● This exquisite house reproduces the architectural details from the 17th-Century. Medieval and Tudor influences, brought to the New World by the first English colonists, distinguish this adaptation. The interior has been designed to serve today's active family.

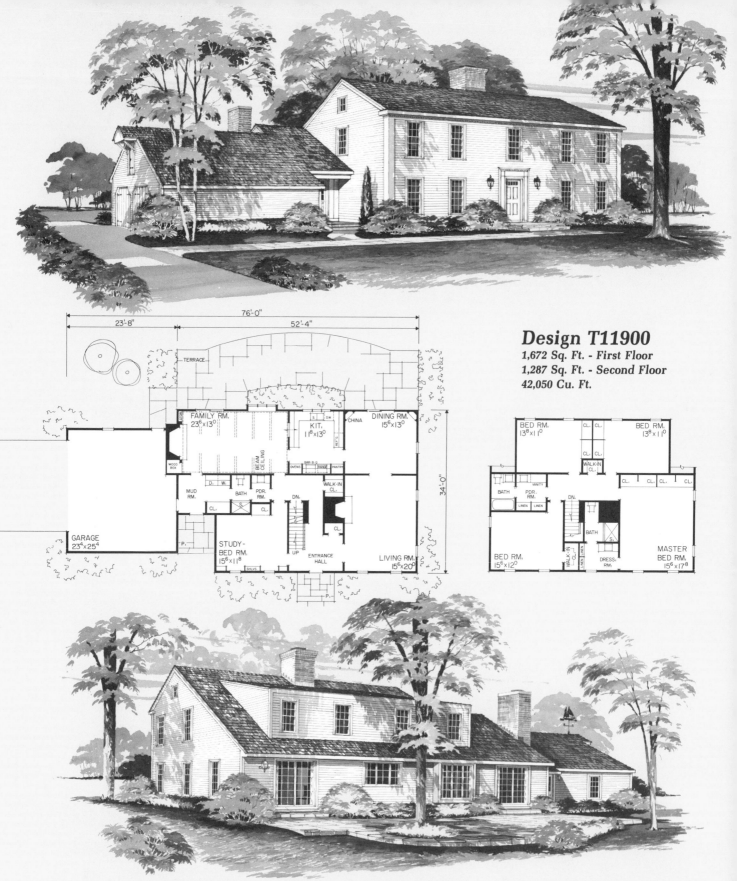

## Design T11900

1,672 Sq. Ft. - First Floor
1,287 Sq. Ft. - Second Floor
42,050 Cu. Ft.

● The history of the Colonial Salt Box goes back some 200 years. This unusually authentic adaptation captures all the warmth and charm of the early days both inside as well as outside. To reflect today's living patterns, an up-dating of the floor plan was inevitable. The result is a room arrangement which will serve the active family wonderfully. Formal living and dining take place at one end of the house which is free of cross-room traffic. Informal living activities will center around the family room and expand through sliding glass doors to the terrace. The mud room area is strategically located and includes the laundry and a full bath. An extra study/bedroom supplements four bedrooms upstairs. Count the closets and the other storage areas.

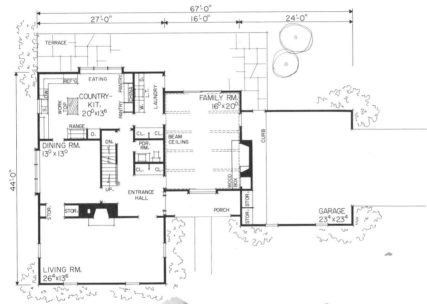

## Design T11887

**1,518 Sq. Ft. - First Floor**
**1,144 Sq. Ft. - Second Floor**
**40,108 Cu. Ft.**

● This Gambrel roof Colonial is steeped in history. And well it should be, for its pleasing proportions are a delight to the eye. The various roof planes, the window treatment, and the rambling nature of the entire house revive a picture of rural New

England. The covered porch protects the front door which opens into a spacious entrance hall. Traffic then flows in an orderly fashion to the end living room, the separate dining room, the cozy family room, and to the spacious country-kitchen. There

is a first floor laundry, plenty of coat closets, and a handy powder room. Two fireplaces enliven the decor of the living areas. Upstairs there is an exceptional master bedroom layout, and abundant storage. Note the walk-in closets.

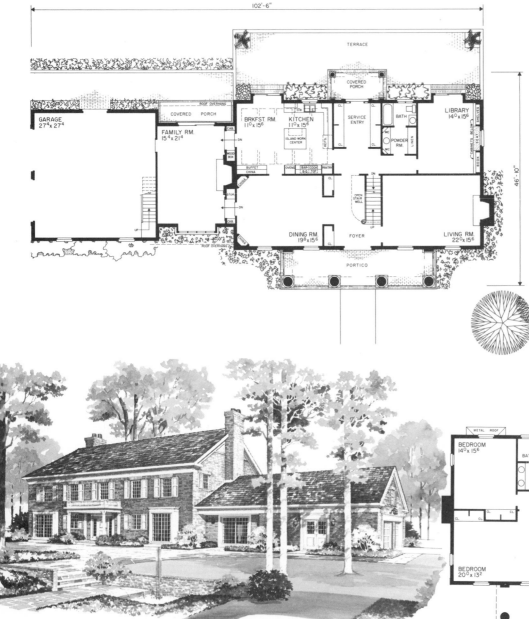

## Design T12230

**2,288 Sq. Ft. - First Floor**
**1,863 Sq. Ft. - Second Floor**
**79,736 Cu. Ft.**

● The gracefulness and appeal of this southern adaptation will be everlasting. The imposing two-story portico is truly dramatic. Notice the authentic detailing of the tapered Doric columns, the balustraded roof deck, the denticulated cornice, the front entrance and the shuttered windows. The architecture of the year is no less appealing. The spacious, formal front entrance hall provides a fitting introduction to the scale and elegance of the interior. The openness of the stairwell provides a view of the curving balusters above.

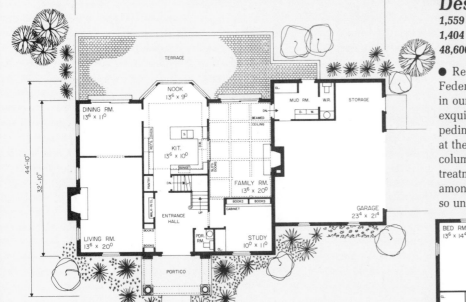

## Design T12283
### 1,559 Sq. Ft. - First Floor
### 1,404 Sq. Ft. - Second Floor
### 48,606 Cu. Ft.

● Reminiscent of the stately character of Federal architecture during an earlier period in our history, this two-story is replete with exquisite detailing. The cornice work, the pediment gable, the dentils, the brick quoins at the corners, the beautifully proportioned columns, the front door detailing, the window treatment and the massive twin chimneys are among the features which make this design so unique and appealing.

# A Charleston Single House

### Design T12660
1,479 Sq. Ft. - First Floor
1,501 Sq. Ft. - Second Floor
912 Sq. Ft. - Third Floor
556 Sq. Ft. - Activities Room Area
57,440 Cu. Ft.

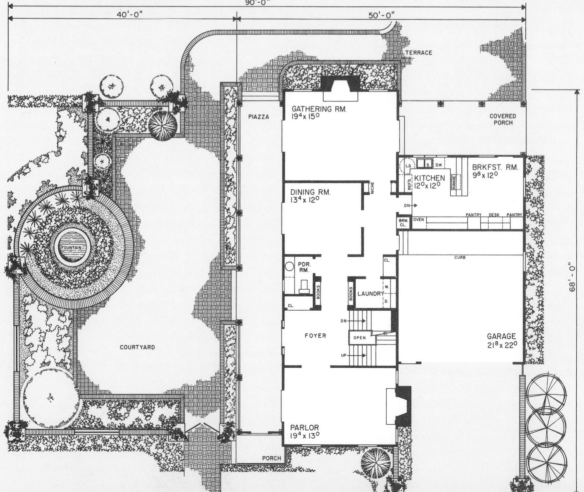

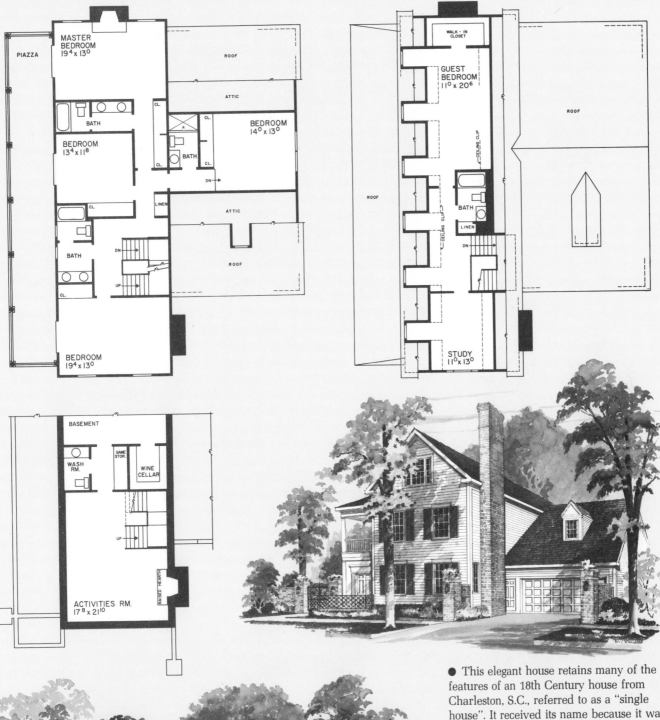

MASTER
BEDROOM
19⁴ x 13⁰

PIAZZA

ROOF

ATTIC

CL.

CL.

BATH

BATH

BEDROOM
14⁰ x 13⁰

BEDROOM
13⁴ x 11⁸

CL.

DN

LINEN

BATH

ATTIC

BATH

DN

UP

CL.

ROOF

BEDROOM
19⁴ x 13⁰

WALK - IN
CLOSET

GUEST
BEDROOM
11⁰ x 20⁶

ROOF

CEILING CLIP

ROOF

CEILING CLIP

BATH

LINEN

DN

STUDY
11⁰ x 13⁰

BASEMENT

GAME
STOR.

WASH
RM.

WINE
CELLAR

UP

RAISED HEARTH

ACTIVITIES RM.
17⁸ x 21¹⁰

● This elegant house retains many of the features of an 18th Century house from Charleston, S.C., referred to as a "single house". It received its name because it was a single room deep. The house is designed to stand narrow-end-to-the-street. The side with the double-tiered porch and courtyard is breathtaking. This design departs from the original plan by adding a wing to the side, to contain the kitchen, breakfast room and two-car garage. The first floor is balanced by having the gathering room and parlor at opposite ends of the plan, each with a fireplace. Four bedrooms and three full baths are on the second floor; another bedroom and study are on the third floor. The basement is developed with an activities room with raised hearth fireplace, wash room and wine cellar.

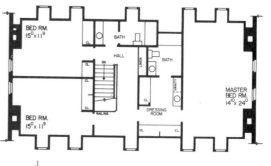

Second Floor plans showing:

**Left plan:**
- BED RM. 15⁰ x 11⁹
- BATH
- HALL
- MASTER BED RM. 14⁴⁰ x 12⁸
- BATH
- LINEN
- DN.
- CL.
- WALK IN CLOSET
- LINEN
- RAILING
- BED RM. 15⁰ x 11⁹
- BED RM. 14¹⁰ x 11⁰

**Right plan:**
- BED RM. 15⁰ x 11⁹
- BATH
- HALL
- LINEN
- BATH
- VANITY
- DN.
- CL.
- DRESSING ROOM
- RAILING
- MASTER BED RM. 14¹⁰ x 24⁰
- BED RM. 15⁰ x 11⁹

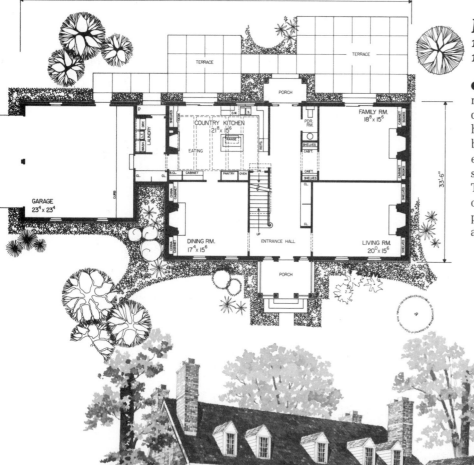

First Floor plan showing:
- 84'-6"
- 33'-6"
- TERRACE
- TERRACE
- PORCH
- COUNTRY KITCHEN 21⁸ x 15⁶
- EATING
- RANGE
- PANTRY
- OVEN
- LAUNDRY
- PDR. RM.
- FAMILY RM. 18⁸ x 15⁶
- SHELVES
- CAB'T.
- CABINET
- GARAGE 23⁴ x 23⁴
- DINING RM. 17⁴ x 15⁶
- ENTRANCE HALL
- UP
- LIVING RM. 20⁰ x 15⁶
- PORCH

## Design T12638
*1,836 Sq. Ft. - First Floor*
*1,323 Sq. Ft. - Second Floor; 57,923 Cu. Ft.*

● The brick facade of this two-story represents the mid-18th-Century design concept. Examine its fine exterior. It has a steeply pitched roof which is broken by two large chimneys at each end and by pedimented dormers. Inside Georgian details lend elegance. Turned balusters and a curved banister ornament the formal staircase. Blueprints include details for both three and four bedroom options.

## Design T12132

**1,958 Sq. Ft. - First Floor**
**1,305 Sq. Ft. - Second Floor**
**51,428 Cu. Ft.**

● Another Georgian adaptation with a great heritage dating back to 18th Century America. Exquisite and symmetrical detailing set the character of this impressive home. Don't overlook such features as the two fireplaces, the laundry, the beamed ceiling, the built-in china cabinets and the oversized garage.

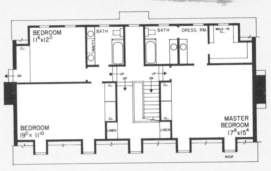

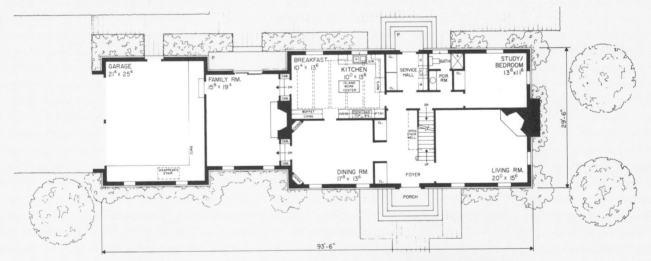

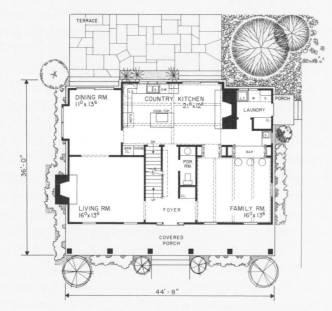

The exterior of this full two-story is highlighted by the covered porch and balcony. Many enjoyable hours will be spent at these outdoor areas. The interior is highlighted by a spacious country kitchen. Be sure to notice its island cook-top, fireplace and the beamed ceiling. A built-in bar is in the family room.

## Design T12664
**1,308 Sq. Ft. - First Floor**
**1,262 Sq. Ft. - Second Floor; 49,215 Cu. Ft.**

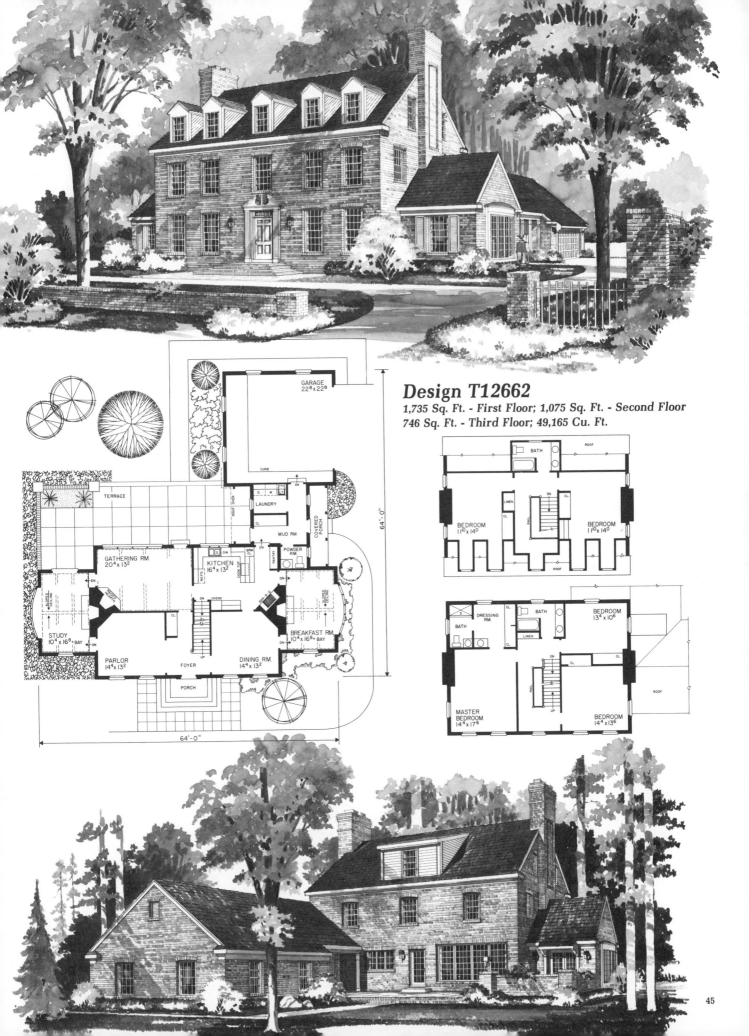

## Design T12662

**1,735 Sq. Ft. - First Floor; 1,075 Sq. Ft. - Second Floor**
**746 Sq. Ft. - Third Floor; 49,165 Cu. Ft.**

GARAGE
22⁸ x 22⁸

CURB

TERRACE

LAUNDRY

MUD RM.

COVERED PORCH

POWDER RM.

GATHERING RM.
20⁴ x 13²

KITCHEN
16⁴ x 13²

PANTRY

STUDY
10⁴ x 16⁸ BAY

SLOPED CEILING

BREAKFAST RM.
10⁴ x 16⁸ BAY

OVENS

PARLOR
14⁴ x 13²

FOYER

UP

DINING RM.
14⁴ x 13²

PORCH

64'-0"

64'-0"

BATH

ROOF

LINEN

CL

BEDROOM
11¹⁰ x 14⁰

BEDROOM
11¹⁰ x 14⁰

DN

RAIL

ROOF

DRESSING RM.

BATH

BATH

LINEN

BEDROOM
13⁴ x 10⁶

MASTER BEDROOM
14⁴ x 17⁶

DN

RAIL

UP

BEDROOM
14⁴ x 13⁶

ROOF

# Design T12668 *1,206 Sq. Ft. - First Floor*
## *1,254 Sq. Ft. - Second Floor; 47,915 Cu. Ft.*

● This elegant exterior houses a very livable plan. Every bit of space has been put to good use. The front country kitchen is a good place to begin. It is efficiently planned with its island cook top, built-ins and pass-thru to the dining room. The large great room will be the center of all family activities. Quiet times can be enjoyed in the front library. Study the second floor sleeping areas.

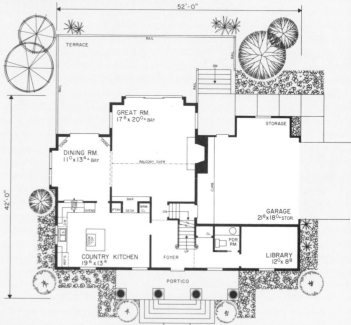

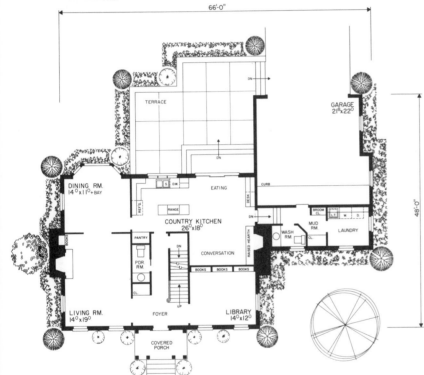

## Design T12688 1,588 Sq. Ft. - First Floor
### 1,101 Sq. Ft. - Second Floor; 44,021 Cu. Ft.

● Here are two floors of excellent livability. Start at the country kitchen. It will be the center for family activities. It has an island, desk, raised hearth fireplace, conversation area and sliding glass doors to the terrace. Adjacent to this area is the washroom and laundry. Quieter areas are available in the living room and library. Three bedrooms are housed on the second floor.

# Georgian Architecture Comes to Life

● You'll not need a curving front drive or formal gardens to insure an impressive setting for this house. The mere statelines of its facade will command the complete and extra-ordinary attention of even the most casual of passers-by. The authentic detailing centers around the fine proportions, the dentils, the window symmetry, the front door and entranceway, the massive chimneys and the masonry work. The rear elevation retains all the grandeur exemplary of exquisite architecture. The projecting wing adds to the breadth of the overall design. This provides for the inclusion of the oversize garage and the family room with its view of both front and rear yards. Surely a fine adaptation from the 18th Century when formality and elegance were by-words. Now study the plan.

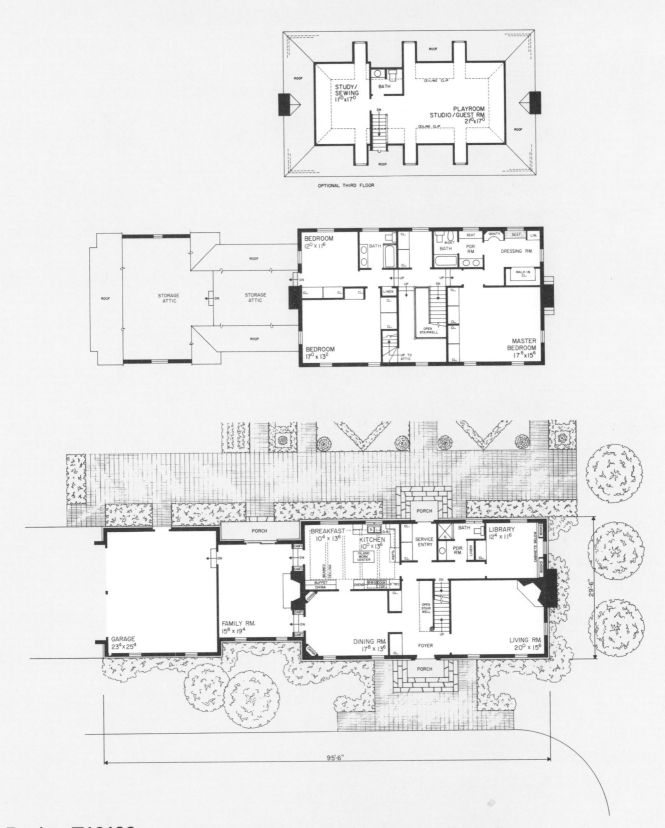

OPTIONAL THIRD FLOOR

STUDY/SEWING 11¹⁰ x 17⁰

BATH

CEILING CLG.

PLAYROOM STUDIO/GUEST RM. 21⁰ x 17⁰

CEILING CLG.

DN

ROOF

BEDROOM 12⁰ x 11⁶

BATH

BIDET

BATH

PDR. RM.

SEAT VANITY SEAT LIN.

DRESSING RM.

WALK-IN CL.

STORAGE ATTIC

STORAGE ATTIC

ROOF

ROOF

ROOF

DN

DN

UP

UP

LINEN

OPEN STAIRWELL

CL.

BEDROOM 17⁰ x 13²

UP TO ATTIC

MASTER BEDROOM 17⁸ x 15⁶

BREAKFAST 10⁴ x 13⁶

KITCHEN 10⁰ x 13⁶

ISLAND WORK CENTER

SERVICE ENTRY

BATH

PDR. RM.

LINEN

LIBRARY 12⁴ x 11⁶

CABINETS BELOW BOOKS

PORCH

PORCH

BEAMED CEILING

BUFFET CHINA

OVENS

REF'S.

PTRY.

OPEN STAIR WELL

DN

GARAGE 23⁴ x 25⁴

FAMILY RM. 15⁸ x 19⁴

DINING RM. 17⁸ x 13⁶

FOYER

UP

LIVING RM. 20⁰ x 15⁶

PORCH

29'-6"

95'-6"

# Design T12192 *1,884 Sq. Ft. - First Floor; 1,521 Sq. Ft. - Second Floor; 58,380 Cu. Ft.*

● The appeal of this outstanding home does not end with its exterior elevations. There are a variety of interior elevations with their own full measure of charm. Consider the formal living room with its corner fireplace. Also, the library with its wall of bookshelves and cabinets. Further, the dining room highlights corner china cabinets The two entrances to the sunken family room each feature storage niches. The work center is reminiscent of the old country-kitchen. There is the beamed ceiling and plenty of breakfast eating area. Notice the service entry and the nearby bath. The second floor has three big bedrooms, including an excellent master bedroom with dressing room and compartmented bath. Folding stairs leading to third floor attic, another area for bulk storage.

## Design T12542 *2,025 Sq. Ft. - First Floor*
*1,726 Sq. Ft. - Second Floor; 61,315 Cu. Ft.*

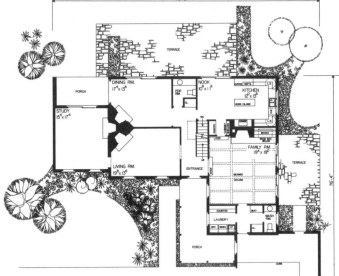

● Here is a fieldstone Farmhouse that has its roots in the rolling countryside of Pennsylvania. In addition to its stone exterior, the charm of such a house is characterized by the various appendages. These additions, of course, came into being as the size of the family fortune increased. The living potential offered by this Farmhouse adaptation can hardly be topped. Imagine, five fireplaces! Study the outstanding livability offered in this house from the past. Surely its floor plan has been up-dated to serve today's contemporary family.

# Design T12633

**1,338 Sq. Ft. - First Floor**
**1,200 Sq. Ft. - Second Floor**
**506 Sq. Ft. - Third Floor**
**44,525 Cu. Ft.**

● This is certainly a pleasing Georgian. Its facade features an atypical porch with a roof supported by simple wooden posts. The garage wing has a sheltered service entry and brick facing which complements the design. Sliding glass doors link the terrace and family room, providing an indoor/outdoor area for entertaining as pictured in the rear elevation. The floor plan has been designed to serve the family efficiently. The stairway in the foyer leads to four second-floor bedrooms. The third floor is windowed and can be used as a studio and study.

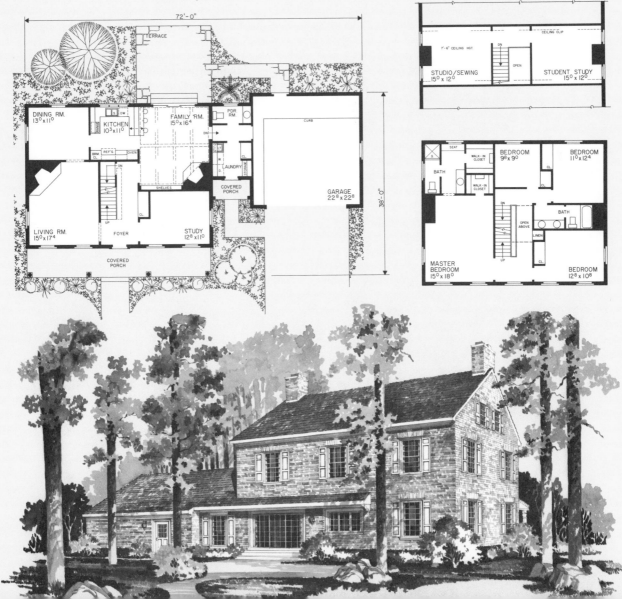

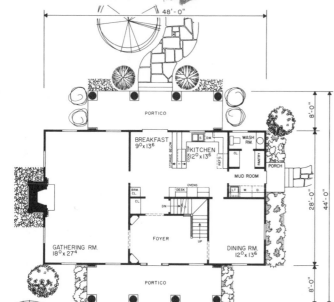

## Design T12663 1,344 Sq. Ft. - First Floor
### 947 Sq. Ft. - Second Floor; 39,790 Cu. Ft.

● Reminiscent of the past, this home reflects the Greek Revival heritage. This is demonstrated in its front and rear porticoes which have graceful columns. While the exterior comes from yesteryear, the floor plan is designed to serve today's active family. Imagine the activities that can be enjoyed in the huge gathering room. It stretches from the front to the rear of the house. Three bedrooms are on the second floor.

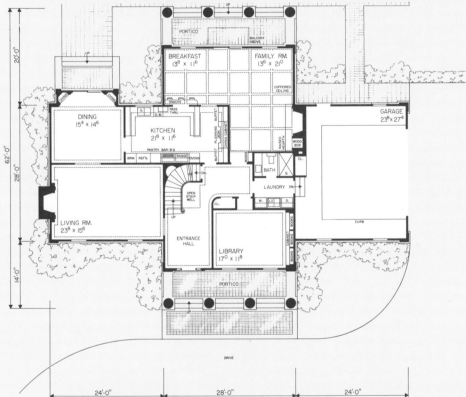

| | | |
|---|---|---|
| 24'-0" | 28'-0" | 24'-0" |
| | 76'-0" | |

## Design T12184

**1,999 Sq. Ft. - First Floor**
**1,288 Sq. Ft. - Second Floor**
**58,441 Cu. Ft.**

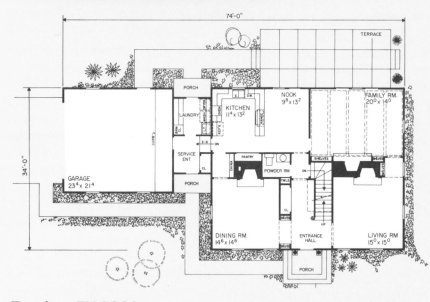

Here is a New England Georgian adaptation with an elevated doorway highlighted by pilasters and a pediment which gives way to a second-story Palladian window, capped in turn by a pediment projecting from the hipped roof. The interior is decidely up-to-date with even an upstairs lounge.

## Design T12639 1,556 Sq. Ft. - First Floor; 1,428 Sq. Ft. - Second Floor; 46,115 Cu. Ft.

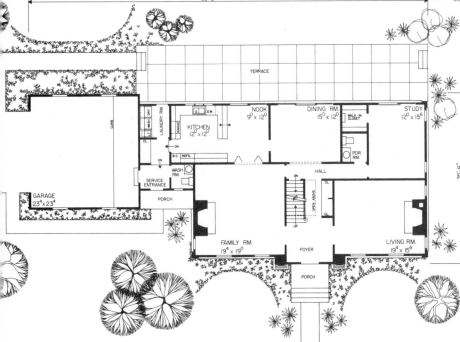

## Design T12522

1,835 Sq. Ft. - First Floor
1,625 Sq. Ft. - Second Floor
58,700 Cu. Ft.

● This wood frame Georgian adaptation revives the architecture of an earlier period in New England. Its formal facade houses an abundance of spacious livability.

# A Mount Vernon Reminiscence

● This magnificent manor's streetview illustrates a centralized mansion connected by curving galleries to matching wings. What a grand presentation this home will make! The origin of this house dates back to 1787 and George Washington's stately Mount Vernon. The underlying aesthetics for this design come from the rational balancing of porticoes, fenestration and chimneys. The rear elevation of this home also deserves mention. Six two-story columns, along with four sets of French doors, highlight this view. Study all of the intricate detailing that is featured all around these exteriors.

The flanking wings create a large formal courtyard where guests of today can park their cars. This home, designed from architecture of the past, is efficient and compact enough to fit many suburban lots. Its interior has been well planned and is ready to serve a family of any size.

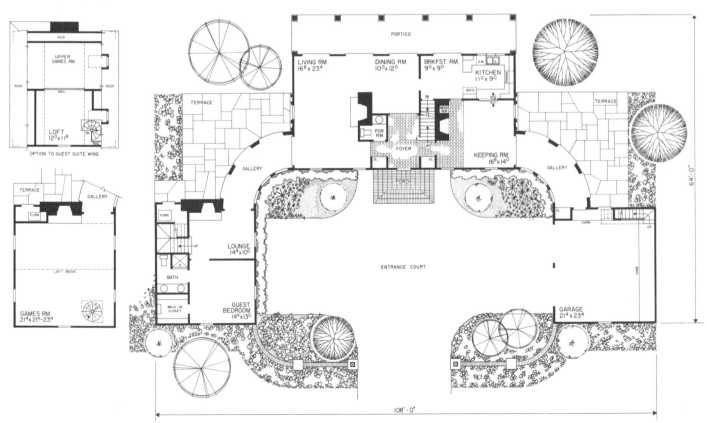

# Design T12665 1,152 Sq. Ft. - First Floor
**1,152 Sq. Ft. - Second Floor; 38,754 Cu. Ft. (Excludes Guest Suite and Galleries)**

● The main, two-story section of this home houses the living areas. First - there is the large, tiled foyer with two closets and powder room. Then there is the living room which is the entire width of the house. This room has a fireplace and leads into the formal dining room. Three sets of double French doors lead to the rear portico from this formal area. The kitchen and breakfast room will function together. There is a pass-thru from the kitchen to the keeping room. All of the sleeping facilities, four bedrooms, are on the second floor. The gallery on the right leads to the garage; the one on the left, to a lounge and guest suite with studio above. The square and cubic footages quoted above do not include the guest suite or gallery areas. The first floor of the guest suite contains 688 sq. ft.; the second floor studio, 306 sq. ft. The optional plan shows a game room with a loft above having 162 sq. ft.

# Design T12658

*1,218 Sq. Ft. - First Floor*
*764 Sq. Ft. - Second Floor; 29,690 Cu. Ft.*

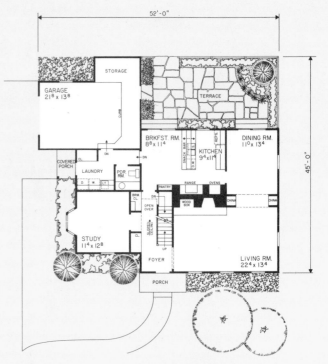

● Traditional charm of yesteryear is exemplified delightfully in this one-and-a-half story home. The garage has been conveniently tucked away in the rear of the house which makes this design ideal for a corner lot. Interior livability has been planned for efficient living. The front living room is large and features a fireplace with wood box. The laundry area is accessible by way of both the garage and a side covered porch. Enter the rear terrace from both eating areas, the formal dining room and the informal breakfast room.

## Design T12656 1,122 Sq. Ft. - First Floor
**884 Sq. Ft. - Second Floor; 31,845 Cu. Ft.**

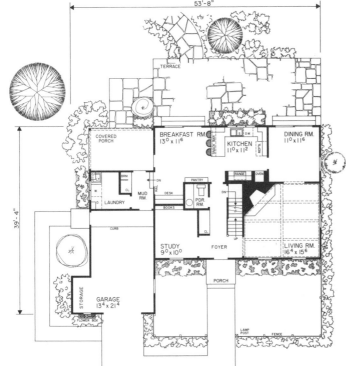

● This charming Cape cottage possesses a great sense of shelter through its gambrel roof. Dormers at front and rear pierce the gambrel roof to provide generous, well-lit living space on the second floor which houses three bedrooms. This design's first floor layout is not far different from that of the Cape cottages of the 18th century. The large kitchen and adjoining dining room recall cottage keeping rooms both in function and in location at the rear of the house.

# Expanding the Half-House

## Design T12682 976 Sq. Ft. - First Floor (Basic Plan)
1,230 Sq. Ft. - First Floor (Expanded Plan); 744 Sq. Ft. - Second Floor (Both Plans)
29,355 Cu. Ft. Basic Plan; 35,084 Cu. Ft. Expanded Plan

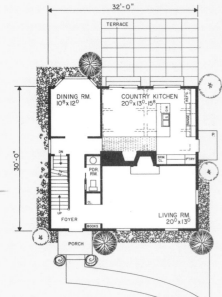

● Here is an expandable Colonial with a full measure of Cape Cod Charm. For those who wish to build the basic house, there is an abundance of low-budget livability. Twin fireplaces serve the formal living room and the informal country kitchen. Note the spaciousness of both areas. A dining room and powder room are also on the first floor of this basic plan. Upstairs three bedrooms and two full baths.

60'-0"

TERRACE

COVERED PORCH

DINING RM. 10⁸ x 12⁰

COUNTRY KITCHEN 20⁰ x 13⁰ - 15⁸

GARAGE 13⁸ x 20⁴

STUDY 13⁶ x 18⁰

PDR. RM.

BRM CL.

FOYER

LIVING RM. 20⁰ x 13⁰

BOOKS

PORCH

35'-0"

ATTIC STORAGE (FUTURE ROOM)

BEDROOM 12¹⁰ x 9⁸

BEDROOM 12¹⁰ x 9⁸

ROOF

ROOF

DN

LINEN

BATH

BATH

CL

MASTER BEDROOM 11⁰ x 14⁰

ROOF

ROOF

● This expanded version of the basic house on the opposite page is equally as reminiscent of Cape Cod. Common in the 17th-Century was the addition of appendages to the main structure. This occurred as family size increased or finances improved. This version provides for the addition of wings to accommodate a large study and a garage. Utilizing the alcove behind the study results in a big, covered porch. Certainly a charming design whichever version you decide to build for your family.

## Design T12687 1,819 Sq. Ft. - First Floor
1,472 Sq. Ft. - Second Floor; 56,820 Cu. Ft.

● Exterior styling of this home is reminiscent of the past but its floor plan is as up-to-date as it can get. Its many unique features include: a greenhouse, 78 square feet, off the country kitchen, a media room for all the modern electronic equipment, a hobby/laundry room with a washroom and a deluxe master bath. Imagine how your family will utilize each of these areas.

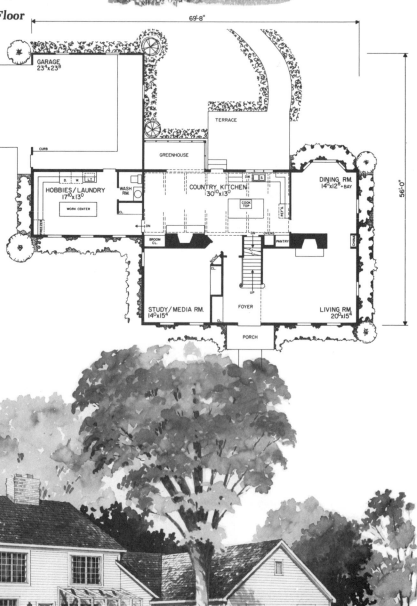

## Design T12659

**1,023 Sq. Ft. - First Floor; 1,008 Sq. Ft. - Second Floor**
**476 Sq. Ft. - Third Floor; 31,510 Cu. Ft.**

● The facade of this three-storied, pitch-roofed house has a symmetrical placement of windows and a restrained but elegant central entrance. The central hall, or foyer, expands midway through the house to a family kitchen. Off the foyer are two rooms, a living room with fireplace and a study. The windowed third floor attic can be used as a study and studio. Three bedrooms are housed on the second floor.

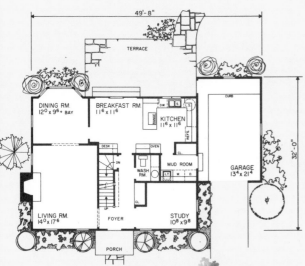

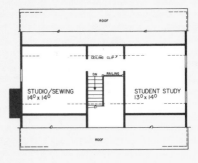

## Design T12650

**1,451 Sq. Ft. - First Floor**
**1,091 Sq. Ft. - Second Floor; 43,555 Cu. Ft.**

● The rear view of this design is just as appealing as the front. The dormers and the covered porch with pillars is a charming way to introduce this house to the on-lookers. Inside, the appeal is also outstanding. Note the size (18 x 25) of the gathering room which is open to the dining room. Kitchen-nook area is very spacious and features an island range, built-in desk and more. It is a great convenience having the laundry in the service area which is close to the kitchen. Imagine, a fireplace in both the gathering room and the master bedroom! Make special note of the front and rear service entrances.

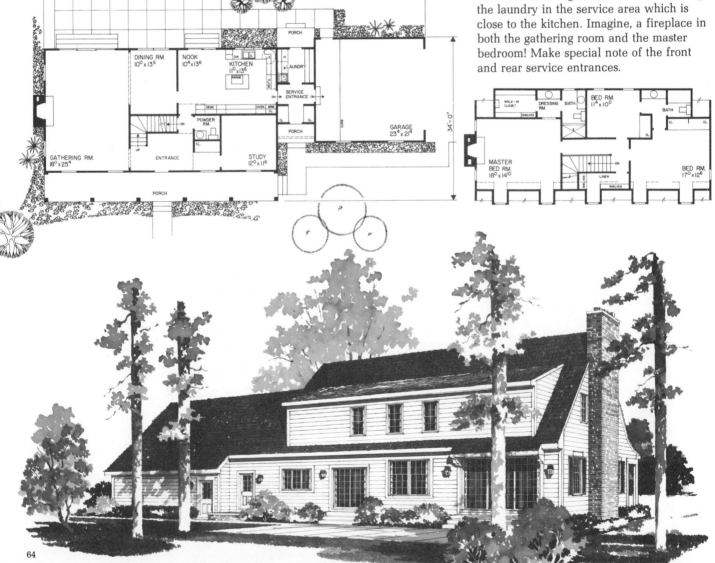

# ONE-STORY HOMES under 2,000 sq. ft. . . . . *Whether*

*its facade be Tudor, Contemporary, Early American, French or Spanish, the one-story home assures a full measure of living convenience for you and your family. The designs in this section are for the modest or restricted building budgets. However, whatever the size, no concession has been made to sound, practical and enjoyable living patterns. Whether it contains 936 or 1994 square feet, your new home can add to the aesthetics of your neighborhood. The delightful exterior appeal can be a major factor in maintaining its long-lasting value.*

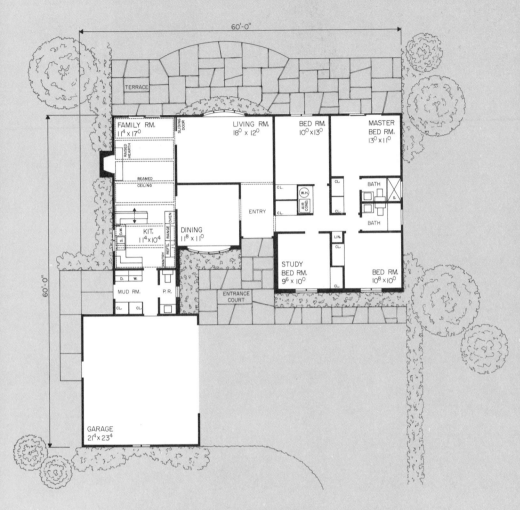

## Design T12170
### 1,646 Sq. Ft.; 22,034 Cu. Ft.

● An L-shaped home with an enchanting Olde English styling. The wavy-edged siding, the simulated beams, the diamond lite windows, the unusual brick pattern and the interesting roof lines all are elements which set the character of authenticity. The center entry routes traffic directly to the formal living and sleeping zones of the house. Between the kitchen-family room area and the attached two-car garage is the mud room. Here is the washer and dryer with the extra powder room nearby. The family room is highlighted by the beamed ceilings, the raised hearth fireplace and sliding glass doors to the rear terrace. The work center with its abundance of cupboard space will be fun in which to function. Four bedrooms, two full baths and good closet space are features of the sleeping area.

## Design T12703
### 1,445 Sq. Ft.; 30,300 Cu. Ft.

● This modified, hip-roofed contemporary design will be the answer for those who want something both practical, yet different, inside and out. The covered front walk sets the stage for entering a modest sized home with tremendous livability. The focal point will be the pleasant conversation lounge. It is sunken, particlaly open to the other living areas and shares the enjoyment of the thru-fireplace with the living room. There are two bedrooms, two full baths and a study. The kitchen is outstanding.

## Design T12753
### 1,539 Sq. Ft.; 31,910 Cu. Ft.

● In this day and age of expensive building sites, projecting the attached garage from the front line of the house makes a lot of economic sense. It also lends itself to interesting roof lines and plan configurations. Here, a pleasing covered walkway to the front door results. A privacy wall adds an extra measure of design appeal and provides a sheltered terrace for the study/bedroom. You'll seldom find more livability in 1,539 square feet. Imagine, three bedrooms, two baths, a spacious living/dining area and a family room.

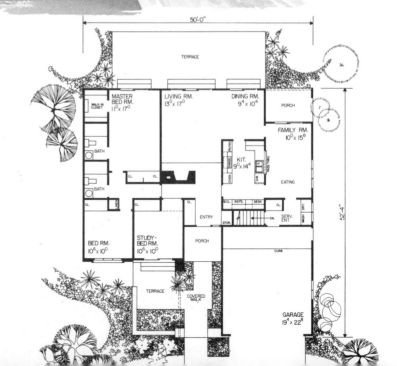

## Design T12744
**1,381 Sq. Ft.; 17,530 Cu. Ft.**

● Here is a practical and an attractive contemporary home for that narrow building site. It is designed for efficiency with the small family or retired couple in mind. Sloping ceilings foster an extra measure of spaciousness. In addition to the master bedroom, there is the study that can also serve as the second bedroom or as an occasional guest room. The single bath is compartmented and its dual access allows it to serve living and sleeping areas more than adequately. Note raised hearth fireplace, snack bar, U-shaped kitchen, laundry, two terraces, etc.

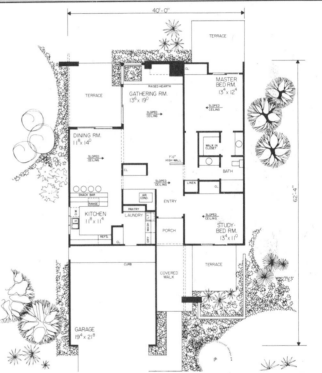

## Design T11337

*1,606 Sq. Ft.; 31,478 Cu. Ft.*

● A pleasantly traditional facade which captures a full measure of warmth. Its exterior appeal results from a symphony of such features as: the attractive window detailing; the raised planter; the paneled door, carriage light and cupola of the garage; the use of both horizontal siding and brick. The floor plan has much to recommend this design to the family whose requirements include formal and informal living areas. There is an exceptional amount of livability in this modest-sized design.

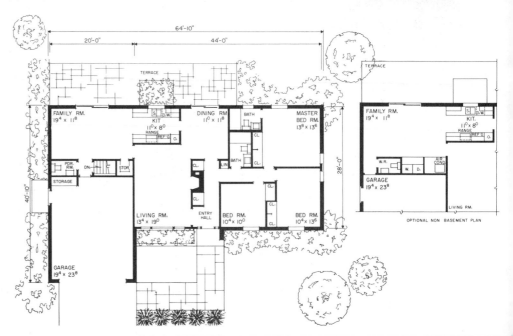

## Design T11890

*1,628 Sq. Ft.; 20,350 Cu. Ft.*

● The pediment gable and columns help set the charm of this modestly sized home. Here is graciousness normally associated with homes twice its size. The pleasant symmetry of the windows and the double front doors complete the picture. Inside, each square foot is wisely planned to assure years of convenient living. There are three bedrooms, each with twin wardrobe closets. There are two full baths economically grouped with the laundry and heating equipment. A fine feature.

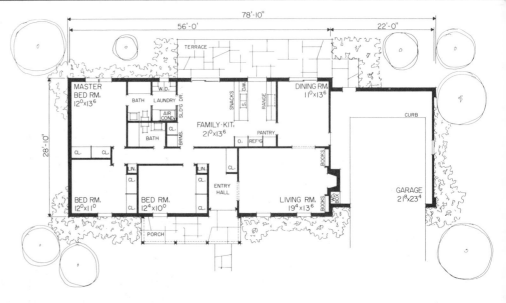

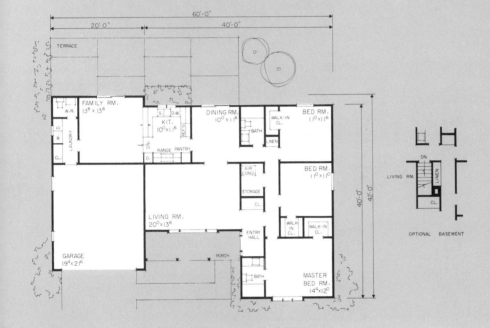

## Design T11920
**1,600 Sq. Ft.; 18,966 Cu. Ft.**

● A charming exterior with a truly great floor plan. The front entrance with its covered porch seems to herald all the outstanding features to be found inside. Study the sleeping zone with its three bedrooms and two full baths. Each of the bedrooms has its own walk-in closet. Note the efficient U-shaped kitchen with the family and dining rooms to each side. Observe the laundry and the extra wash room. Blueprints for this design include details for both basement and non-basement construction.

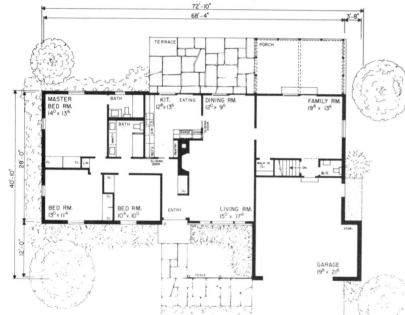

## Design T11100
**1,752 Sq. Ft.; 34,304 Cu. Ft.**

● This modest sized, brick veneer home has a long list of things in its favor—from its appealing exterior to its feature-packed interior. All of the elements of its exterior complement each other to result in a symphony of attractive design features. The floor plan features three bedrooms, two full baths, an extra wash room, a family room, kitchen eating space, a formal dining area, two sets of sliding glass doors to the terrace and one set to the covered porch, built-in cooking equipment, a pantry and vanity with twin lavatories. Further, there is the living room fireplace, attached two-car garage with a bulk storage unit and a basement for extra storage and miscellaneous recreational activities. A fine investment.

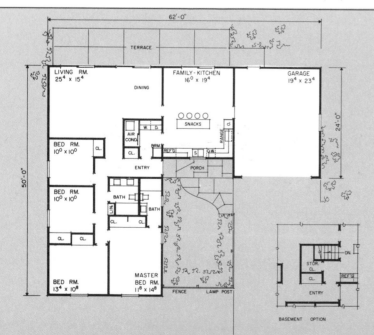

## Design T11343
**1,620 Sq. Ft.; 18,306 Cu. Ft.**

● This is truly a prize-winner! The traditional, L-shaped exterior with its flower court and covered front porch is picturesque, indeed. The formal front entry routes traffic directly to the three distinctly zoned areas—the quiet sleeping area; the spacious; formal living and dining area; the efficient, informal family-kitchen. A closer look at the floor plan reveals four bedrooms, two full baths, good storage facilities, a fine snack bar and sliding glass doors to the rear terrace. The family-kitchen is ideally located. In addition to being but a few steps from both front and rear entrances, one will enjoy the view of both yards. Blueprints include basement and non-basement details.

# Design T11896
**1,690 Sq. Ft.; 19,435 Cu. Ft.**

● Complete family livability is provided by this exceptional floor plan. Further, this design has a truly delightful traditional exterior. The fine layout features a center entrance hall with storage closet in addition to the wardrobe closet. Then, there is the formal, front living room and the adjacent, separate dining room. The U-shaped kitchen has plenty of counter and cupboard space. There is even a pantry. The family room functions with the kitchen and is but a step from the outdoor terrace. The mud room has space for storage and laundry equipment. The extra wash room is nearby. The large family will find those four bedrooms and two full baths just the answer to sleeping and bath accommodations.

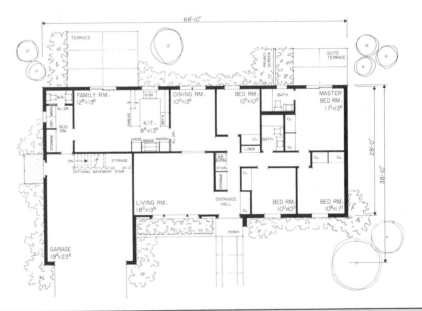

## Design T12605
**1,775 Sq. Ft.; 34,738 Cu. Ft.**

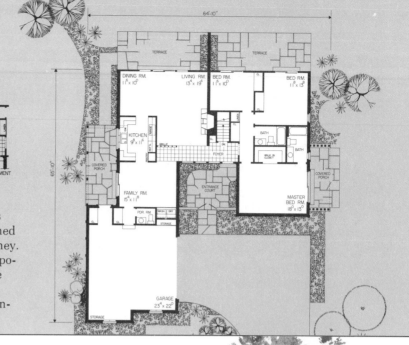

● Here are three modified L-shaped Tudor designs with tremendous exterior appeal and efficient floor plans. While each plan features three bedrooms and 2½ baths, the square footage differences are interesting. Note that each design may be built with or without a basement. This appealing exterior is highlighted by a variety of roof planes, patterned brick, wavy-edged siding and a massive chimney. The garage is oversized and has good storage potential. In addition to the entrance court, there are two covered porches and two terraces for outdoor living. Most definitely a home to be enjoyed by all family members.

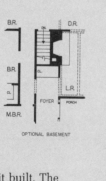

## Design T12206
**1,769 Sq. Ft.; 25,363 Cu. Ft.**

● The charm of Tudor adaptations has become increasingly popular in recent years. And little wonder. Its freshness of character adds a unique touch to any neighborhood. This interesting one-story home will be a standout wherever you choose to have it built. The covered front porch leads to the formal front entry–the foyer. From this point traffic flows freely to the living and sleeping areas. The outstanding plan features a separate dining room, a beamed ceiling living room, an efficient kitchen and an informal family room.

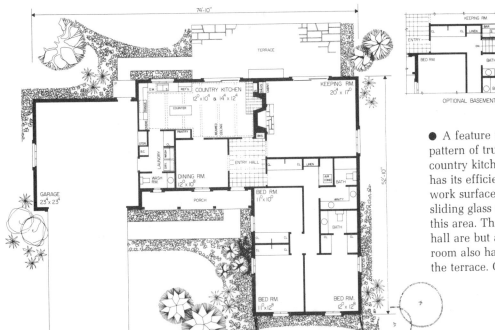

**Design T12604**
**1,956 Sq. Ft.; 28,212 Cu. Ft.**

● A feature that will set the whole wonderful pattern of true living will be the 26 foot wide country kitchen. The spacious, L-shaped kitchen has its efficiency enhanced by the island counter work surface. Beamed ceilings, fireplace and sliding glass doors add to the cozy atmosphere of this area. The laundry, dining room and entry hall are but a step or two away. The big keeping room also has a fireplace and can function with the terrace. Observe the 2½ baths.

## Design T12277
**1,903 Sq. Ft.; 25,087 Cu. Ft.**

● Tudor design front and center! And what an impact this beautifully proportioned L-shaped home does deliver. Observe the numerous little design features which make this such an attractive home. The half-timber work, the window styling, the front door detailing, the covered porch post brackets and the chimney are all among the delightful highlights. Well-zoned, the dining and living rooms are openly planned for formal dining and living.

OPTIONAL BASEMENT

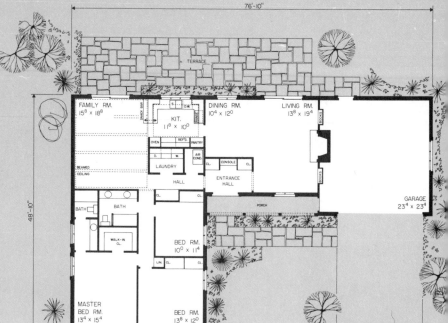

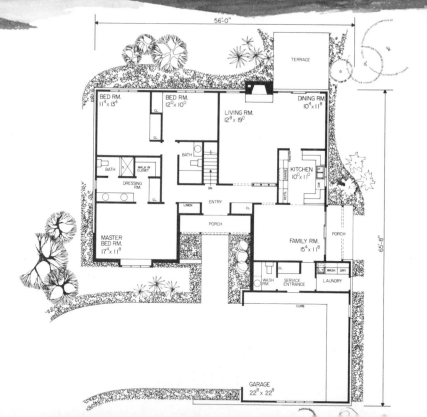

## Design T12728
**1,825 Sq. Ft.; 38,770 Cu. Ft.**

● Your family's new lifestyle will surely flourish in this charming, L-shaped English adaptation. The curving front driveway produces an impressive approach. A covered front porch shelters the centered entry hall which effectively routes traffic to all areas. The fireplace is the focal point of the spacious, formal living and dining area. The kitchen is strategically placed to service the dining room and any informal eating space developed in the family room. In addition to the two full baths of the sleeping area, there is a handy wash room at the entrance from the garage. A complete, first floor laundry is nearby and has direct access to the yard. Sliding glass doors permit easy movement to the outdoor terrace and side porch. Don't overlook the basement and its potential for the development of additional livability and/or storage.

## Design T12374
### 1,919 Sq. Ft.; 39,542 Cu. Ft.

● This English adaptation will never grow old. There is, indeed, much here to please the eye for many a year to come. The wavy-edged siding contrasts pleasingly with the diagonal pattern of brick below. The diamond lites of the windows create their own special effect. The projecting brick wall creates a pleasant court outside the covered front porch. The floor plan is well-zoned with the three bedrooms and two baths comprising a distinct sleeping wing. Flanking the entrance hall is the formal living room and the informal, multi-purpose family room. The large dining room is strategically located. The mud room area is adjacent to the extra wash room and the stairs to the basement.

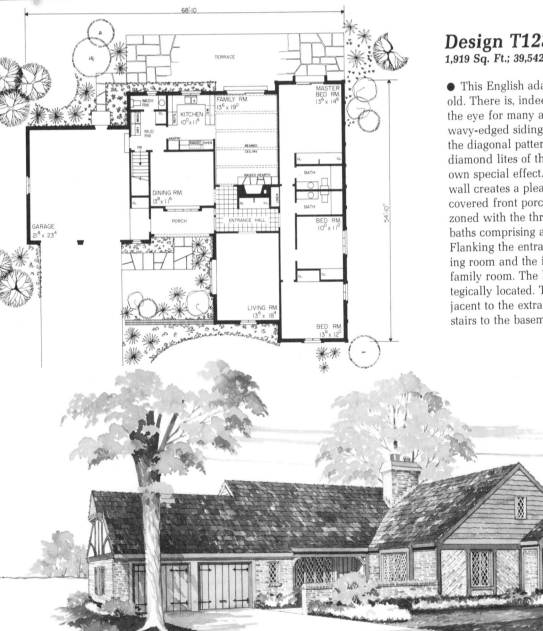

# Design T11802
**1,315 Sq. Ft.; 24,790 Cu. Ft.**

● A small house which includes a full measure of big house livability features. The master bedroom has its extra washroom. In addition to the two bedrooms for the children, there is a study, or fourth bedroom. (This extra room offers the option to serve as a sewing, TV, music or even a guest room.) The living room is well situated and will not be bothered by cross-room traffic. The kitchen functions conveniently with the family-dining area. The stairs to the basement are just inside the entrance from the attached garage.

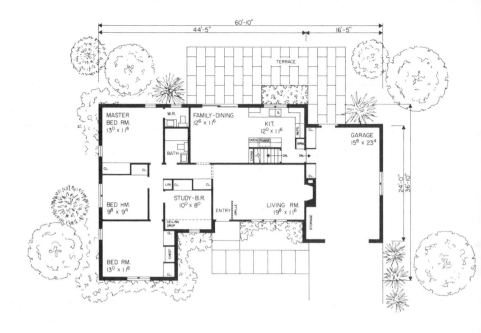

# Design T12671
**1,589 Sq. Ft.; 36,210 Cu. Ft.**

● A rustic exterior of this one-story home features vertical wood siding. The entry foyer is floored with flagstone and leads to the three areas of the plan: sleeping, living and work center. The sleeping area has three bedrooms, the master bedroom has sliding glass doors to the rear terrace. The living area, consisting of gathering and dining rooms, also has access to the terrace. The work center is efficiently planned. It houses the kitchen with snack bar, breakfast room with built-in china cabinet and stairs to the basement. This is a very livable plan.

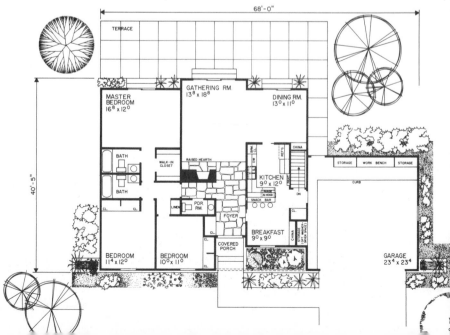

## Design T12606
### 1,499 Sq. Ft.; 19,716 Cu. Ft.

● This modest sized house with its 1,499 square feet could hardly offer more in the way of exterior charm and interior livability. Measuring only 60 feet in width means it will not require a huge, expensive piece of property. The orientation of the garage and the front drive court are features which promote an economical use of property. In addition to the formal, separate living and dining rooms, there is the informal kitchen/family room area. Note the beamed ceiling, the fireplace, the sliding glass doors and the eating area of the family room.

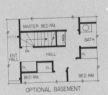

OPTIONAL BASEMENT

# Design T12737
**1,796 Sq. Ft.; 43,240 Cu. Ft.**

● You will be able to build this distinctive, modified U-shaped one-story home on a relatively narrow site. But, then, if you so wished, with the help of your architect and builder you may want to locate the garage to the side of the house. Inside, the living potential is just great. The interior U-shaped kitchen handily services the dining and family rooms and nook. A rear covered porch functions ideally with the family room while the formal living room has its own terrace. Three bedrooms and two baths highlight the sleeping zone (or make it two bedrooms and a study). Notice the strategic location of the wash room, laundry, two storage closets and the basement stairs.

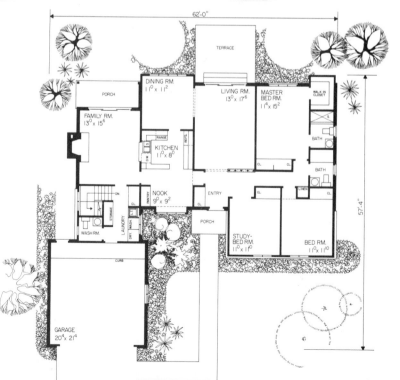

## Design T12742
**1,907 Sq. Ft.; 38,950 Cu. Ft.**

● Colonial charm is expressed in this one-story design by the vertical siding, the post pillars, the cross fence, paned glass windows and the use of stone. A 19' wide living room, a sloped ceilinged family room with a raised hearth fireplace and its own terrace, a kitchen with many built-ins and a dining room with built-in china cabinets are just some of the highlights. The living terrace is accessible from the dining room and master bedroom. There are two more bedrooms and a full bath in addition to the master bedroom.

## Design T12738
**1,898 Sq. Ft.; 36,140 Cu. Ft.**

● Impressive architectural work is indeed apparent in this three bedroom home. The three foot high entrance court wall, the high pitched roof and the paned glass windows all add to this home's appeal. It is also apparent that the floor plan is very efficient with the side U-shaped kitchen and nook with two pantry closets, the rear dining and gathering rooms and the three (or make it two with a study) bedrooms and two baths of the sleeping wing. Indoor-outdoor living also will be enjoyed in this home with a dining terrace off the nook and a living terrace off the gathering room and master bedroom. Note the fireplace in the gathering room and bay window in dining room.

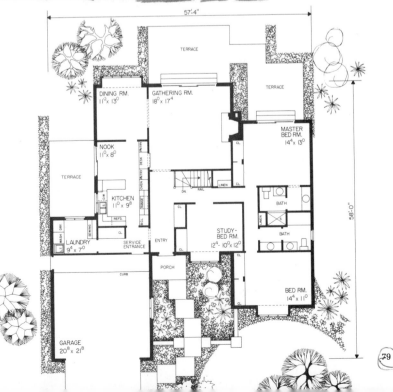

## Design T11075
**1,232 Sq. Ft.; 24,123 Cu. Ft.**

● This picturesque traditional one-story home has much to offer the young family. Because of its rectangular shape and its predominantly frame exterior, construction costs will be economical. Passing through the front entrance, visitors will be surprised to find so much livability in only 1,232 square feet. Consider these features: spacious formal living and dining area; two full baths; efficient kitchen; and large, rear family room. In addition there is the full basement for further recreational facilities and bulk storage. The attached garage is extra long to accommodate the storage of garden equipment, lawn furniture, bicycles, etc.

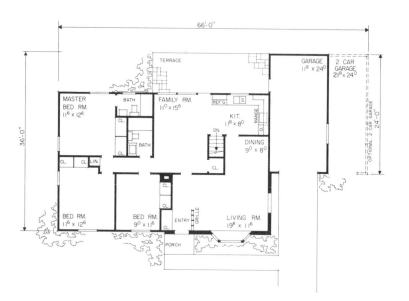

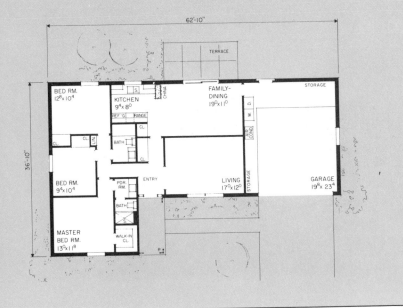

# Design T11366
## 1,280 Sq. Ft.; 14,848 Cu. Ft.

● The extension of the main roof, along with the use of ornamental iron, vertical siding and glass side lites flanking the paneled door, all contribute to a delightful and inviting front entrance to this L-shaped design. There is much to recommend this design—from the attached two-car garage to the walk-in closet of the master bedroom. Don't overlook the compartmented master bath with its stall shower and powder room; the built-in china cabinet with an attractive planter above or the two closets right in the center of the house.

# Design T11191
## 1,232 Sq. Ft.; 15,400 Cu. Ft.

● A careful study of the floor plan for this cozy appearing traditional home reveals a fine combination of features which add tremendously to convenient living. For instance, observe the wardrobe and storage facilities of the bedroom area. A built-in chest in the one bedroom and also one in the family room. Then, notice the economical plumbing of the two full back-to-back baths. Postively a great money saving feature for today and in the future. Further, don't overlook the location of the washer and dryer which have cupboards above the units themselves. Observe storage facilities. Optional two-car garage is available if necessary.

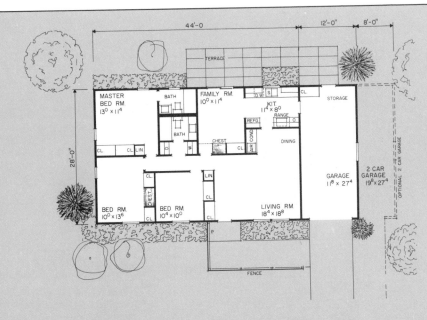

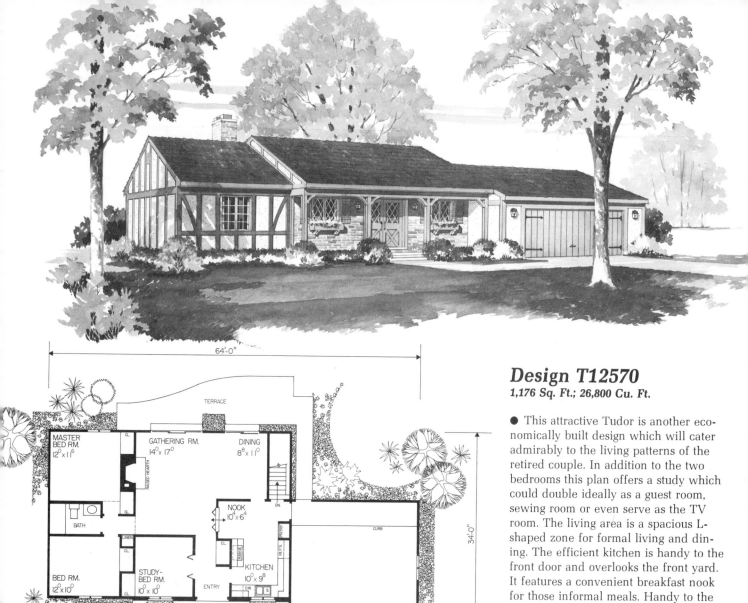

## Design T12570
### 1,176 Sq. Ft.; 26,800 Cu. Ft.

● This attractive Tudor is another economically built design which will cater admirably to the living patterns of the retired couple. In addition to the two bedrooms this plan offers a study which could double ideally as a guest room, sewing room or even serve as the TV room. The living area is a spacious L-shaped zone for formal living and dining. The efficient kitchen is handy to the front door and overlooks the front yard. It features a convenient breakfast nook for those informal meals. Handy to the entry from the garage and the yard are the stairs to the basement. Don't overlook the attractive front porch.

## Design T12864
### 1,387 Sq. Ft.; 29,160 Cu. Ft.

● Projecting the garage to the front of a house is very economical in two ways. One, it reduces the required lot size for building (in this case the overall width is under 50 feet). And, two, it will protect the interior from street noise and unfavorable winds. Many other characteristics about this design deserve mention, too. The entrance court and covered porch are a delightful way to enter this home. Upon entering, the foyer will take you to the various areas. The interior kitchen has an adjacent breakfast room and a snack bar on the gathering room side. Here, one will enjoy a sloped ceiling and a fireplace. A study with a wet bar is adjacent. If need be, adjust the plan and make the study the third bedroom. Sliding glass doors in the study and master bedroom open to the terrace.

## Design T12607
**1,208 Sq. Ft.; 15,183 Cu. Ft.**

● Here is an English Tudor retirement cottage. Its byword is "convenience". There are two sizable bedrooms, a full bath, plus an extra washroom. The living and dining areas are spacious and overlook both front and rear yards. Sliding glass doors in both these areas lead to the outdoor terrace. Note the fireplace in the living room. In addition to the formal dining area with its built-in china cabinet, there is a delightful breakfast eating alcove in the kitchen. The U-shaped work area is wonderfully efficient. The laundry is around the corner. Blueprints include optional basement details.

OPTIONAL BASEMENT

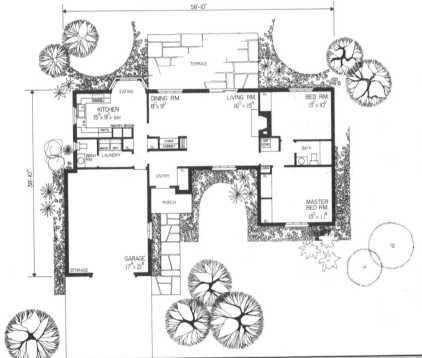

# Design T11311 1,050 Sq. Ft.; 11,370 Cu. Ft.

● Delightful design and effective, flexible planning comes in little packages, too. This fine traditional exterior with its covered front entrance features an alternate basement plan. Note how the non-basement layout provides a family room and mud room, while the basement option shows kitchen eating and dining room. Sensible planning.

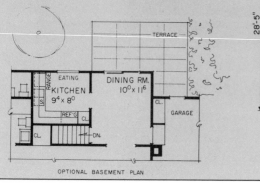

OPTIONAL BASEMENT PLAN

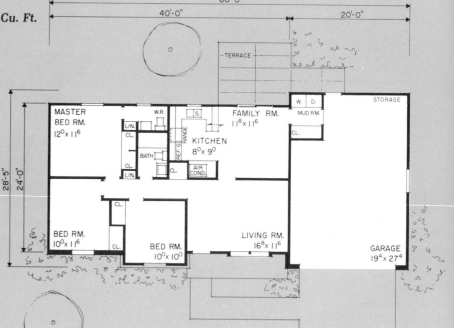

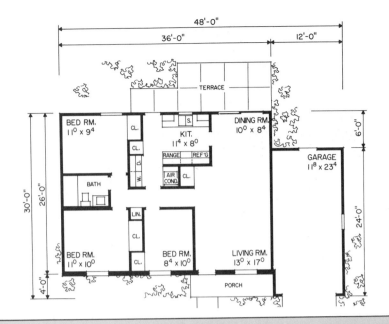

## Design T11531
**936 Sq. Ft.; 12,252 Cu. Ft.**

● This is but another example of delightful custom design applied to a small home. The detailing of the windows and the door, plus the effective use of siding and brick contribute to the charm. The attached garage helps make the house appear even bigger than it really is. The front-to-rear living/dining area opens onto the rear terrace through sliding glass doors. The washer and dryer with wall cabinets above complete the efficient work center area. Observe extra kitchen closet.

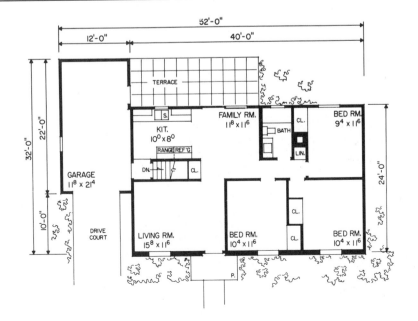

## Design T11522
**960 Sq. Ft.; 18,077 Cu. Ft.**

● Certainly a home to make its occupants proud. The front exterior is all brick veneer, while the remainder of the house and garage is horizontal siding. The slightly overhanging roof, the wood shutters and the carriage lights flanking the front door are among the features that will surely catch the eyes of the passer-by. The living room has excellent wall space for furniture placement. The family room, the full basement and the attached garage are other features. Don't miss the sliding glass doors.

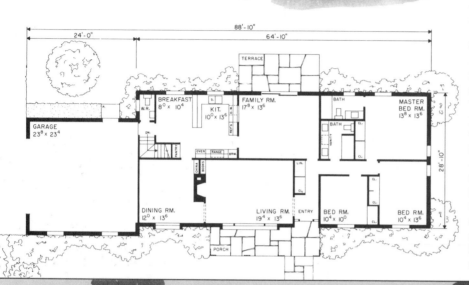

## Design T11130
### 1,856 Sq. Ft.; 36,044 Cu. Ft.

● A delightfully impressive and formal ranch home. The brick veneer, the ornamental iron columns supporting the overhanging gable, the window treatment and the cupola are among the features that contribute to the charm of this almost perfectly rectangular home. A study of the floor plan reveals excellent room relationships. The formal areas, the living and dining rooms, are adjacent to each other and overlook the front yard. The efficient kitchen is flanked by the informal breakfast area and the all-purpose family room.

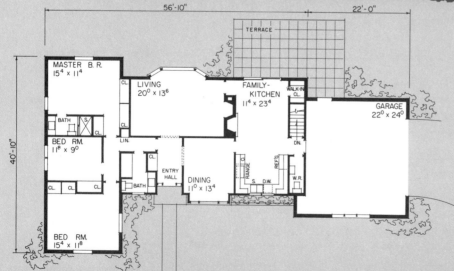

## Design T11091
### 1,666 Sq. Ft.; 28,853 Cu. Ft.

● What could be finer than to live in a delightfully designed home with all the charm of the exterior carried right inside. The interior points of interest are many. However, the focal point will surely be the family-kitchen. The work center is U-shaped and most efficient. The family activity portion of the kitchen features an attractive fireplace which will contribute to a feeling of warmth and fellowship. Nearby is the wash room and stairs to the basement.

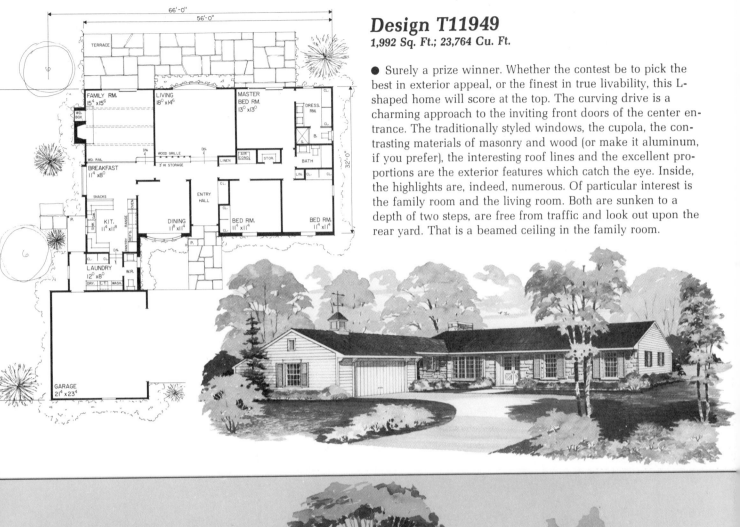

## Design T11949
**1,992 Sq. Ft.; 23,764 Cu. Ft.**

● Surely a prize winner. Whether the contest be to pick the best in exterior appeal, or the finest in true livability, this L-shaped home will score at the top. The curving drive is a charming approach to the inviting front doors of the center entrance. The traditionally styled windows, the cupola, the contrasting materials of masonry and wood (or make it aluminum, if you prefer), the interesting roof lines and the excellent proportions are the exterior features which catch the eye. Inside, the highlights are, indeed, numerous. Of particular interest is the family room and the living room. Both are sunken to a depth of two steps, are free from traffic and look out upon the rear yard. That is a beamed ceiling in the family room.

## Design T11346
**1,644 Sq. Ft.; 19,070 Cu. Ft.**

● Whether you enter through the service door of the attached garage, or through the centered front entry your appreciation of what this plan has to offer will grow. The mud room area is certainly an outstanding feature. Traffic flows from this area to the informal family room with its fireplace and access to the rear terrace.

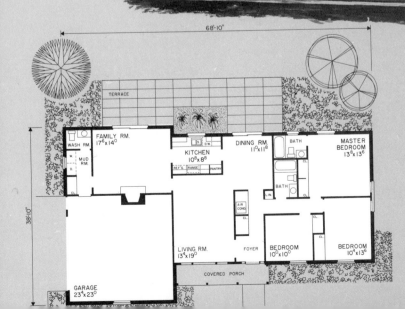

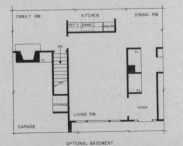

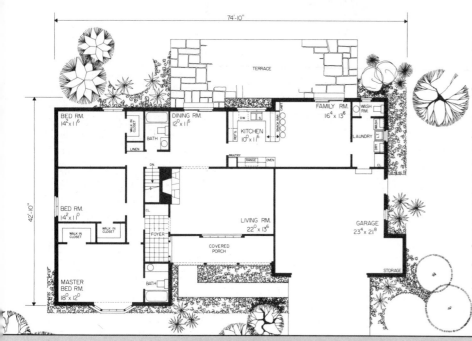

## Design T12603
**1,949 Sq. Ft.; 41,128 Cu. Ft.**

● Surely it would be difficult to beat the appeal of this traditional one-story home. Its slightly modified U-shape with the two front facing gables, the bay window, the covered front porch and the interesting use of exterior materials all add to the exterior charm. Besides, there are three large bedrooms serviced by two full baths and three walk-in closets. The excellent kitchen is flanked by the formal dining room and the informal family room. Don't miss the pantry, the built-in oven and the pass-thru to the snack bar. The handy first floor laundry is strategically located to act as a mud room. The extra wash room is but a few steps away. The sizable living room highlights a fireplace and a picture window. Note the location of the basement stairs.

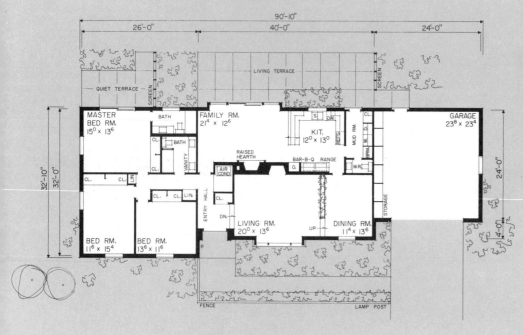

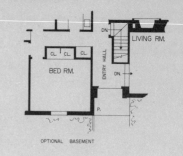

OPTIONAL BASEMENT

## Design T11748
**1,986 Sq. Ft.; 23,311 Cu. Ft.**

● A sunken living room, two fireplaces, 2½ baths, a rear family room, a formal dining room, a mud room and plenty of storage facilities are among the features of this popular design. Blueprints include optional basement details.

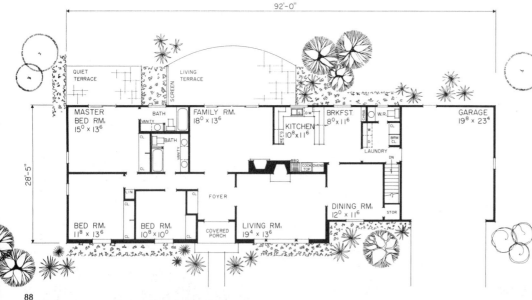

## Design T11325
**1,942 Sq. Ft.; 35,384 Cu. Ft.**

● The large front entry hall permits direct access to the formal living room, the sleeping area and the informal family room. Both of the living areas have a fireplace. When formal dining is the occasion of the evening, the separate dining room is but a step from the living room. The U-shaped kitchen is strategically flanked by the family room and the breakfast area.

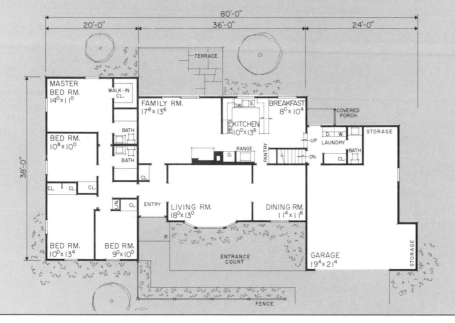

Floor plan labels for Design T11829:

80'-0" · 20'-0" · 36'-0" · 24'-0" · 38'-0"

TERRACE

MASTER BED RM. 14⁰ x 11⁰ · WALK-IN CL. · FAMILY RM. 17⁸ x 13⁶ · KITCHEN 10⁰ x 13⁶ · BREAKFAST 8⁰ x 10⁴ · COVERED PORCH

BED RM. 10⁸ x 10⁰ · BATH · BATH · REFG · DW · S · STORAGE · D. W. · LAUNDRY · UP · DN · BATH · CL.

CL. CL. CL. · O · RANGE · PANTRY

BED RM. 10⁰ x 13⁴ · BED RM. 9⁰ x 10⁰ · LIN · CL · ENTRY · LIVING RM. 18⁴ x 13⁰ · DINING RM. 11⁴ x 11⁶

P. · ENTRANCE COURT · GARAGE 19⁴ x 21⁴ · STORAGE

FENCE

## Design T11829
### 1,800 Sq. Ft.; 32,236 Cu. Ft.

● All the charm of a traditional heritage is wrapped up in this U-shaped home with its narrow, horizontal siding, delightful window treatment and high-pitched roof. The massive center chimney, the bay window and the double front doors are plus features. Inside, the living potential is outstanding. The sleeping wing is self-contained and has four bedrooms and two baths. The large family and living rooms cater to the divergent age groups.

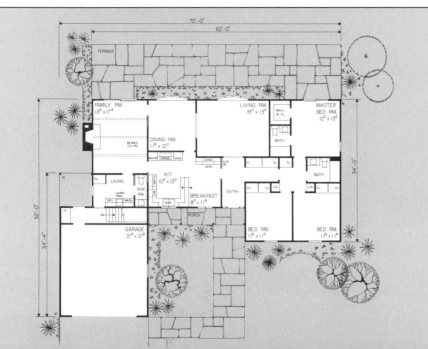

Floor plan labels for Design T11980:

70'-0" · 62'-0" · 34'-0" · 52'-0" · 34'-4"

TERRACE

FAMILY RM. 13⁴ x 17⁴ · DINING RM. 11⁸ x 12⁰ · BEAMED CEILING · LIVING RM. 18⁰ x 13⁴ · WALK-IN CL. · MASTER BED RM. 12⁰ x 13⁴ · BATH

PANTRY · RANGE · OVEN · CHINA · SLID. DR. · DESK · CL. · CL. · CL. · BATH

CL. · LAUND. · LAUND. TRAY · DRY · WASH · POR. RM. · KIT. 10⁰ x 13⁰ · ENTRY · CL. · CL. · LIN · LIN · CL.

CL. · ON · BREAKFAST 8⁰ x 11⁸ · PORCH · BED RM. 11⁶ x 11⁴ · BED RM. 11⁶ x 11⁴

GARAGE 21⁴ x 21⁸ · ENTRY

## Design T11980
### 1,901 Sq. Ft.; 36,240 Cu. Ft.

● Planned for easy living, the daily living patterns of the active family will be pleasant ones, indeed. All the elements are present to assure a wonderful family life. The impressive exterior is enhanced by the recessed front entrance area with its covered porch. The center entry results in a convenient and efficient flow of traffic. A secondary entrance leads from the covered side porch, or the garage, into the first floor laundry. Note the powder room nearby.

## Design T12360
*1,936 Sq. Ft.; 37,026 Cu. Ft.*

● There is no such thing as taking a fleeting glance at this charming home. Fine proportion and pleasing lines assure a long and rewarding study. Inside, the family's everyday routine will enjoy all the facilities which will surely guarantee pleasurable living. Note the sunken living room with its fireplace flanked by storage cabinets and book shelves. Observe the excellent kitchen just a step from the dining room and the nook.

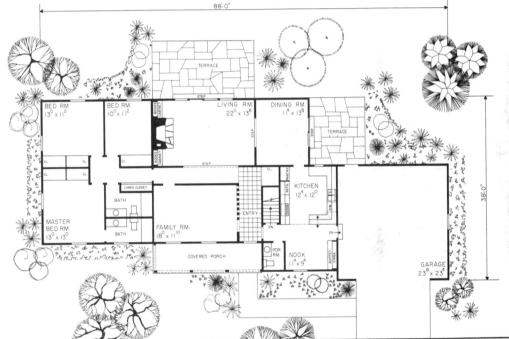

## Design T12741
**1,842 Sq. Ft.; 37,045 Cu. Ft.**

● Here is another example of what 1,800 square feet can deliver in comfort and convenience. The setting reminds one of the sun country of Arizona. However, this design would surely be an attractive and refreshing addition to any region. The covered front porch with its adjacent open trellis area shelters the center entry. From here traffic flows efficiently to the sleeping, living and kitchen zones. There is much to recommend each area. The sleeping with its fine bath and closet facilities; the living with its spaciousness, fireplace and adjacent dining room; the kitchen with its handy nook, excellent storage, nearby laundry and extra wash room.

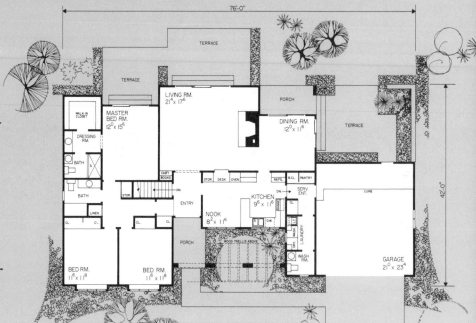

## Design T12386
**1,994 Sq. Ft.; 22,160 Cu. Ft.**

● This distinctive home may look like the Far West, but don't let that inhibit you from enjoying the great livability it has to offer. Wherever built, you will surely experience a satisfying pride of ownership. Imagine, an entrance court in addition to a large side courtyard! A central core is made up of the living, dining and family rooms, plus the kitchen. Each functions with an outdoor living area. The younger generation has its sleeping zone divorced from the master bedroom. The location of the attractive attached garage provides direct access to the front entry. Don't miss the vanity, the utility room with laundry equipment, the snack bar and the raised hearth fireplace. Note three pass-thrus from the kitchen. Observe the beamed and sloping ceilings of the living areas.

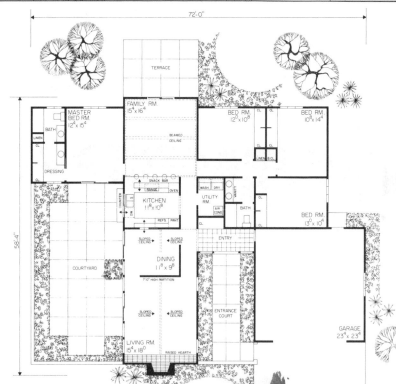

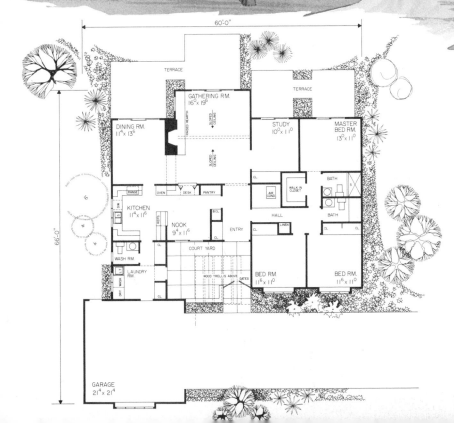

## Design T12743
### 1,892 Sq. Ft.; 23,300 Cu. Ft.

● For those who feel they really don't require both a living and a family room, this refreshing contemporary will serve its occupants well, indeed. Ponder deeply its space and livability; for this design makes a lot of economic sense, too. First of all, placing the attached garage at the front cuts down on the size of a site required. It also represents an appealing design factor. The privacy wall and overhead trellis provide a pleasant front courtyard. Inside, the gathering room satisfies the family's more gregarious instincts, while there is always the study nearby to serve as a more peaceful haven. The separate dining room and the nook offer dining flexibility. The two full baths highlight the economical back-to-back plumbing feature. Note the rear terraces.

## Design T12232
### 1,776 Sq. Ft.; 17,966 Cu. Ft.

● This appealing, flat roof design has its roots in the Spanish Southwest. The arched, covered porch with its heavy beamed ceiling sets the note of distinction. The center foyer routes traffic effectively to the main zones of the house. Down a step is the sunken living room. Privacy will be the byword here. The cluster of three bedrooms features two full baths and good storage facilities.

## Design T12200
### 1,695 Sq. Ft.; 18,916 Cu. Ft.

● If you have a penchant for something delightfully different this Spanish adaptation may be just what you've been waiting for. This ranch home with an L-shape will go well on any site - large or small. A popular feature will be the entry court. Of great interest is the indoor-outdoor relationships. Observe how the major rooms function through sliding glass doors with the terraces.

## Design T11726
1,910 Sq. Ft.; 19,264 Cu. Ft.

● The U-shaped plan has long been honored for its excellent zoning. As the floor plan for this fine Spanish adaptation illustrates, it not only provides separation between parents' area and children's wing, but also it places a buffer area in the center. This makes the kitchen the "control center" for the home - handy to the family room, living room and the dining alcove.

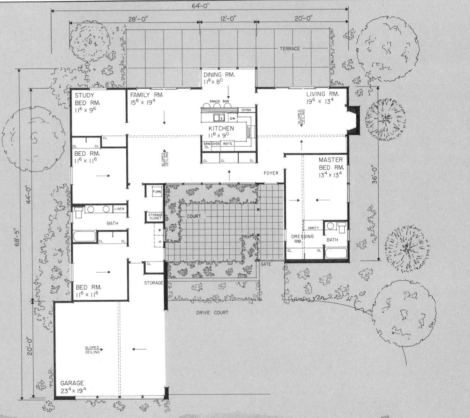

## Design T12707
**1,267 Sq. Ft.; 27,125 Cu. Ft.**

50'-0"

TERRACE

BATH
MASTER
BED RM.
12⁰ x 11⁰

LIVING RM.
18⁴ x 16⁸

RAISED HEARTH

DINING RM
13⁰ x 10⁴

BATH

EATING

KITCHEN
13⁵-9⁰ x 12⁸

HALL

CL

LIN

ENTRY

STORAGE

DN

OVENS RANGE

BED RM.
9⁸ x 10⁴

CL

BED RM-
STUDY
9⁸ x 10⁴

PORCH

CURB

46'-0"

GARAGE
21⁴ x 21⁸

● Here is a charming Early American adaptation that will serve as a picturesque and practical retirement home. Also, it will serve admirable those with a small family in search of an efficient, economically built home. The living area, highlighted by the raised hearth fireplace, is spacious. The kitchen features eating space and easy access to the garage and basement. The dining room is adjacent to the kitchen and views the rear yard. Then, there is the basement for recreation and hobby pursuits. The bedroom wing offers three bedrooms and two full baths. Don't miss the sliding doors to the terrace from the living room and the master bedroom. The storage units are plentiful including a pantry cabinet in the eating area of the kitchen.

## Design T12597
**1,515 Sq. Ft.; 32,000 Cu. Ft.**

71'-8"

TERRACE

TERRACE

STORAGE

WALK IN CLOSET

MASTER
BED RM.
11⁰ x 15⁶

GATHERING RM.
26⁸ x 15⁶

DINING

BATH

CURB

BATH

CL

CL

R.D.
RANGE OVEN

DN

REF'S.

36'-0"

LINEN

HALL

STOR

ENTRY

KITCHEN
10⁰ x 11⁶

NOOK
8⁴ x 11⁶

GARAGE
23⁴ x 23⁴

BED RM.
11⁰ x 11²

BED RM.
10⁰ x 11²

PORCH

● Whether it be a starter house you are after, or one in which to spend your retirement years, this pleasing frame home will provide a full measure of pride of ownership. The contrast of vertical and horizontal lines, the double front doors and the coach lamp post at the garage create an inviting exterior. The floor plan functions in an orderly and efficient manner. The 26 foot gathering room has a delightful view of the rear yard and will take care of those formal dining occasions. Two full baths serve the three bedrooms. Plenty of storage facilities, two sets of glass doors to the terraces, a fireplace in the gathering room, a basement and an attached two-car garage to act as a buffer against the wind highlight this traditional design. A delightful home, indeed.

# 1½-STORY HOMES

The low profile of the 1½-story home is so often associated with the traditional Cape Cod design. Here is a selection offering variations of the Williamsburg and New England themes. In addition, there is an interesting representation of Tudor and Contemporary styles. Designs for low to expanded budgets range from 1200 to 3477 square feet. Many with first floor bedrooms offer expansible potential. A study of the floor plans will reveal a delightful array of living patterns.

## Design T12520 1,419 Sq. Ft. - First Floor
1,040 Sq. Ft. - Second Floor; 39,370 Cu. Ft.

● From Tidewater Virginia comes this historic adaptation, a positive reminder of the charm of Early American architecture. Note how the center entrance gives birth to fine traffic circulation. List the numerous features.

# Design T12569

**1,102 Sq. Ft. - First Floor**
**764 Sq. Ft. - Second Floor; 29,600 Cu. Ft.**

● What an enchanting updated version of the popular Cape Cod cottage. There are facilities for both formal and informal living pursuits. Note first floor laundry.

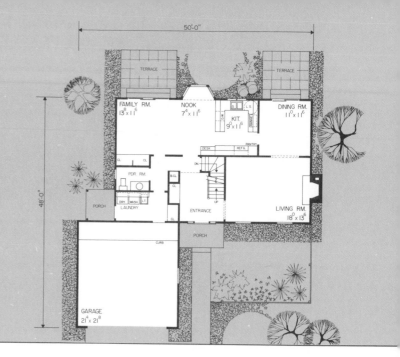

# Design T12559

**1,388 Sq. Ft. - First Floor**
**809 Sq. Ft. - Second Floor; 36,400 Cu. Ft.**

● Imagine, a 26 foot living room with fireplace, a quiet study with built-in bookshelves and excellent dining facilities. Within such an appealing exterior, too.

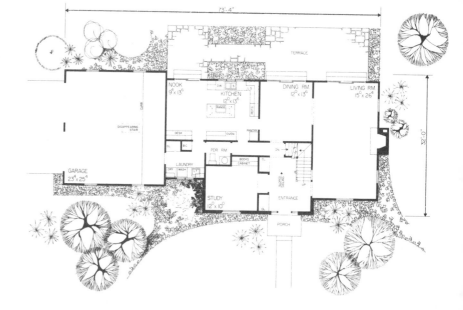

# Design T12563

**1,500 Sq. Ft. - First Floor**
**690 Sq. Ft. - Second Floor; 38,243 Cu. Ft.**

● You'll have all kinds of fun deciding just how your family will function in this dramatically expanded half-house. There is lots of attic storage, too. Observe three-car garage.

## Design T11365
*975 Sq. Ft. - First Floor*
*583 Sq. Ft. - Second Floor*
*20,922 Cu. Ft.*

● Here are three wonderfully livable houses. Each provides facilities to function as either three or four bedroom, two bath homes. Compare each of the three designs. Consider them in light of your building budget and your family's living requirements. Whichever design you choose it will be a credit to your family's design taste.

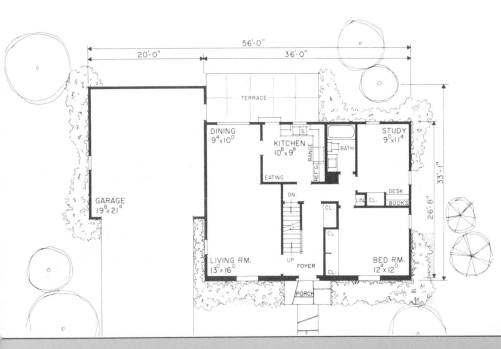

## Design T12395
*1,481 Sq. Ft. - First Floor*
*861 Sq. Ft. - Second Floor*
*34,487 Cu. Ft.*

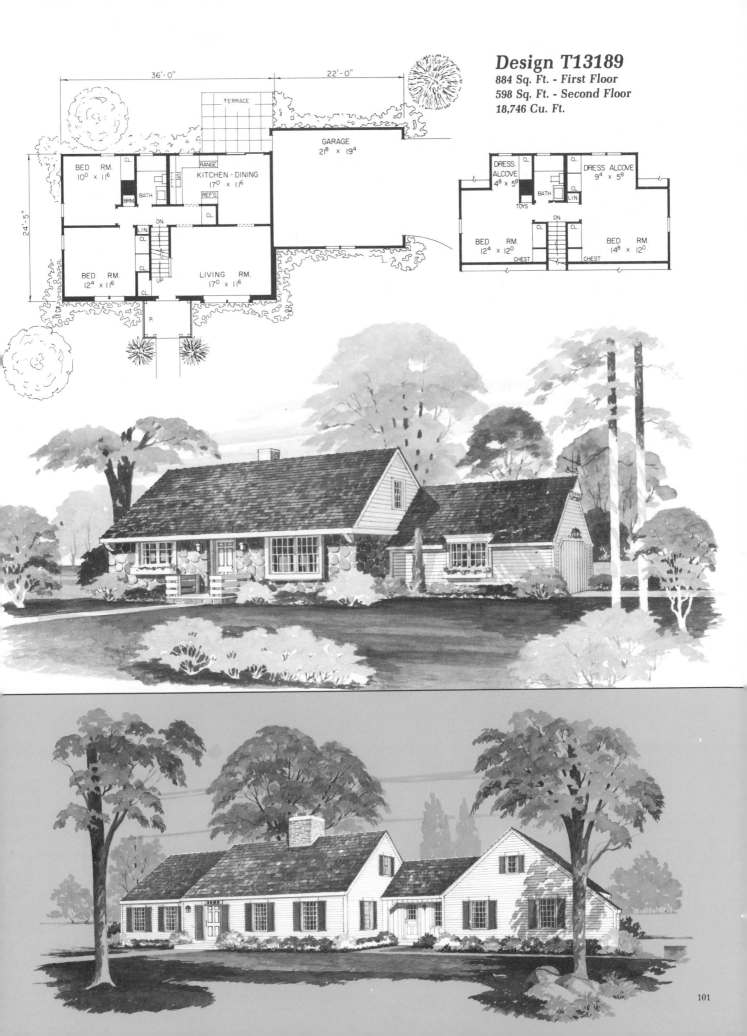

## Design T13189
884 Sq. Ft. - First Floor
598 Sq. Ft. - Second Floor
18,746 Cu. Ft.

36'-0"

22'-0"

TERRACE

GARAGE
21⁸ x 19⁴

BED RM.
10⁰ x 11⁶

RANGE

KITCHEN - DINING
17⁰ x 11⁶

BATH

REF'G

CL.

BRM.

CL.

24'-5"

LIN
CL.

DN.

CL.

CL.

BED RM.
12⁴ x 11⁶

UP

LIVING RM.
17⁰ x 11⁶

CL.

P.

DRESS.
ALCOVE
4⁸ x 5⁸

CL.

CL.

DRESS ALCOVE
9⁴ x 5⁸

BATH

LIN.

TOYS

BED RM.
12⁴ x 12⁰

CL.

DN.

CL.

CL.

BED RM.
14⁸ x 12⁰

CHEST

CHEST

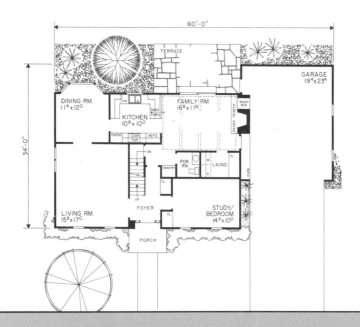

## Design T11791
**1,157 Sq. Ft. - First Floor**
**875 Sq. Ft. - Second Floor**
**27,790 Cu. Ft.**

● Wherever you build this moderately sized house an aura of Cape Cod is sure to unfold. The symmetry is pleasing, indeed. The authenic center entrance seems to project a beckoning call.

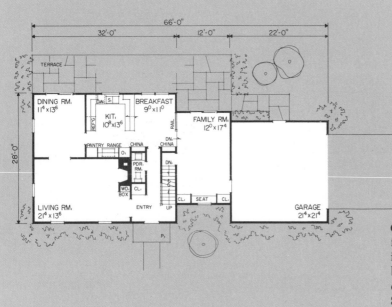

## Design T11870
**1,136 Sq. Ft. - First Floor**
**936 Sq. Ft. - Second Floor**
**26,312 Cu. Ft.**

● Besides an enchanting exterior, this home has formal dining and living rooms, plus informal family and breakfast rooms. Built-ins are located in both of these informal rooms. U-shaped, the kitchen will efficiently service both of the dining areas. Study the sleeping facilities of the second floor.

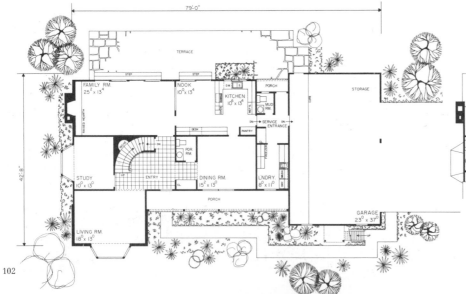

## Design T12513
**1,799 Sq. Ft. - First Floor**
**1,160 Sq. Ft. - Second Floor**
**47,461 Cu. Ft.**

● What an appealing story-and-a-half design. Delightful, indeed, is the colonial detailing of the garage. The large entry hall with its open curving staircase is dramatic.

102

**Design T11766** 1,638 Sq. Ft. - First Floor; 1,006 Sq. Ft. - Second Floor; 35,352 Cu. Ft.

● Here is a home that truly fits the description of traditional charm. The symmetry is, indeed, delightful. A certain magnetic aura seems to reach out with a whisper of welcome. Observe the spacious family-kitchen area, the study, the separate dining room and the extra bath.

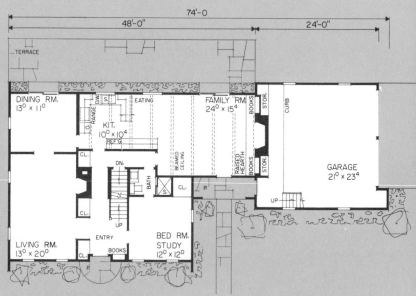

**Design T12124**
1,176 Sq. Ft. - First Floor
922 Sq. Ft. - Second Floor; 29,854 Cu. Ft.

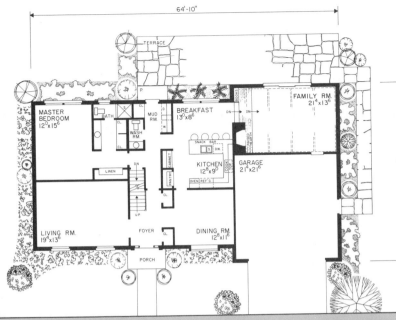

● This cozy home has over 2,600 square feet of livable floor area! And the manner in which this space is put to work to function conveniently for the large family is worth studying. Imagine five bedrooms, three full baths, living, dining and family rooms. Note large kitchen.

**Design T11701** 1,344 Sq. Ft. - First Floor; 948 Sq. Ft. - Second Floor; 33,952 Cu. Ft.

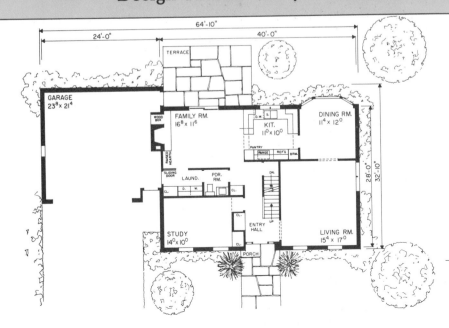

● Surely your list of favorite features will be fun to compile. It certainly will be a long one. The center entry hall helps establish excellent traffic patterns and good zoning. The formal living and dining rooms function well together, as do the kitchen and family room. Note laundry and study.

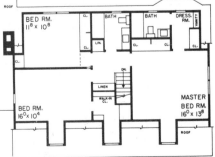

105

## Design T12776 1,134 Sq. Ft. - First Floor
874 Sq. Ft. - Second Floor; 31,600 Cu. Ft.

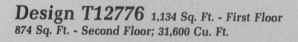

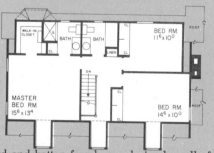

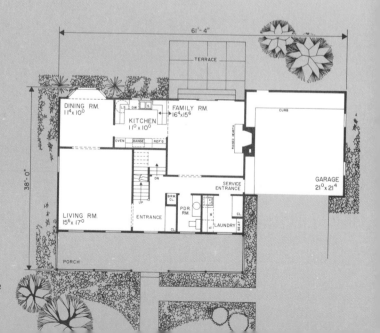

● This board-and-batten farmhouse design has all of the country charm of New England. The large, front covered porch will be appreciated during the beautiful warm weather months. Immediately off the front entrance is the delightful corner living room. The dining room with bay window will be easily served by the U-shaped kitchen. The second floor houses all of the sleeping facilities.

## Design T12500
**1,851 Sq. Ft. - First Floor**
**762 Sq. Ft. - Second Floor**
**43,052 Cu. Ft.**

● The large family will enjoy the wonderful living patterns offered by this charming home. Don't miss the covered rear porch and the many features of the family room.

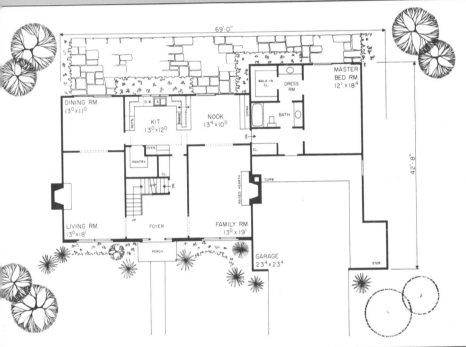

## Design T12501
**1,699 Sq. Ft. - First Floor**
**758 Sq. Ft. - Second Floor**
**37,693 Cu. Ft.**

● Whether you build this inviting home with a fieldstone front, or substitute with a different material of your choice, you can be assured that you've selected a great home for your family.

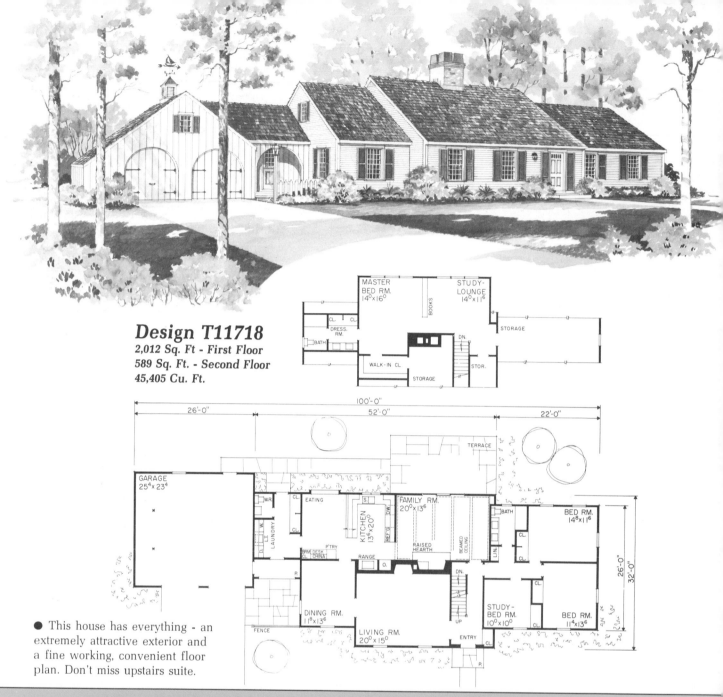

## Design T11718

2,012 Sq. Ft - First Floor
589 Sq. Ft. - Second Floor
45,405 Cu. Ft.

Second floor plan labels:
MASTER BED RM. 14⁰x16⁰ · STUDY-LOUNGE 14⁰x11⁶ · BOOKS · CL. · CL. · DRESS. RM. · BATH · DN. · STORAGE · WALK-IN CL · STORAGE · STOR.

First floor plan labels:
100'-0" · 26'-0" · 52'-0" · 22'-0" · TERRACE · GARAGE 25⁴x23⁴ · W.R. · CL. · EATING · S. · FAMILY RM. 20⁰x13⁶ · BATH · BED RM. 14⁸x11⁶ · CL. · D. · W. · LT. LAUNDRY · CL. · KITCHEN 13⁶x20⁰ · REF'G · DW · CL. · LIN. · CL. · DN. · BRK DESK · CL. CHINA · RANGE · RAISED HEARTH · BEAMED CEILING · CL. · P'TRY · P. · RANGE · O. · DN. · STUDY-BED RM. 10⁰x10⁰ · CL. · BED RM. 11⁴x13⁶ · 26'-0" · 32'-0" · DINING RM. 11⁸x13⁶ · FENCE · LIVING RM. 20⁰x15⁰ · UP · ENTRY · CL. · P.

● This house has everything - an extremely attractive exterior and a fine working, convenient floor plan. Don't miss upstairs suite.

## Design T11794

**2,122 Sq. Ft. - First Floor**
**802 Sq. Ft. - Second Floor**
**37,931 Cu. Ft.**

● The inviting warmth of this delightful story-and-a-half home catches the eye of even the most casual observer. Imagine, four big bedrooms! Formal and informal living can be enjoyed throughout this charming plan. Two fireplaces. One has a raised hearth and an adjacent wood box. A very private, formal dining room for those very special occasions. A U-shaped kitchen pass-thru to family room. Note the two distinct rear terraces.

## Design T11987

**1,632 Sq. Ft. - First Floor**
**980 Sq. Ft. - Second Floor**
**35,712 Cu. Ft.**

● The comforts of home will surely be endless and enduring when experienced and enjoyed in this Colonial adaptation. What's your favorite feature?

● A versatile plan, wrapped in a pleasing traditional facade, to cater to the demands of even the most active of families. There is plenty of living space for both formal and informal activities. With two bedrooms upstairs and two down, sleeping accommodations are excellently planned to serve all.

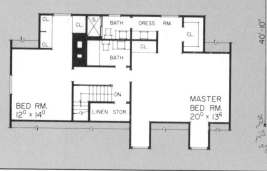

● A great plan! The large family will find its living requirements satisfied admirably all throughout those active years of growing up. This would make a fine expansible house. The upstairs may be finished off as the size of the family increases and budget permits. Complete living requirements can be obtained on the first floor.

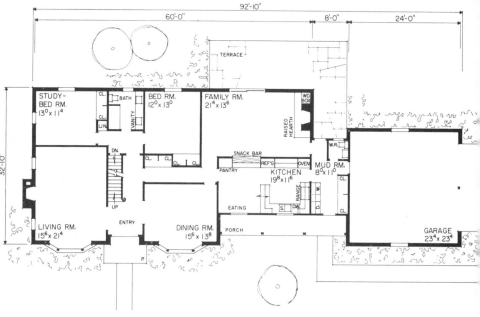

● A study of the first and second floors of this charming design will reveal that nothing has been omitted to assure convenient living. List your family's living requirements and then observe how this house will proceed to satisfy them. Features galore.

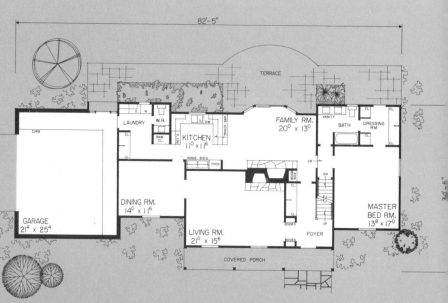

**Design T11790** 1,782 Sq. Ft. - First Floor; 920 Sq. Ft. - Second Floor; 37,359 Cu. Ft.

**Design T11793** 1,986 Sq. Ft. - First Floor; 944 Sq. Ft. - Second Floor; 35,800 Cu. Ft.

**Design T11736** 1,618 Sq. Ft. - First Floor; 952 Sq. Ft. - Second Floor; 34,106 Cu. Ft.

## Design T12661

*1,020 Sq. Ft. - First Floor*
*777 Sq. Ft. - Second Floor; 30,745 Cu. Ft.*

● Any other starter house or retirement home couldn't have more charm than this design. Its compact frame houses a very livable plan. An outstanding feature of the first floor is the large country kitchen. Its fine attractions include a beamed ceiling, raised hearth fireplace, built-in window seat and a door leading to the outdoors. A living room is in the front of the plan and has another fireplace which shares the single chimney. The rear dormered second floor houses the sleeping and bath facilities.

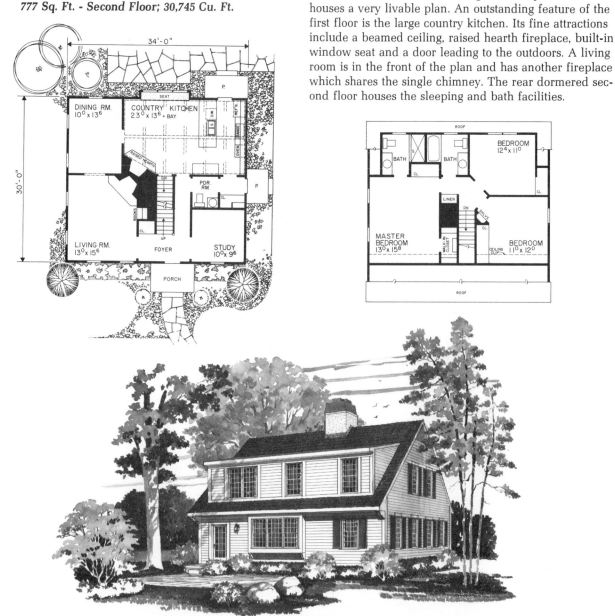

## Design T12655

893 Sq. Ft. - First Floor
652 Sq. Ft. - Second Floor; 22,555 Cu. Ft.

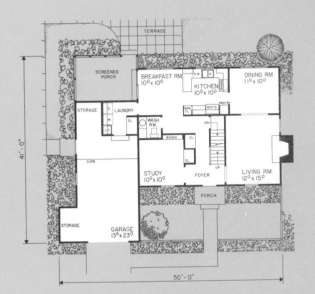

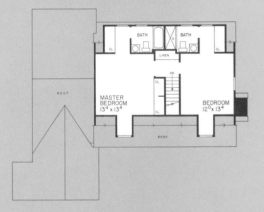

● Wonderful things can be enclosed in small packages. This is the case for this one-and-a-half story design. The total square footage is a mere 1,545 square feet yet its features are many, indeed. Its exterior appeal is very eye-pleasing with horizontal lines and two second story dormers. Livability will be enjoyed in this plan. The front study is ideal for a quiet escape. Nearby is a powder room also convenient to the kitchen and breakfast room. Two bedrooms and two full baths are located on the second floor.

## Design T11372
**768 Sq. Ft. - First Floor**
**432 Sq. Ft. - Second Floor**
**17,280 Cu. Ft.**

● Low cost livability could hardly ask for more. Here, is an enchanting exterior and a four bedroom floor plan. Note stairs to basement.

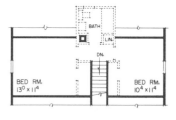

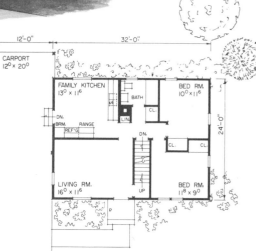

## Design T12162
**741 Sq. Ft. - First Floor**
**504 Sq. Ft. - Second Floor**
**17,895 Cu. Ft.**

● This economical design delivers great exterior appeal and fine livability. In addition to kitchen eating space there is a separate dining room.

# Design T11394

832 Sq. Ft. - First Floor
512 Sq. Ft. - Second Floor
18,453 Cu. Ft.

● The growing family with a restricted building budget will find this a great investment - a convenient living floor plan inside an attractive facade.

# Design T12510

1,191 Sq. Ft. - First Floor
533 Sq. Ft. - Second Floor
27,500 Cu. Ft.

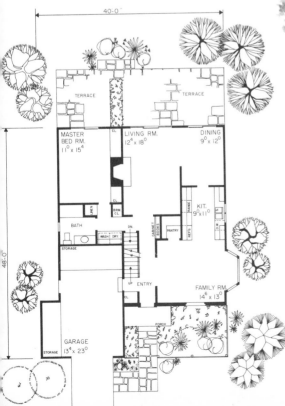

● The pleasant in-line kitchen is flanked by a separate dining room and a family room. The master bedroom is on the first floor with two more bedrooms upstairs.

# Design T12571

**1,137 Sq. Ft. - First Floor**
**795 Sq. Ft. - Second Floor; 28,097 Cu. Ft.**

● Cost-efficient space! That's the bonus with this attractive Cape Cod. An efficient kitchen! With a pass-through to the family room and a large storage pantry. Three bedrooms on second floor.

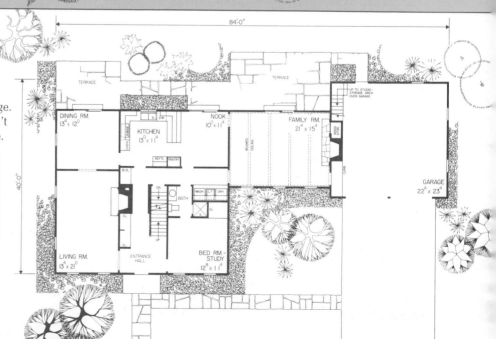

# Design T12596

**1,489 Sq. Ft. - First Floor**
**982 Sq. Ft. - Second Floor; 38,800 Cu. Ft.**

● Captivating as a New England village! From the weathervane atop the garage to the roofed side entry and paned windows, this home is perfectly detailed.

# Design T12396

**1,616 Sq. Ft. - First Floor**
**993 Sq. Ft. - Second Floor**
**30,583 Cu. Ft.**

● Another picturesque facade right from the pages of our Colonial heritage. The authentic features are many. Don't miss the stairs to area over the garage.

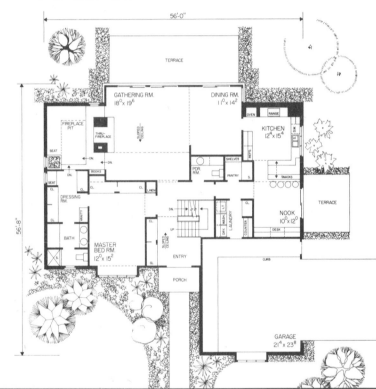

### Design T12718
**1,941 Sq. Ft. - First Floor**
**791 Sq. Ft. - Second Floor; 49,895 Cu. Ft.**

● You and your family will just love the new living patterns you'll experience in this story-and-a-half home. Livability will be equally as great on the second floor as well as the first.

## Design T12757

**2,052 Sq. Ft. - First Floor**
**1,425 Sq. Ft. - Second Floor; 56,775 Cu. Ft.**

● An L-shaped story-and-a-half with a traditional facade is hard to beat for pure charm. Here, the use of contrasting exterior materials - fieldstone, brick, vertical siding - along with delightful window treatment, recessed front door, carriage lamps, two massive chimneys and a cupola all make a contribution to outright appeal.

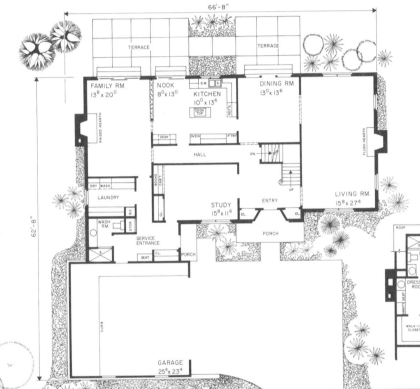

## Design T12174    1,506 Sq. Ft. - First Floor
**1,156 Sq. Ft. - Second Floor; 37,360 Cu. Ft.**

● Your building budget could hardly buy more charm, or greater livability. The appeal of the exterior is wrapped up in a myriad of design features. The livability of the interior is represented by a long list of features.

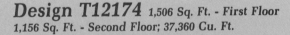

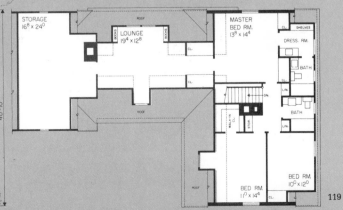

## Design T12854 1,261 Sq. Ft. - First Floor
**950 Sq. Ft. - Second Floor; 36,820 Cu. Ft.**

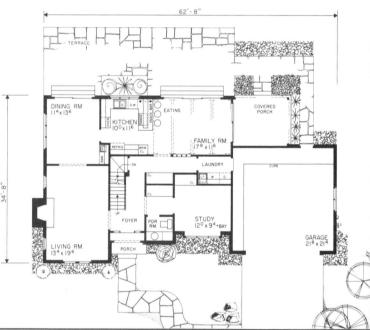

● The flair of old England has been captured in this outstanding one-and-a-half story design. The first floor offers both formal and informal areas along with the work centers. Note some of the various features which include a wet-bar in the dining room, the kitchen's snack bar, first floor laundry and rear covered porch to mention a few. Don't miss the uniqueness of the lounge/nursery area which is attached to the master bedroom.

## Design T11991

**1,262 Sq. Ft. - First Floor**
**1,108 Sq. Ft. - Second Floor**
**31,073 Cu. Ft.**

● Put yourself and your family in this English cottage adaptation and you'll all rejoice over your new home for many a year. The pride of owning and living in a home that is distinctive will be a constant source of satisfaction. Count the features that will serve your family well for years.

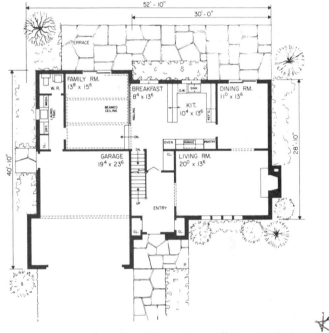

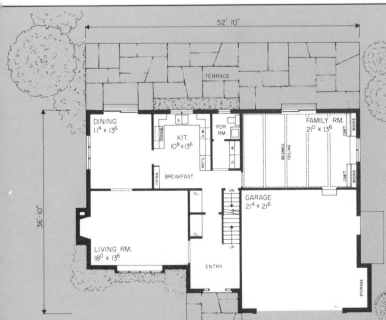

## Design T12175 1,206 Sq. Ft. - First Floor

**1,185 Sq. Ft. - Second Floor; 32,655 Cu. Ft.**

● An English adaptation with all the amenities for gracious living. Note built-ins.

121

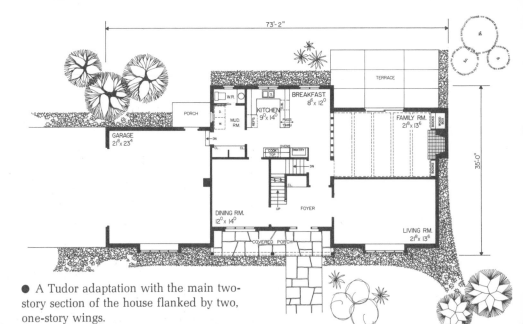

## Design T12242

**1,327 Sq. Ft. - First Floor**
**832 Sq. Ft. - Second Floor**
**35,315 Cu. Ft.**

● A Tudor adaptation with the main two-story section of the house flanked by two, one-story wings.

● This is a most interesting home; both inside and out. Its L-shape with covered porch and diamond lite windows is appealing.

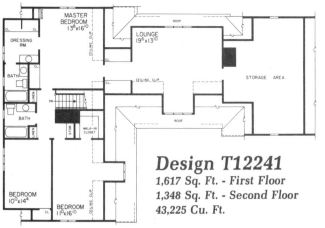

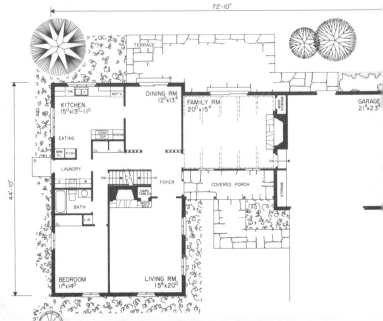

## Design T12241

**1,617 Sq. Ft. - First Floor**
**1,348 Sq. Ft. - Second Floor**
**43,225 Cu. Ft.**

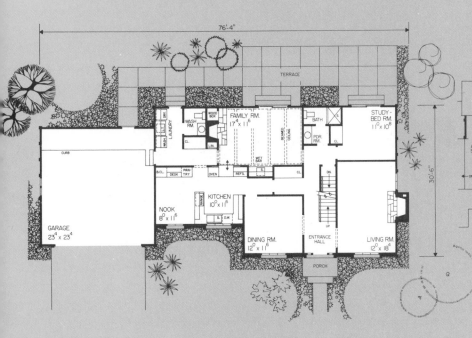

## Design T12626
**1,420 Sq. Ft. - First Floor**
**859 Sq. Ft. - Second Floor; 34,974 Cu. Ft.**

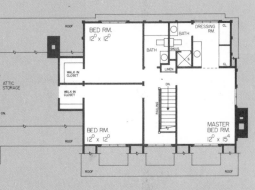

● This charming, one-and-a-half story home surely elicits thoughts of an English countryside. It has a beckoning warmth that seems to foretell a friendly welcome. The exterior features are appealing, indeed.

## Design T12780
**2,006 Sq. Ft. - First Floor**
**718 Sq. Ft. - Second Floor; 42,110 Cu. Ft.**

● This 1½-story contemporary has more fine features than one can imagine. The livability is outstanding and can be appreciated by the whole family. Note the fine indoor-outdoor living relationships.

## Design T12772
**1,579 Sq. Ft. - First Floor**
**1,240 Sq. Ft. - Second Floor; 39,460 Cu. Ft.**

● This four-bedroom two-story contemporary design is sure to suit your growing family needs. The rear U-shaped kitchen, flanked by the family and dining rooms, will be very efficient to the busy homemaker. Parents will enjoy all the convenience of the master bedroom suite.

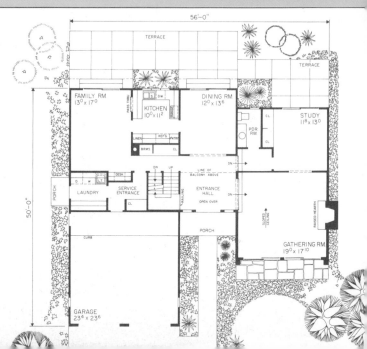

## Design T12771

**2,087 Sq. Ft. - First Floor**
**816 Sq. Ft. - Second Floor; 53,285 Cu. Ft.**

● This design will provide an abundance of livability for your family. The second floor is highlighted by an open lounge which overlooks both the entry and the gathering room below.

## Design T12708

2,108 Sq. Ft. - First Floor
824 Sq. Ft. - Second Floor; 52,170 Cu. Ft.

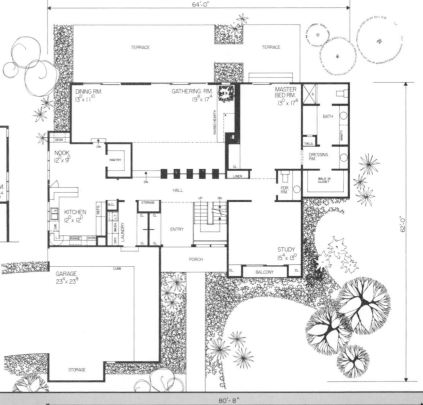

● Here is a one-and-a-half story home whose exterior is distinctive. It has a contemporary feeling, yet it retains some of the fine design features and proportions of traditional exteriors. Inside the appealing double front doors there is livability galore. The sunken rear living-dining area is delightfully spacious. The open end fireplace with its raised hearth and planter is the living area's focal point.

## Design T12782

2,060 Sq. Ft. - First Floor
897 Sq. Ft. - Second Floor; 47,750 Cu. Ft.

## Design T12581 2,125 Sq. Ft. - First Floor
903 Sq. Ft. - Second Floor; 54,476 Cu. Ft.

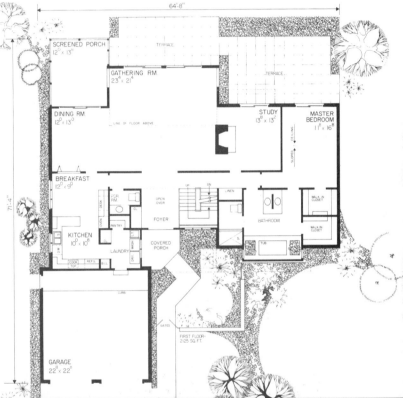

● The exterior of this contemporary design has a projecting, front entrance garage. This feature in itself is significant since it results in the need of a much smaller building site; perhaps an important consideration in this day of high land costs. Pay special attention to the bathroom off the master bedroom. It features a walk-in closet, two lavatories, double entrance and a tub plus a stall shower. Don't miss the sizable screened-in porch.

● You don't need a mansion to live graciously. What you do need is a practical floor plan which takes into consideration the varied activities of the busy family. This story-and-a-half design will not require a large piece of property. Its living potential is tremendous.

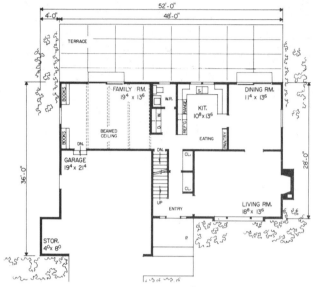

## Design T11241
### 1,064 Sq. Ft. - First Floor
### 898 Sq. Ft. - Second Floor; 24,723 Cu. Ft.

● Positively outstanding. From the delightful flower court to the upstairs storage room, this New England adaptation has much about which to talk. There is the U-shaped kitchen, the family-dining room, the four bedrooms, the two full baths, the fireplace, the numerous closets, the covered porch and two-car garage.

## Design T13126
### 1,141 Sq. Ft. - First Floor
### 630 Sq. Ft. - Second Floor; 25,533 Cu. Ft.

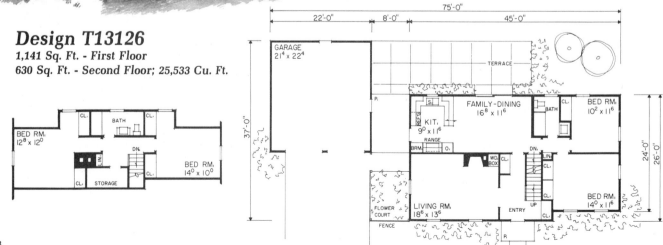

# OPTIONAL EXTERIORS & PLANS . . .

*Occasionally, one's enthusiasm for a favorite floor plan may not be matched by a similar feeling about that plan's exterior styling. And, of course, within families, members may differ about their style preferences. The designs in this section offer an excellent opportunity to observe how (with minor modifications) a given floor plan can have different exteriors. This presents an option of which exterior to build. As shown, different types of houses can include variations of Early American, Tudor, Contemporary, French, Spanish and Western as styling options.*

## Design T11715 1,276 Sq. Ft. - First Floor; 1,064 Sq. Ft. - Second Floor; 31,295 Cu. Ft.

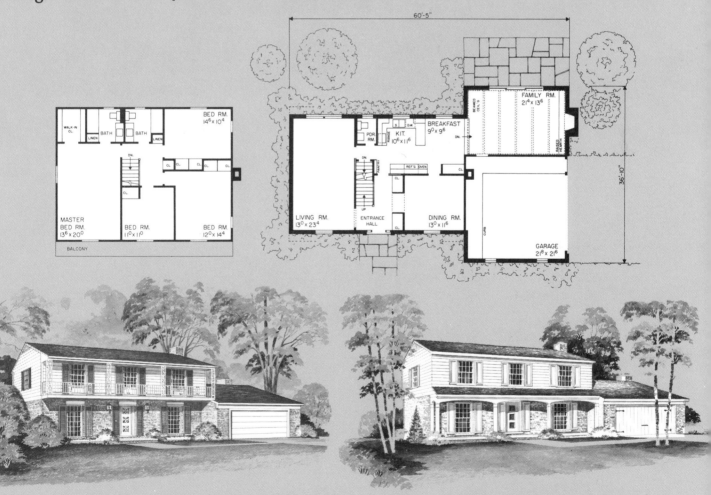

● The blueprints you order for this design show details for building each of these three appealing exteriors. Which do you like best? Whatever your choice, the interior will provide the growing family with all the facilities for fine living.

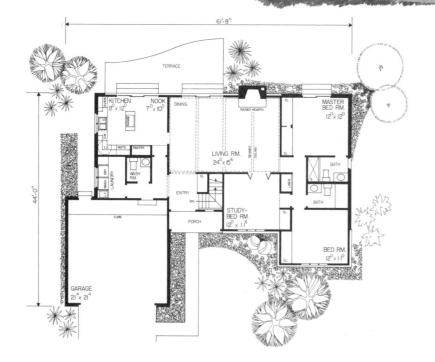

## Design T12565
### 1,540 Sq. Ft.; 33,300 Cu. Ft.

● This modest sized floor plan has much to offer in the way of livability. It may function as either a two or three bedroom home. The living room is huge and features a fine, raised hearth fireplace. The open stairway to the basement is handy and will lead to what may be developed as the recreation area. In addition to the two full baths, there is an extra wash room. Adjacent is the laundry room and the service entrance from the garage. The blueprints you order for this design will show details for each of the three delightful elevations above. Which is your favorite? The Tudor, the Colonial or the Contemporary?

## Design T12505
**1,366 Sq. Ft.; 29,329 Cu. Ft.**

● This design offers you a choice of three distinctively different exteriors. Which is your favorite? Blueprints show details for all three optional elevations. A study of the floor plan reveals a fine measure of livability. In less than 1,400 square feet there are features galore. An excellent return on your construction dollar. In addition to the two eating areas and the open planning of the gathering room, the indoor-outdoor relationships are of great interest. The basement may be developed for recreational activities. Be sure to note the storage potential, particularly the linen closet, the pantry, the china cabinet and the broom closet.

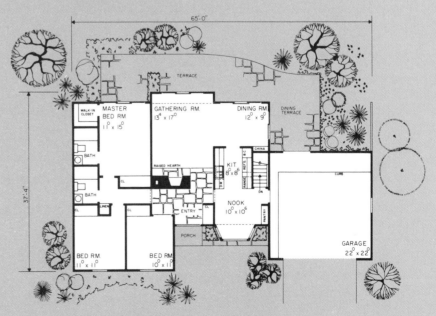

## Design T12802
### 1,729 Sq. Ft.; 42,640 Cu. Ft.

● The three exteriors shown at the left house the same, efficiently planned one-story floor plan shown below. Be sure to notice the design variations in the window placement and roof pitch. The Tudor design to the left is delightful. Half-timbered stucco and brick comprise the facade of this English Tudor variation of the plan. Note authentic bay window in the front bedroom.

## Design T12803
### 1,679 Sq. Ft.; 36,755 Cu. Ft.

● Housed in varying facades, this floor plan is very efficient. The front foyer leads to each of the living areas. The sleeping area of two, or optional three, bedrooms is ready to serve the family. Then there is the gathering room. This room is highlighted by its size, 16 x 20 feet. A contemporary mix of fieldstone and vertical wood siding characterizes this exterior. The absence of columns or posts gives a modern look to the covered porch.

## Design T12804
### 1,674 Sq. Ft.; 35,465 Cu. Ft.

● Stuccoed arches, multi-paned windows and a gracefully sloped roof accent the exterior of this Spanish-inspired design. Like the other two designs, the interior kitchen will efficiently serve the dining room, covered dining porch and breakfast room with great ease. Blueprints for all three designs include details for an optional non-basement plan.

OPTIONAL NON-BASEMENT

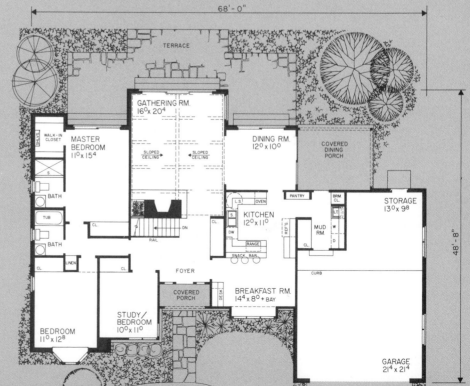

## Design T12805

**1,547 Sq. Ft.; 40,880 Cu. Ft.**

● Three completely different exterior facades share one compact, practical and economical floor plan. The major design variations are roof pitch, window placement and garage openings. Each design will hold its own when comparing the three exteriors. The design to the right is a romantic stone-and-shingle cottage design. This design, along with the other two designs presented here, make outstanding one-story homes.

## Design T12806

**1,584 Sq. Ft.; 41,880 Cu. Ft.**

● Even though these exteriors are extremely different in their styling and also have a few design variations, their floor plans are identical. Each will provide the family with a very livable plan. In this brick and half-timbered stucco Tudor version, like the other two, the living-dining room expands across the rear of the plan and has direct access to the skylite covered porch. Notice the built-in planter adjacent to the open staircase leading to the basement.

## Design T12807

**1,576 Sq. Ft.; 35,355 Cu. Ft.**

● Along with the living-dining areas of the other two plans, this sleek contemporary styled home's breakfast room also will have a view of the covered porch. A desk, snack bar and mud room housing the laundry facilities are near the U-shaped kitchen. Clustering these work areas together is very convenient. The master bedroom has a private bath and walk-in closet.

OPTIONAL NON-BASEMENT

## Design T11305 1,382 Sq. Ft.; 16,584 Cu. Ft.

● Order blueprints for any one of the three exteriors shown on this page and you will receive details for building this outstanding floor plan. You'll find the appeal of these exteriors difficult to beat. As for the plan, in less than 1,400 square feet there are three bedrooms, two full baths, a separate dining room, a formal living room, a fine kitchen overlooking the rear yard and an informal family room. In addition, there is the attached two-car garage. Note the location of the stairs when this plan is built with a basement. Each of the exteriors is predominantly brick - the front of Design T11305 (above) features both stone and vertical boards and battens with brick on the other three sides. Observe the double front doors of the French design, T11382 (below) and the Contemporary design, T11383 (bottom). Study the window treatment.

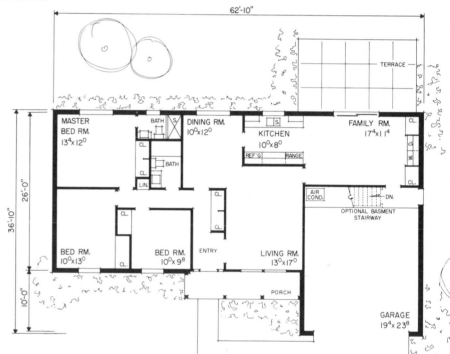

## Design T11382
1,382 Sq. Ft.; 17,164 Cu. Ft.

## Design T11383
1,382 Sq. Ft.; 15,448 Cu. Ft.

# Design T11307 1,357 Sq. Ft.; 14,476 Cu. Ft.

● These three stylish exteriors have the same practical, L-shaped floor plan. Design T11307 (above) features a low-pitched, wide-overhanging roof, a pleasing use of horizontal siding and brick and an enclosed front flower court. Design T11380 (below) has its charm characterized by the pediment gables, the effective window treatment and the masses of brick. Design T11381 (bottom) is captivating because of its hip-roof, its dentils, panelled shutters and lamp post. Each of these three designs has a covered front porch. Inside, there is an abundance of livability. The formal living and dining area is spacious, and the U-shaped kitchen is efficient. There is informal eating space, a separate laundry and a fine family room. Note the sliding glass doors to the terrace. The blueprints include details for building either with or without a basement. Observe the pantry of the non-basement plan.

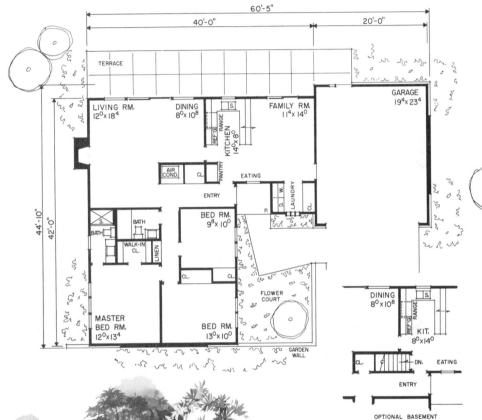

# Design T11380
### 1,399 Sq. Ft.; 17,709 Cu. Ft.

# Design T11381
### 1,399 Sq. Ft.; 17,937 Cu. Ft.

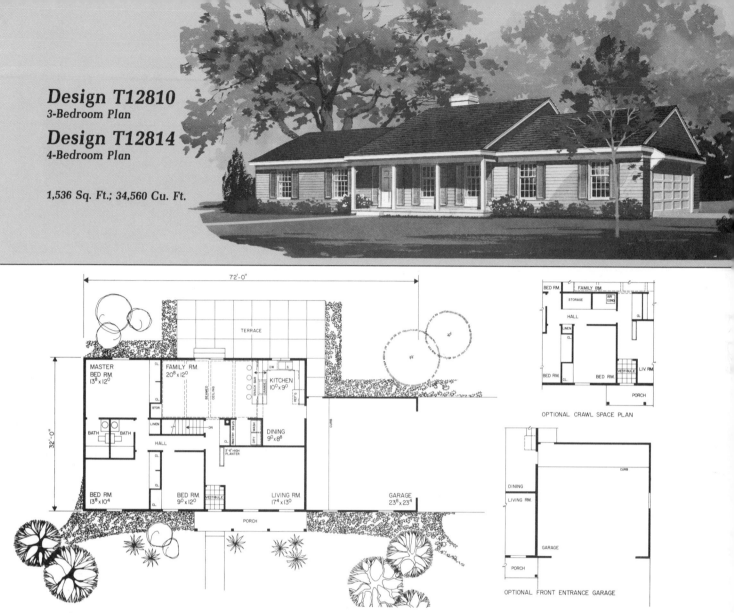

## Design T12810
**3-Bedroom Plan**

## Design T12814
**4-Bedroom Plan**

1,536 Sq. Ft.; 34,560 Cu. Ft.

OPTIONAL CRAWL SPACE PLAN

OPTIONAL FRONT ENTRANCE GARAGE

● 2 x 6 stud wall construction front and center! The designs on these two pages are particularly energy-efficient minded. All exterior walls employ the use of the larger size stud (in preference to the traditional 2 x 4 stud) to permit the installation of extra thick insulation. The high cornice design also allows for more ceiling insulation. In addition to the insulation factor, 2 x 6 studs are practical from an economic standpoint. According to many experts, the use of 2 x 6's spaced 24 inches O.C. results in the need for less lumber and saves construction time. However, the energy-efficient features of this series do not end with the basic framing members. Efficiency begins right at the front door where the vestibule acts as an airlock restricting the flow of cold air to the interior. The basic rectangular shape of the house spells efficiency. No complicated and costly construction here. Yet, there has been no sacrifice of delightful exterior appeal. Efficiency and economy are also embodied in such features as back-to-back plumbing, centrally located furnace, minimal window and door openings and, most important of all - size.

## Design T12811
**3-Bedroom Plan**

## Design T12815
**4-Bedroom Plan**

1,581 Sq. Ft.; 36,694 Cu. Ft.

# Design T12812
**3-Bedroom Plan**

# Design T12816
**4-Bedroom Plan**

**1,581 Sq. Ft.; 35,040 Cu. Ft.**

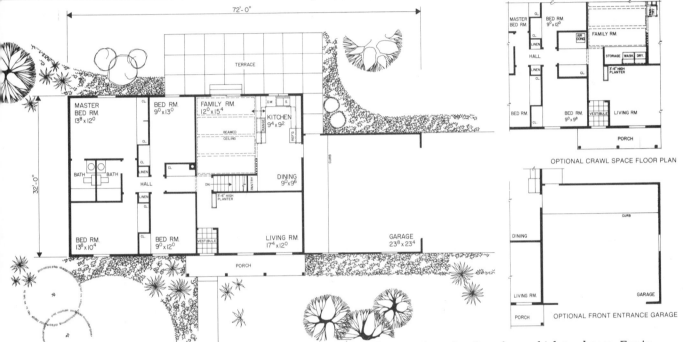

OPTIONAL CRAWL SPACE FLOOR PLAN

OPTIONAL FRONT ENTRANCE GARAGE

● Within 1,536 square feet there is outstanding livability and a huge variety of options from which to choose. For instance, of the four stylish exteriors, which is your favorite? The cozy, front porch Farmhouse adaptation; the pleasing Southern Colonial version, the French creation, or the rugged Western facade? Further, do you prefer a three or a four bedroom floor plan? With or without a basement? Front or side-opening garage? If you wish to order blueprints for the hip-roofed design with three bedrooms, specify Design T12812; for the four bedroom option specify T12816. To order blueprints for the three bedroom Southern Colonial, request Design T12811; for the four bedroom model, ask for Design T12815, etc. All blueprints include the optional non-basement and front opening garage details. Whatever the version you select, you and your family will enjoy the beamed ceiling of the family room, the efficient, U-shaped kitchen, the dining area, the traffic-free living room and the fine storage facilities. Truly, a fine design series created to give each home buyer the maximum amount of choice and flexibility.

# Design T12813
**3-Bedroom Plan**

# Design T12817
**4-Bedroom Plan**

**1,536 Sq. Ft.; 33,334 Cu. Ft.**

## Design T11389
**1,488 Sq. Ft.; 18,600 Cu. Ft.**

● Your choice of exterior goes with this outstanding floor plan. If your tastes include a liking for French Provincial, Design T11389, above, will provide a lifetime of satisfaction. On the other hand, should you prefer the simple straightforward lines of contemporary design, the exterior for Design T11387, below, will be your favorite. For those who enjoy the warmth of Colonial adaptations, the charming exterior for Design T11388, bottom, will be perfect. Of interest is a comparison of these three exteriors. Observe the varying design treatment of the windows, the double front doors, the garage doors and the roof lines. Don't miss other architectural details. Study each exterior and the floor plan carefully. Three charming designs you won't want to miss.

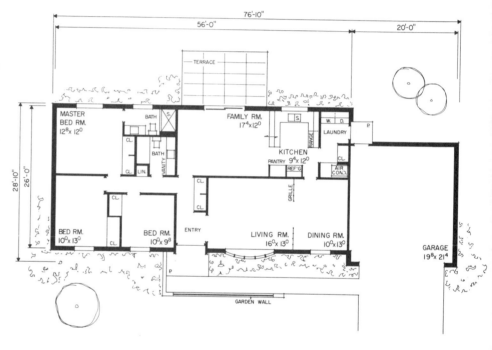

## Design T11387
**1,488 Sq. Ft.; 16,175 Cu. Ft.**

## Design T11388
**1,488 Sq. Ft.; 18,600 Cu. Ft.**

## Design T11864
**1,598 Sq. Ft.; 27,611 Cu. Ft.**

● What's your favorite exterior? The one above which has a distinctive colonial appearance, or that below with its sleek contemporary look? Maybe you prefer the more formal hip-roof exterior (bottom) with its French feeling. Whatever your choice, you'll know your next home will be one that is delightfully proportioned and is sure to be among the most attractive in the neighborhood. It is interesting to note that each exterior highlights an effective use of wood siding and stone (or brick, as in the case of Design T11866). The floor plan features three bedrooms, 2½ baths, a formal living and dining room, a snack bar and a mud room. The master bedroom of the contemporary design has its window located in the left side elevation wall.

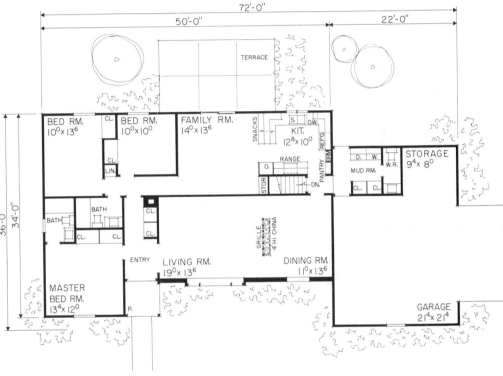

## Design T11865
**1,598 Sq. Ft.; 25,626 Cu. Ft.**

## Design T11866
**1,598 Sq. Ft.; 27,248 Cu. Ft.**

## Design T11938 1,428 Sq. Ft.; 29,702 Cu. Ft.

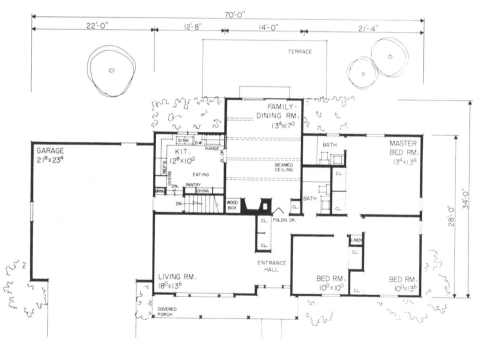

● A fine efficient plan designed to fit each of the three delightful exteriors above. You can reserve your choice of exterior until you receive the blueprints. Each set you order contains the details for the construction of all three. Note the differences in exterior materials, window treatment, car storage facilities and roof lines. Observe the beamed ceiling, all purpose family room and the kitchen eating space. There is a lot of living in under 1,400 square feet.

## Design T11323 1,344 Sq. Ft.; 17,472 Cu. Ft.

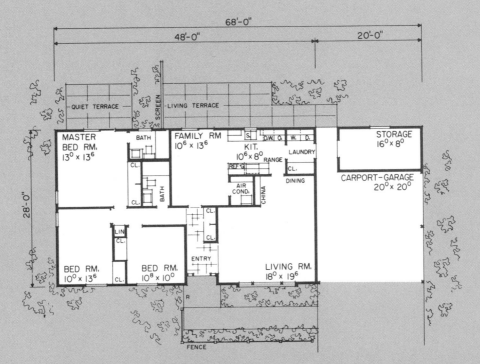

● Incorporated in the set of blueprints for this design are details for building each of the three charming, traditional exteriors. Each of the three alternate exteriors has a distinction all its own. A study of the floor plan reveals fine livability. There are two full baths, a fine family room, an efficient work center, a formal dining area, bulk storage facilities and sliding glass doors to the quiet and living terraces. Laundry is strategically located near the kitchen.

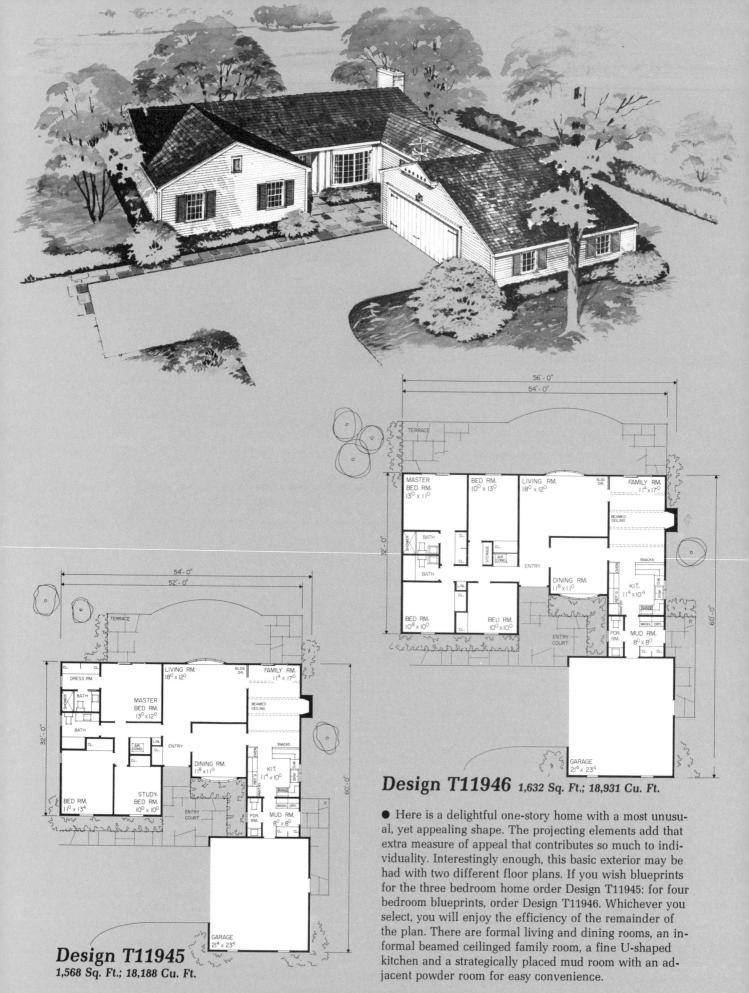

**Design T11946** 1,632 Sq. Ft.; 18,931 Cu. Ft.

● Here is a delightful one-story home with a most unusual, yet appealing shape. The projecting elements add that extra measure of appeal that contributes so much to individuality. Interestingly enough, this basic exterior may be had with two different floor plans. If you wish blueprints for the three bedroom home order Design T11945; for four bedroom blueprints, order Design T11946. Whichever you select, you will enjoy the efficiency of the remainder of the plan. There are formal living and dining rooms, an informal beamed ceilinged family room, a fine U-shaped kitchen and a strategically placed mud room with an adjacent powder room for easy convenience.

**Design T11945**
1,568 Sq. Ft.; 18,188 Cu. Ft.

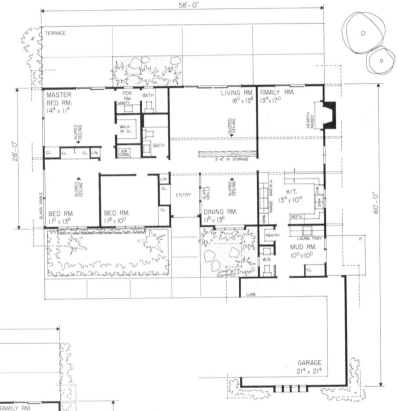

## Design T11947 1,764 Sq. Ft.; 18,381 Cu. Ft.

● When it comes to housing your family, if you are among the contemporary-minded, you'll want to give this L-shaped design a second, then even a third, or fourth, look. It is available as either a three or four bedroom home. If you desire the three bedroom, 58 foot wide design order blueprints for T11947; for the four bedroom, 62 foot wide design, order T11948. Inside, you will note a continuation of the contemporary theme with sloping ceilings, exposed beams and a practical 42 inch high storage divider between the living and dining rooms. Don't miss the mud rooms.

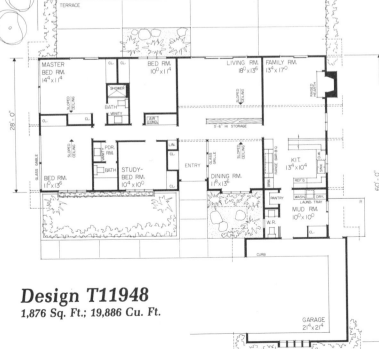

## Design T11948
### 1,876 Sq. Ft.; 19,886 Cu. Ft.

## Design T12704
**1,746 Sq. Ft.; 38,000 Cu. Ft.**

● Three different exteriors! But inside it's all the same livable house. Begin with the impressive entry hall which is more than 19' long and offering double entry to the gathering room. Now the gathering room which is notable for its size and design. Notice how the fireplace is flanked by sliding glass doors leading to the terrace.

## Design T12705
**1,746 Sq. Ft.; 37,000 Cu. Ft.**

● There's a formal dining room, too! The right spot for special birthday dinners as well as supper parties for friends. And an efficient kitchen that makes meal preparation easy whatever the occasion. Look for a built-in range and oven here plus a bright dining nook with sliding glass doors to a second terrace.

## Design T12706
**1,746 Sq. Ft.; 36,800 Cu. Ft.**

● Three large bedrooms! All located to give family members the utmost of privacy. Including a master suite with a dressing room, bath and sliding glass doors opening onto the main terrace. For blueprints of the Colonial adaptation (top) order Design T12704; the hip-roof French version (middle) Design T12705; and the Contemporary, (bottom) order Design T12706.

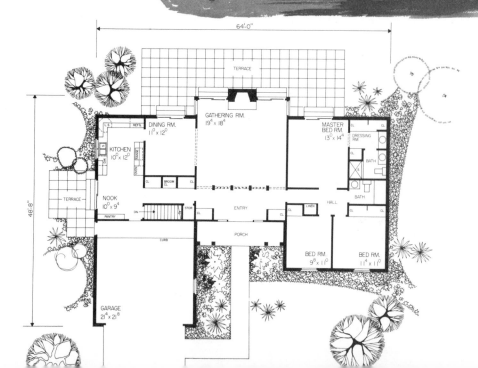

● Here is a unique series of designs with three charming exterior adaptations-Southern Colonial, Western Ranch, French Provincial - and two distinctive floor plans. Each plan has a different design number and is less than 1,600 square feet.

If yours is a preference for the floor plan featuring the 26 foot keeping room, you should order blueprints for Design T12611. Of course, the details for each of the three delightful exteriors will be included. On the other hand, should the plan with the living, dining and family rooms be your favorite, order blueprints for Design T12612 and get details for all three exteriors.

There are many points of similarity in the two designs. Each has a fireplace, 2½ baths, sliding glass doors to the rear terrace, master bedroom with walk-in closet and private bath with stall shower and a basement. It is interesting to note that two of the exteriors have covered porches. Don't miss the beamed ceilings, the various storage facilities and the stall showers.

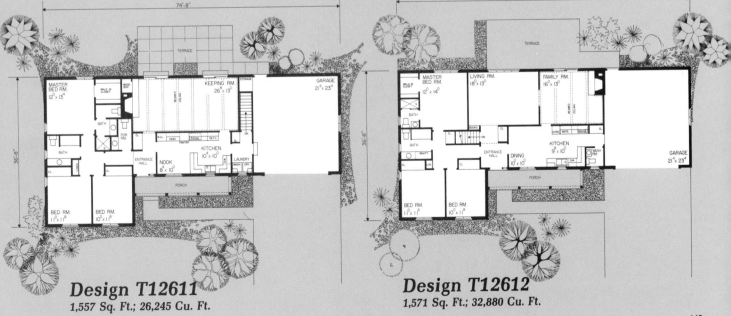

## Design T12611
1,557 Sq. Ft.; 26,245 Cu. Ft.

## Design T12612
1,571 Sq. Ft.; 32,880 Cu. Ft.

## Design T11322 1,478 Sq. Ft.; 28,969 Cu. Ft.

## Design T11321
1,478 Sq. Ft.
30,447 Cu. Ft.

## Design T11320
1,478 Sq. Ft.
27,195 Cu. Ft.

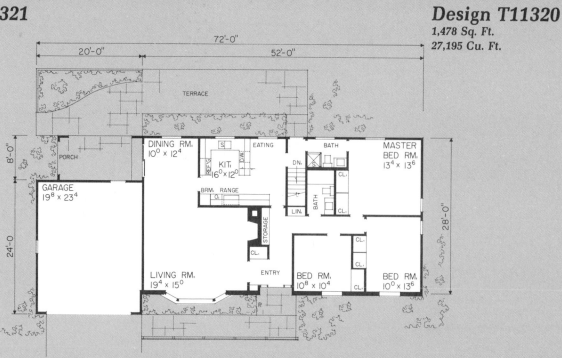

● Three totally different front elevations which have the same basic floor plan layout. There is a separate set of blueprints for each attractive front exterior. The economically built plan, because of its simplicity, is outstanding.

## Design T11352 1,592 Sq. Ft.; 29,554 Cu. Ft.

## Design T11351
1,592 Sq. Ft.
31,328 Cu. Ft.

## Design T11350
1,592 Sq. Ft.
29,855 Cu. Ft.

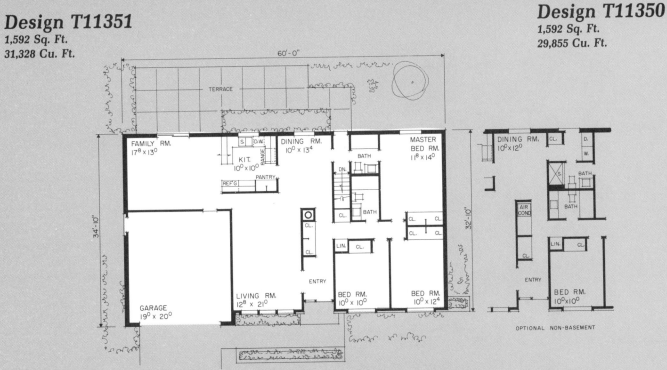

● When you order blueprints for the exterior that appeals to you the most, you'll receive details for building with or without a basement. Note the family room and the arrangements of the two full baths.

## Design T12349
### *1,863 Sq. Ft.; 17,505 Cu. Ft.*

● This plan can be built with two-strikingly contemporary facades. The living patterns of this refreshingly simple design will be delight-fully different. From the formal sunken front living room to the informal beamed ceilinged rear family room, this interior has much to of-fer. There is a formal dining room with a con-venient pass-thru from the efficient kitchen. Then there is the snack bar, also but an arms reach from the kitchen. Back-to-back plumb-ing is an economical feature of the two full baths. The focal point of the family room is the raised hearth fireplace flanked by bookshelves, cabinet and wood box. Sliding glass doors provide easy access to the outdoor patio from the master bedroom and family room. The blueprints ordered for this design show details for both exteriors as well as for basement and non-basement construction.

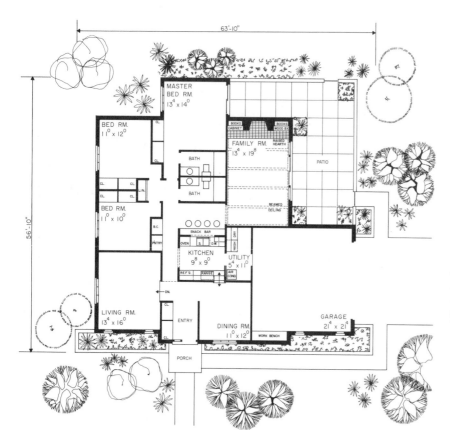

## Design T12525

919 Sq. Ft. - First Floor
1,019 Sq. Ft. - Second Floor
29,200 Cu. Ft.

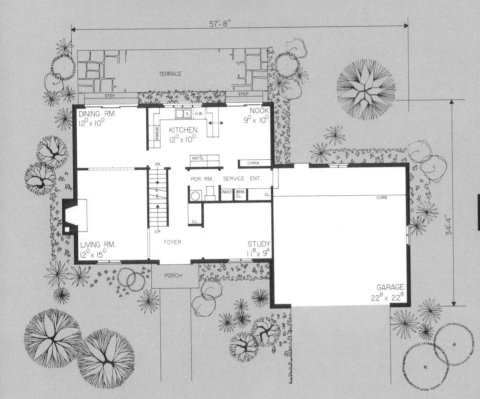

● Here is an economically built home that can be constructed with either of the two illustrated exteriors. Which is your favorite? The two study areas provide plenty of multi-purpose, informal living space.

## Design T12585

**990 Sq. Ft. - First Floor**
**1,011 Sq. Ft. - Second Floor; 30,230 Cu. Ft.**

● A traditional Colonial, a stately Tudor and an elegant French facade house this two-story floor plan. The exteriors are highlighted with large paned-glass windows. Note that the second floor overhangs in the front to extend the size of the master bedroom. After entering through the front door one can either go directly to the formal area or to the informal area.

## Design T12586

**984 Sq. Ft. - First Floor**
**1,003 Sq. Ft. - Second Floor; 30,080 Cu. Ft.**

● The formal area consists of the living and dining rooms. These two areas stretch from the front to the rear of the house. Together they offer the correct setting for the most formal occasion. The informal area is the front family room. A fireplace will warm this casual, family living area. The work center is easily accessible from all areas, including the garage and terrace.

## Design T12587

**984 Sq. Ft. - First Floor**
**993 Sq. Ft. - Second Floor; 30,090 Cu. Ft.**

● The second floor has been designed to please all of the family. Four good-sized bedrooms, plenty of closet space and two baths are available. Not a bit of wasted space will be found in these sleeping facilities. Choose your favorite facade to go with this floor plan. Order Design T12585 for the Colonial; Design T12586 for the Tudor and for the French, order Design T12587.

# Design T12617

**1,223 Sq. Ft. - First Floor**
**1,018 Sq. Ft. - Second Floor; 30,784 Cu. Ft.**

● This Gambrel roof version shares the two-story floor plan below with the Tudor and the hip-roofed design from the Southwest. Each of these exterior facades, housing the same practical plan, will be an outstanding investment for a lifetime of proud ownership. Don't miss the delightful symmetry of the window treatment and the front opening garage of Design T12617.

# Design T12618

**1,269 Sq. Ft. - First Floor**
**1,064 Sq. Ft. - Second Floor; 33,079 Cu. Ft.**

● Tudor design has become very popular in recent years; if this is your choice, order Design T12618. Inside, the large family will enjoy all of the features that will aide a family to easy living. Note the large 13 x 23 foot formal end-living room. It is assured excellent privacy. A separate dining room, too. It has easy access to the kitchen for ease in serving.

# Design T12619

**1,269 Sq. Ft. - First Floor**
**1,064 Sq. Ft. - Second Floor; 29,195 Cu. Ft.**

● The Southwest is captured ideally in this hip-roofed house. To receive this elevation, order Design T12619. Along with the other two designs, the informal area is a sunken family room. It features a raised hearth fireplace and access to the terrace, as does the nook. Four bedrooms and two bathrooms with economical back-to-back plumbing are on the second floor.

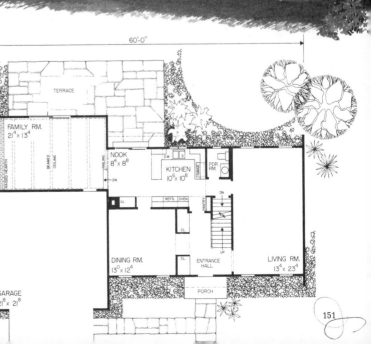

## Design T11957 1,042 Sq. Ft. - First Floor; 780 Sq. Ft. - Second Floor; 24,982 Cu. Ft.

● When you order your blueprints for this design you will receive details for the construction of each of the three charming exteriors pictured above. Whichever the exterior you finally decide to build, the floor plan will be essentially the same except the location of the windows. This will be a fine home for the growing family. It will serve well for many years. There are four bedrooms and two full baths (one with a stall shower) upstairs.

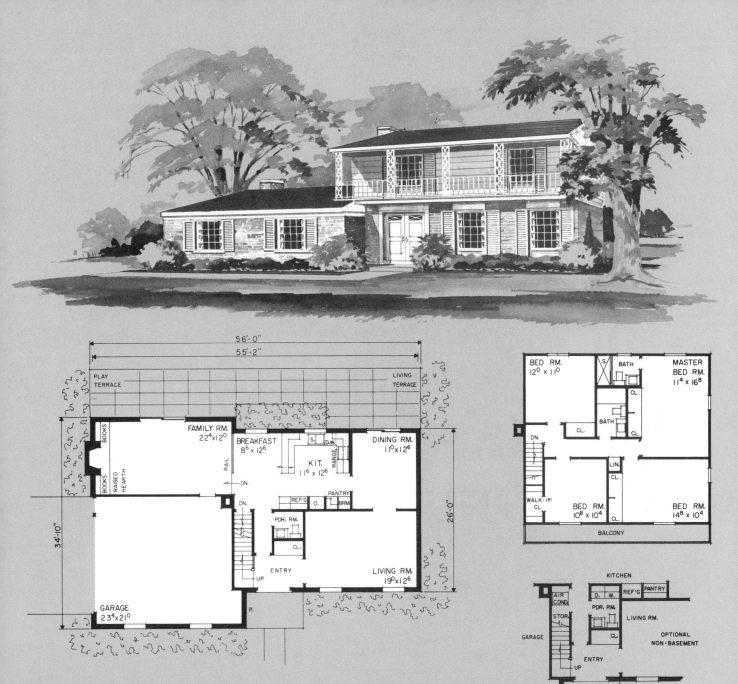

## Design T11371 *1,172 Sq. Ft. - First Floor; 896 Sq. Ft. - Second Floor; 28,726 Cu. Ft.*

First Floor:

- PLAY TERRACE
- LIVING TERRACE
- FAMILY RM. 22⁴ x 12⁰
- BREAKFAST 8⁶ x 12⁶
- KIT. 11⁶ x 12⁶
- DINING RM. 11⁰ x 12⁶
- BOOKS
- RAISED HEARTH
- REF'G
- O.
- PANTRY
- BRM
- PDR. RM.
- CL.
- ENTRY
- LIVING RM. 19⁰ x 12⁶
- GARAGE 23⁴ x 21⁰
- UP / DN.
- 56'-0"
- 55'-2"
- 34'-10"
- 26'-0"

Second Floor:

- BED RM. 12⁰ x 11⁰
- BATH
- MASTER BED RM. 11⁴ x 16⁸
- CL.
- WALK-IN CL.
- DN.
- LIN.
- CL.
- BED RM. 10⁸ x 10⁴
- BED RM. 14⁸ x 10⁴
- BALCONY

Optional Non-Basement:

- GARAGE
- AIR COND.
- STOR.
- KITCHEN
- D. / W.
- REF'G
- PANTRY
- PDR. RM.
- LIVING RM.
- CL.
- ENTRY
- UP
- OPTIONAL NON-BASEMENT

● If you like traditional charm and the tried and true living patterns of the conventional two-story idea, you'll not go wrong in selecting this design as your next home. In fact, when you order blueprints for T11371 you'll receive details for building all three optional elevations. So, you needn't decide which front exterior is your favorite right now. Any one of these will surely add a touch of class to your new neighborhood.

### Design T12149
**988 Sq. Ft. - First Floor**
**952 Sq. Ft. - Second Floor; 30,438 Cu. Ft.**

● Any one of these exteriors can be built with the floor plan below. If you like the traditional version to the left, order blueprints for T12149; if you prefer the Farmhouse adaptation below, order T12150; should your choice be for the Tudor variation at the bottom, order T12151. Whatever your selection, you'll know that your new home will be finely proportioned.

### Design T12150
**991 Sq. Ft. - First Floor**
**952 Sq. Ft. - Second Floor; 27,850 Cu. Ft.**

● In each design the attached two-car garage adds to the appeal as its roof continues to provide shelter for the front doors. A professional builder could hardly do better than to find a place for these charming houses in his subdivision. The basically rectangular shape of the main house will mean economical construction.

### Design T12151
**991 Sq. Ft. - First Floor**
**952 Sq. Ft. - Second Floor; 28,964 Cu. Ft.**

● The blueprints you order will show details for building either the four or the five bedroom version. Which will serve your family best? In addition to the two baths of the second floor, there is an extra powder room. Further, there is a laundry, separate dining room, family room, U-shaped kitchen and basement. A great plan for the modest budget.

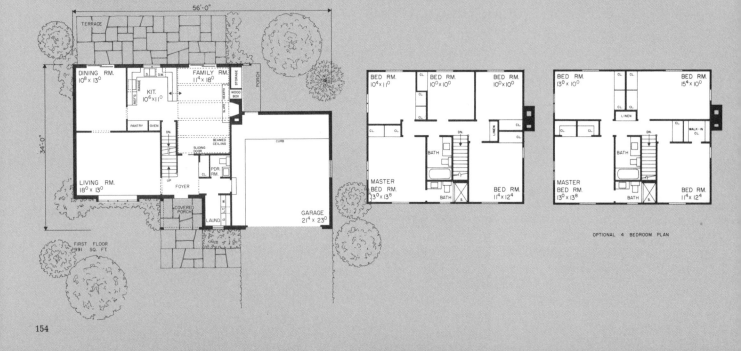

## Design T12750
**1,209 Sq. Ft. - First Floor**
**965 Sq. Ft. - Second Floor; 32,025 Cu. Ft.**

● These impressive two-story homes will catch the eye of the on-lookers. The extended one-story wings at each end of the house add appeal to the exterior. The covered porch also is a charming feature. No matter which of these delightful exteriors that you choose, you will receive a home to serve your family for a lifetime.

## Design T12751
**1,202 Sq. Ft. - First Floor**
**964 Sq. Ft. - Second Floor; 33,830 Cu. Ft.**

● Now take a walk through the efficient floor plan. The living/dining room is L-shaped with the dining room being convenient to the kitchen. The kitchen has a pass-thru to the breakfast nook plus many built-ins to help ease kitchen duties. The nook, along with the family room, has sliding glass doors to the terrace.

## Design T12752
**1,209 Sq. Ft. - First Floor**
**960 Sq. Ft. - Second Floor; 34,725 Cu. Ft.**

● Also on the first floor is a powder room and laundry. The second floor houses the three family bedrooms, bath and the master bedroom suite with all the extras. Order Design T12750 for the Mansard roofed exterior; Design T12751 for the Colonial with the Gambrel roof and for the Farmhouse type design, order T12752.

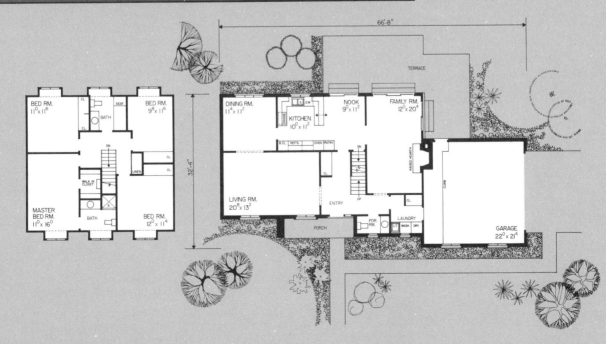

# Design T11831 1,108 Sq. Ft. - First Floor; 992 Sq. Ft. - Second Floor; 31,075 Cu. Ft.

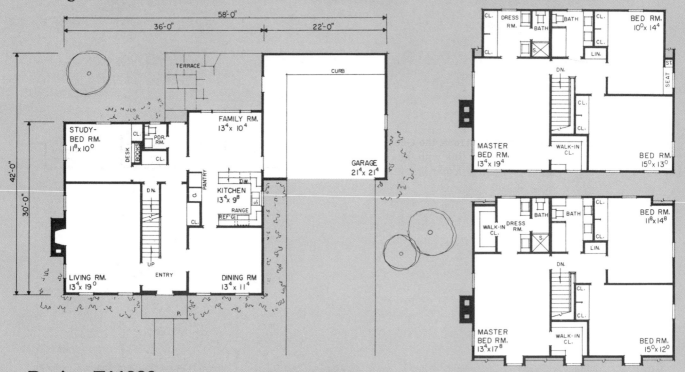

# Design T11832 1,108 Sq. Ft. - First Floor; 1,018 Sq. Ft. - Second Floor; 31,342 Cu. Ft.

## Design T11833 *1,152 Sq. Ft. - First Floor; 958 Sq. Ft. - Second Floor; 31,386 Cu. Ft.*

## Four Authentic Exteriors Go With This Practical Family Living Plan . . .

● . . . which one do you prefer? Each of these delightful exteriors - the New England Salt Box, T11831; the Connecticut Gambrel, Design T11832; the French Mansard, T11833; the Georgian, Design T11834 - will provide you with a proud link with the past. Pride of ownership will be yours forever! The efficient first floor plan is common to each of these four designs. The second floor, however, varies with each exterior style. While each house features three sizeable bedrooms, excellent bath facilities and fine storage potential, a study of the various bedroom dimensions reveals difference in sizes. This is due to the varying characteristics of the roof structures. Observe the center entrance and how the main hall effectively routes traffic to all areas. The efficient work center is strategically located between the separate dining room and the informal family room. The formal living room will be entirely free of unnecessary traffic. Note the fireplace and all that blank space for flexible furniture placement. Don't miss the extra room which may be used as a study or fourth bedroom.

## Design T11834 *1,150 Sq. Ft. - First Floor; 1,120 Sq. Ft. - Second Floor; 34,460 Cu. Ft.*

# Your Choice Of Contemporary - Plus Your 2 Floor Plans

● The bi-level, or split foyer design has become increasingly popular. Here are six alternate elevations – three Traditional and three Contemporary – which may be built with either of two basic floor plans. One plan contains 960 square feet on each level and is 24 feet in depth; the other contains 1,040 square feet on each level and is 26 feet in depth. Plans for traditional and contemporary series include each of the three optional elevations.

### Design T11377 Traditional Exteriors
24 Foot Depth Plan (18,960 Cu. Ft.)

### Design T11375 Traditional Exteriors
26 Foot Depth Plan (20,778 Cu. Ft.)

960 Sq. Ft. - Upper Level; 960 Sq. Ft. - Lower Level

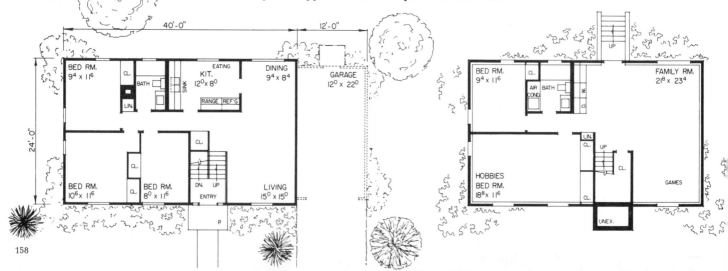

# Traditional or Exterior Styling - Choice of For Each Style

● The popularity of the bi-level design can be traced to the tremendous amount of the livable space that such a design provides per construction dollar. While the lower level is partially below grade, it enjoys plenty of natural light and, hence, provides a bright, cheerful atmosphere for total livability. While these two basic floor plans are essentially the same, it is important to note that the larger of the two features a private bath for the master bedroom. Study the plans.

**Design T11376** Contemporary Exteriors
*24 Foot Depth Plan (18,000 Cu. Ft.)*

**Design T11378** Contemporary Exteriors
*26 Foot Depth Plan (19,624 Cu. Ft.)*

**1,040 Sq. Ft. - Upper Level; 1,040 Sq. Ft. - Lower Level**

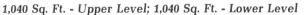

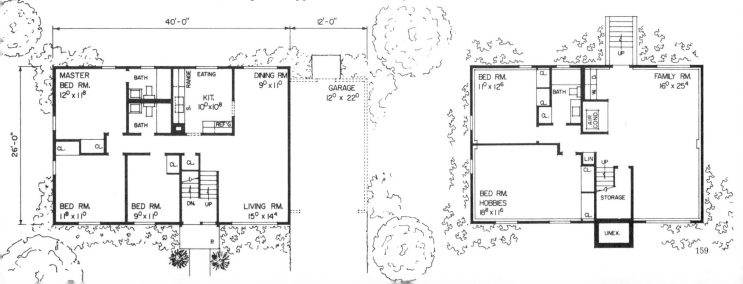

● Here are three optional elevations that function with the same basic floor plan. No need to decide now which is your favorite since the blue-prints for this design include details for each optional exterior.

If yours is a restricted building budget, your construction dollar could hardly return greater dividends in the way of exterior appeal and interior livability. Also, you won't need a big, expensive site on which to build.

In addition to the four bedrooms and 2½ baths, there are two living areas, two places for dining, a fireplace and a basement. Notice the fine accessibility of the rear outdoor terrace.

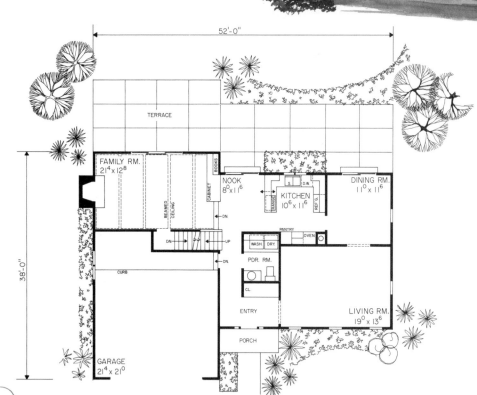

### Design T12366
1,078 Sq. Ft. - First Floor
880 Sq. Ft. - Second Floor
27,242 Cu. Ft.

# ONE-STORY HOMES over 2,000 sq. ft. . . . . *As a home's*

*square footage increases, so does the opportunity to develop a wide variety of features that contribute to more enjoyable living patterns. Of course, as the size of the home escalates so does its cost. The objective should be to make the benefits of increased size cost-effective. This group of one-story homes will cater to the needs of large, active families with expanded building budgets. Square footages range upward to 2889 with four bedrooms predominating. Formal and informal living and dining facilities are represented. Extra baths, laundry rooms, large kitchens and additional storage are among the convenient living highlights of these larger homes.*

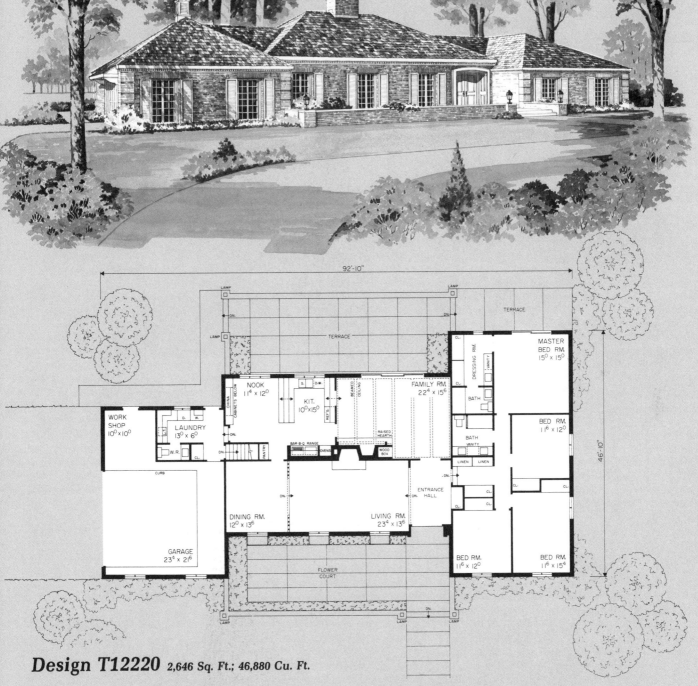

## Design T12220 2,646 Sq. Ft.; 46,880 Cu. Ft.

● The gracious formality of this home is reminiscent of a popularly accepted French styling. The hip-roof, the brick quoins, the cornice details, the arched window heads, the distinctive shutters, the recessed double front doors, the massive center chimney, and the de-

lightful flower court are all features which set the dramatic appeal of this home. This floor plan is a favorite of many. The four bedroom, two bath sleeping wing is a zone by itself. Further, the formal living and dining rooms are ideally located. For enter-

taining they function well together and look out upon the pleasant flower court. Overlooking the raised living terrace at the rear are the family and breakfast rooms and work center. Don't miss the laundry, extra wash room and work shop in garage.

# Design T12527 2,392 Sq. Ft.; 42,579 Cu. Ft.

● Vertical boards and battens, field-stone, bay window, a dovecote, a gas lamp and a recessed front entrance are among the appealing exterior features of this U-shaped design. Through the double front doors, flanked by glass side lites, one enters the spacious foyer. Straight ahead is the cozy sunken gathering room with its sloping, beamed ceiling, raised hearth fireplace and two sets of sliding glass doors to the rear terrace. To the right of the foyer is the sleeping wing with its three bedrooms, study (make it the fourth bedroom if you wish) and two baths. To the left is the strategically located powder room and large kitchen with its delightful nook and bay window.

● What a pleasing, traditional exterior. And what a fine, convenient living interior! The configuration of this home leads to interesting roof planes and even functional outdoor terrace areas. The front court and the covered porch with its stolid pillars strike an enchanting note. The gathering room will be just that. It will be the family's multi-purpose living area. Sunken to a level of two steps, its already spacious feeling is enhanced by its open planning with the dining room and study. This latter room may be closed off for more privacy if desired. Just adjacent to the foyer is the open stairwell to the basement level. Here will be the possibility of developing recreation space.

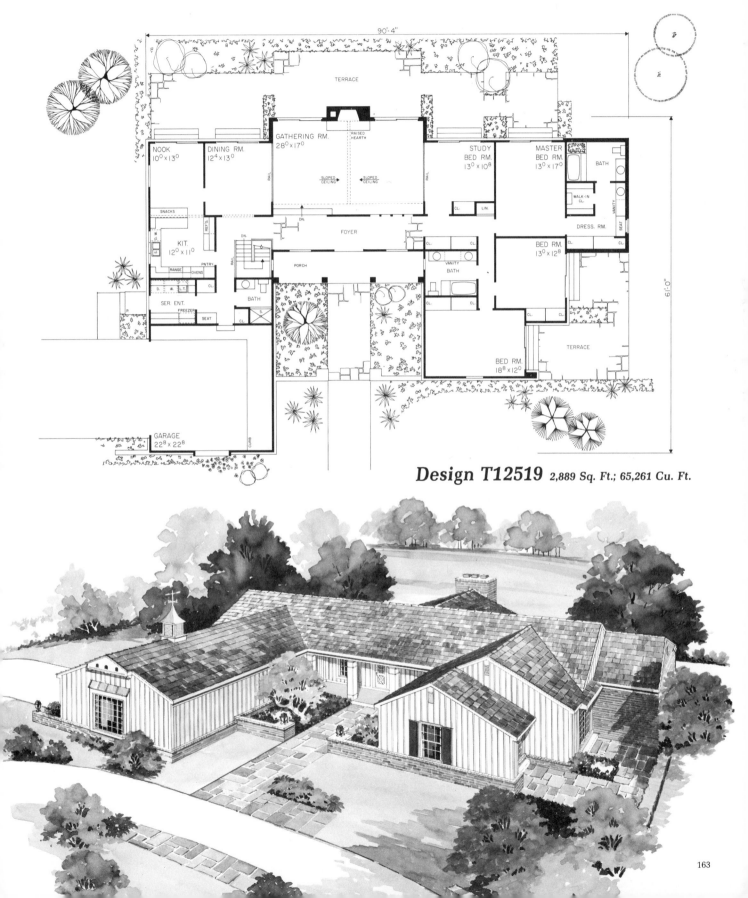

**Design T12519** 2,889 Sq. Ft.; 65,261 Cu. Ft.

# Design T11149

**2,040 Sq. Ft.; 35,290 Cu. Ft.**

● The very shape of this traditional adaptation seems to spell, "welcome". A study of the floor plan reflects excellent zoning. The sleeping area consists of four bedrooms and two full baths. The formal area, located to the front of the house, consists of a separate dining room with built-in china cabinet and living room with fireplace and accompanying woodbox. Study the work center of the kitchen, laundry and wash room. An informal family room. It is only a couple of steps from the kitchen and functions with the outdoor terrace.

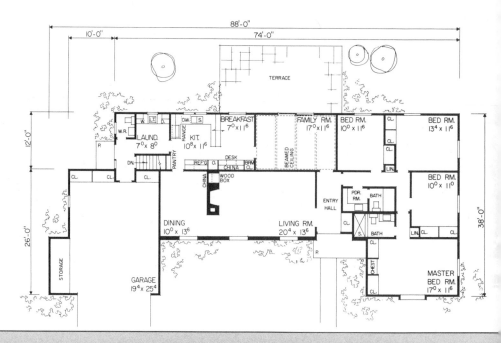

# Design T12316

**2,000 Sq. Ft.; 25,242 Cu. Ft.**

● Here is a basic floor plan which is the favorite of many. It provides for the location, to the front of the plan, of the more formal areas (living and dining rooms); while the informal areas (family room and kitchen) are situated to the rear of the plan and function with the terrace. To the left of the center entrance is the four bedroom, two bath sleeping zone. Adjacent to the kitchen is the utility room with a wash room nearby. The garage features a storage room and work shop area with more storage.

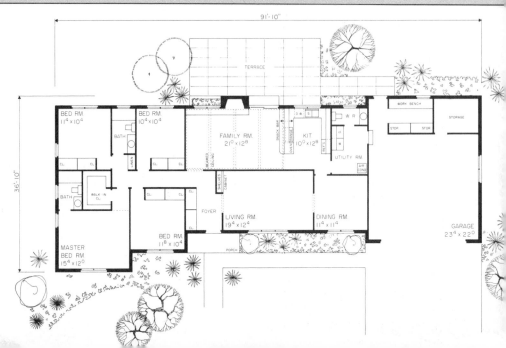

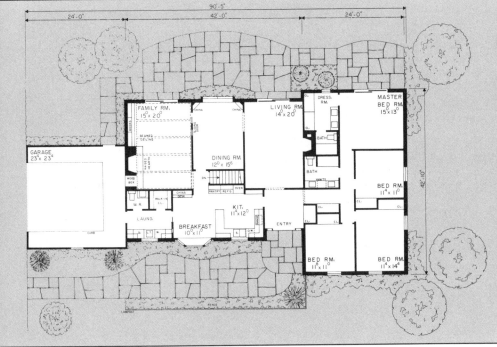

## Design T12144
**2,432 Sq. Ft.; 42,519 Cu. Ft.**

● Have you ever wished you lived in a house in which the living, dining and family rooms all looked out upon the rear terrace? Further, have you ever wished your home had its kitchen located to the front so that you could see approaching callers? Or, have you ever wished for a house where traffic in from the garage was stopped right in the laundry so that wet, snowy, dirty and muddy apparel could be shed immediately? If these have been your wishes, this plan may be just for you.

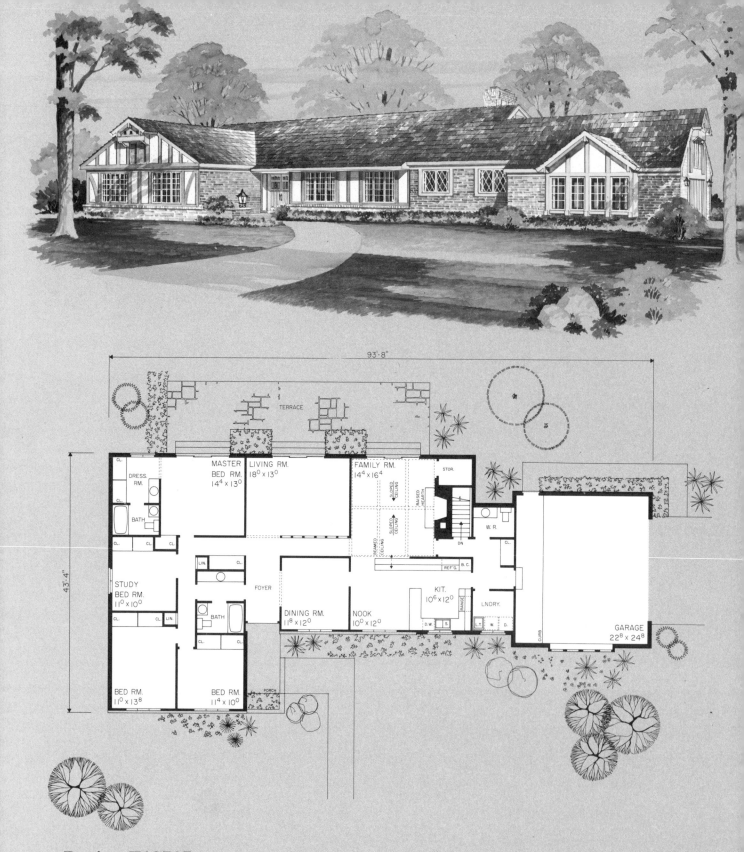

# Design T12515 2,363 Sq. Ft.; 46,676 Cu. Ft.

● Another Tudor adaptation with all the appeal that is inherent in this design style. The brick veneer exterior is effectively complimented by the beam work, the stucco, and the window treatment. The carriage lamp perched on the planter wall adds a delightful touch as do the dovecotes of the bedroom wing and over the garage door. The livability of the interior is just great. The kitchen, nook, and dining room overlook the front yard. Around the corner from the kitchen is the laundry with an extra wash room not far away. Sloping, beamed ceiling and raised hearth fireplace are highlights of the family room. Like the living room and master bedroom it functions with rear terrace. Note vanity outside main bath. Stolid wood posts on 3 foot wall separate living room and hall.

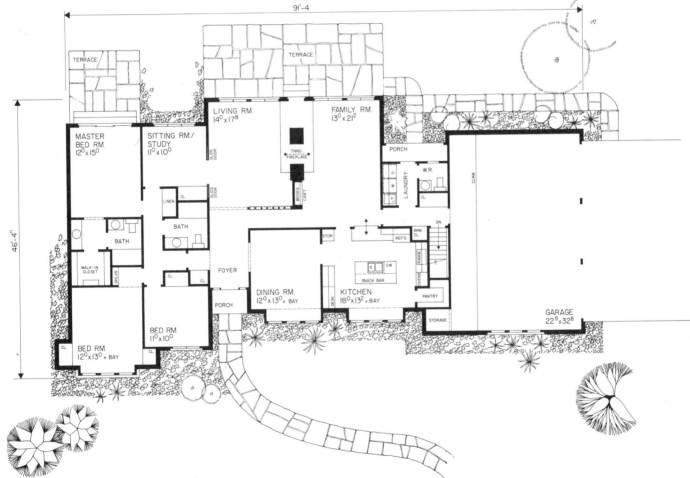

# Design T12785 *2,375 Sq. Ft.; 47,805 Cu. Ft.*

● Exceptional Tudor design! Passersby will surely take a second glance at this fine home wherever it may be located. And the interior is just as pleasing. As one enters the foyer and looks around, the plan will speak for itself in the areas of convenience and efficiency. Cross room traffic will be avoided. There is a hall leading to each of the three bedrooms and study of the sleeping wing and another leading to the living room, family room, kitchen and laundry with wash room. The formal dining room can be entered from both the foyer and the kitchen. Efficiency will surely be the by-word when describing the kitchen. Note the fine features: a built-in desk, pantry, island snack bar with sink and pass-thru to the family room. The fireplace will be enjoyed in the living and family rooms.

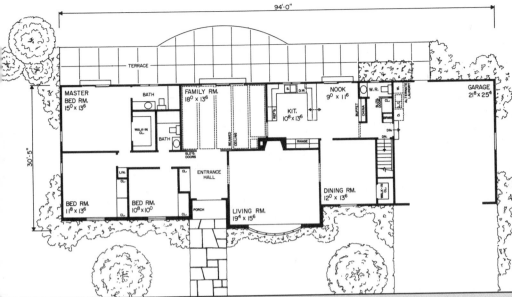

## Design T12204
**2,016 Sq. Ft.; 34,289 Cu. Ft.**

● Your life's investment could hardly be more wisely made than for the choice of this delightful traditional as your family's next home. Over the years its charm will hardly diminish. It will be as impressive as ever. It establishes a quiet sleeping zone, a formal living-dining zone to the front and an informal family-kitchen zone to the rear. Sliding glass doors permit the master bedroom, the family room and the breakfast nook to have access to the rear terrace.

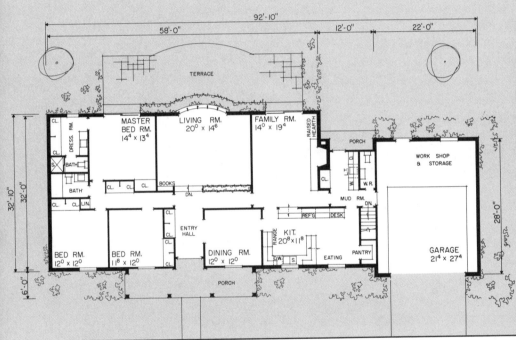

## Design T11788
**2,218 Sq. Ft.; 36,002 Cu. Ft.**

● Charm is but one of the many words which may be used to correctly describe this fine design. In addition to its attractive facade, it has a practical and smoothly functioning one-story floor plan. The detail of the front entrance which is highlighted by columns, supporting the projecting pediment gable, is outstanding. Observe the window treatment and the double front doors. Also the sunken living room with the large bay window overlooking the rear yard.

## Design T11950
**2,076 Sq. Ft.; 27,520 Cu. Ft.**

● If you were to count the various reasons that will surely cause excitement over the prospect of moving into this home, you would certainly be able to compile a long list. You might head your list with the grace and charm of the front exterior. You'd certainly have to comment on the delightful entry court, the picket fence and lamp post, and the recessed front entrance. Comments about the interior obviously would begin with the listing of such features as: spaciousness galore, sunken living room, separate dining room, beamed ceiling family room, excellent kitchen with pass-thru to breakfast room, two full baths plus wash room, etc.

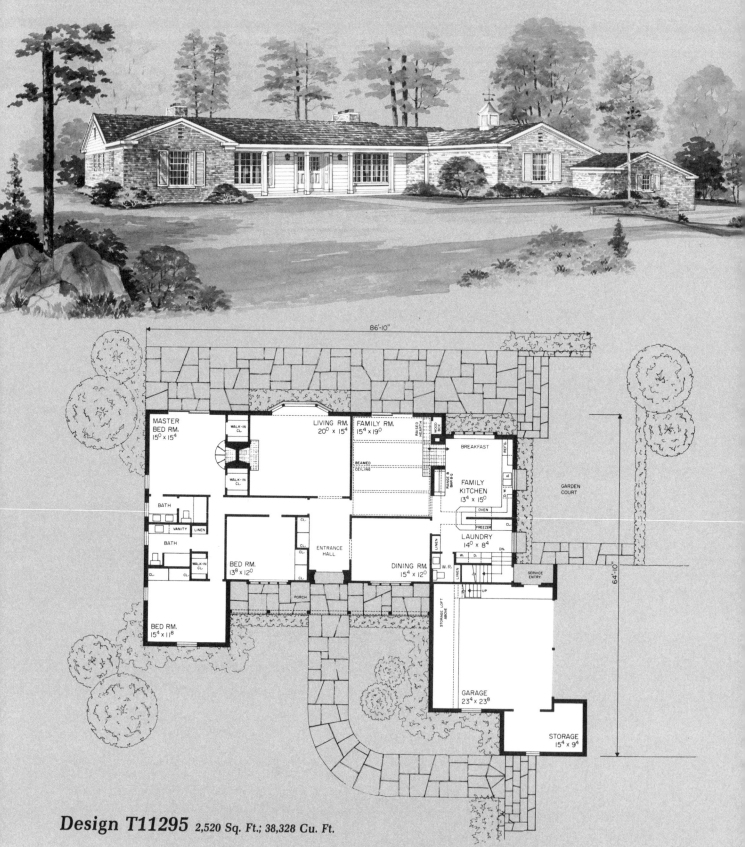

Plan labels:

MASTER BED RM. 15⁰ x 15⁴
WALK-IN CL.
WALK-IN CL.
BATH
VANITY
LINEN
BATH
WALK-IN CL.
CL.
CL.
BED RM. 13⁸ x 12⁰
LIVING RM. 20⁰ x 15⁴
FAMILY RM. 15⁴ x 19⁰
BEAMED CEILING
RAISED HEARTH
WOOD BOX
BREAKFAST
REF'G.
FAMILY KITCHEN 13⁴ x 15⁰
RANGE & BAR-B-Q
OVEN
FREEZER
D. W.
GARDEN COURT
ENTRANCE HALL
CL.
CL.
CL.
DINING RM. 15⁴ x 12⁰
LAUNDRY 14⁰ x 8⁴
LINEN
W.R.
DN.
LINEN
W.
D.
SERVICE ENTRY
UP
BED RM. 15⁴ x 11⁸
PORCH
STORAGE LOFT ABOVE
GARAGE 23⁴ x 23⁸
STORAGE 15⁴ x 9⁴

86'-10"
64'-10"

## Design T11295  2,520 Sq. Ft.; 38,328 Cu. Ft.

● A custom home is one tailored to fit the needs and satisfy the living patterns of a particular family. Here is a traditional home which stands ready to serve its occupants ideally. The overhanging roof allows for the covered porch with its attractive wood columns. The center entrance leads to an interior which will cater to the formal as well as the informal activities of the family. Two fireplaces, back-to-back, serve the master bedroom and the quiet, formal living room. A two-way fireplace can be enjoyed from the large, beamed ceiling family room and the gaily, informal family kitchen. Note the laundry, the powder room and the garage storage. Of particular interest, is the storage room and the storage balcony. No storage problems here.

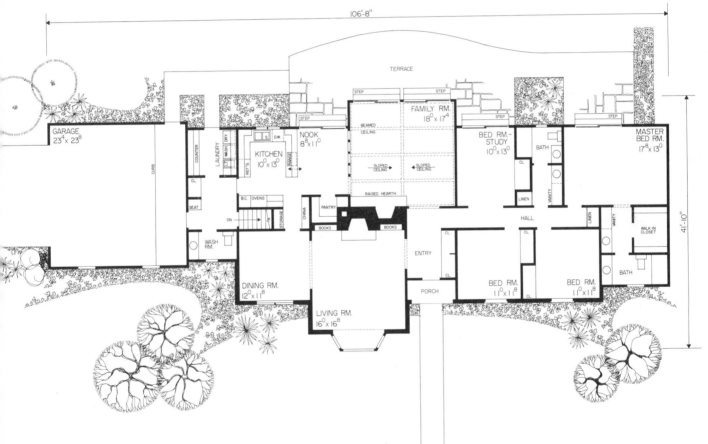

# Design T12544 2,527 Sq. Ft.; 61,943 Cu. Ft.

● A fine blend of exterior materials enhance the beauty of this fine home. Here, the masonry material used is fieldstone to contrast effectively with the horizontal siding. You may substitute brick or quarried stone if you wish. Adding to the appeal are the various projections and their roof planes, the window treatment and the recessed front entrance. Two large living areas highlight the interior. Each has a fireplace. The homemaking effort will be easily and enjoyably dispatched with such features as the efficient kitchen, the walk-in pantry, the handy storage areas, the first floor laundry and extra washroom. The sleeping zone has four bedrooms, two baths with vanities and good closet accommodations. There's a basement for additional storage and recreation.

## Design T11835
**2,144 Sq. Ft.; 33,310 Cu. Ft.**

● Cedar shakes and quarried natural stone, are the exterior materials which adorn this irregularly shaped traditional ranch home. Adding to the appeal of the exterior are the cut-up windows, the shutters, the pediment gable, the cupola and the double front doors. The detail of the garage door opening adds further interest. Inside, this favorite among floor plans, reflects all the features neccessary to provide complete livability for the large family. The sleeping zone is a 24' x 40' rectangle which contains four bedrooms and two full baths. A dressing room with a vanity and a wall of wardrobe storage highlights the master bedroom. Both the informal family room and the formal living room have a fireplace.

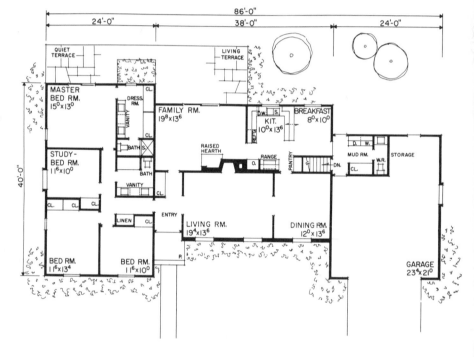

● Whatever the setting, here is a traditional, one story home that is truly impressive. Zoned in a most practical manner, the floor plan features an isolated bedroom wing, formal living and dining rooms and, across the rear of the house, the informal living areas.

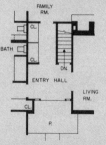

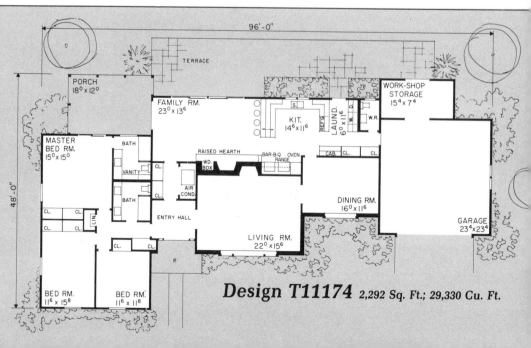

## Design T11174  2,292 Sq. Ft.; 29,330 Cu. Ft.

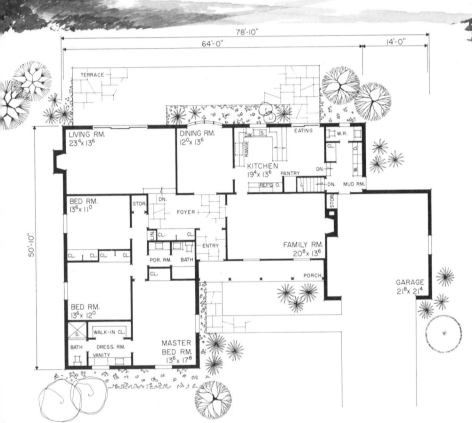

## Design T11786
### 2,370 Sq. Ft.; 37,170 Cu. Ft.

● Like this? If the answer is, yes, it is easy to understand. This is an extremely appealing design, highlighted by its brick masses, its window detailing, its interesting shape, and its inviting covered front entrance. The foyer is centrally located and but a step or two from all areas. The house, while it features all the facilities for family living, assures a full measure of privacy for all. The bedroom wing is distinctly defined. The quiet, sunken living room is off by itself. There is a separate, formal dining room. The family room is one which will function alone and cater to numerous activities. The kitchen, with its eating space, is of good size. The mud-room area is a true convenient living feature.

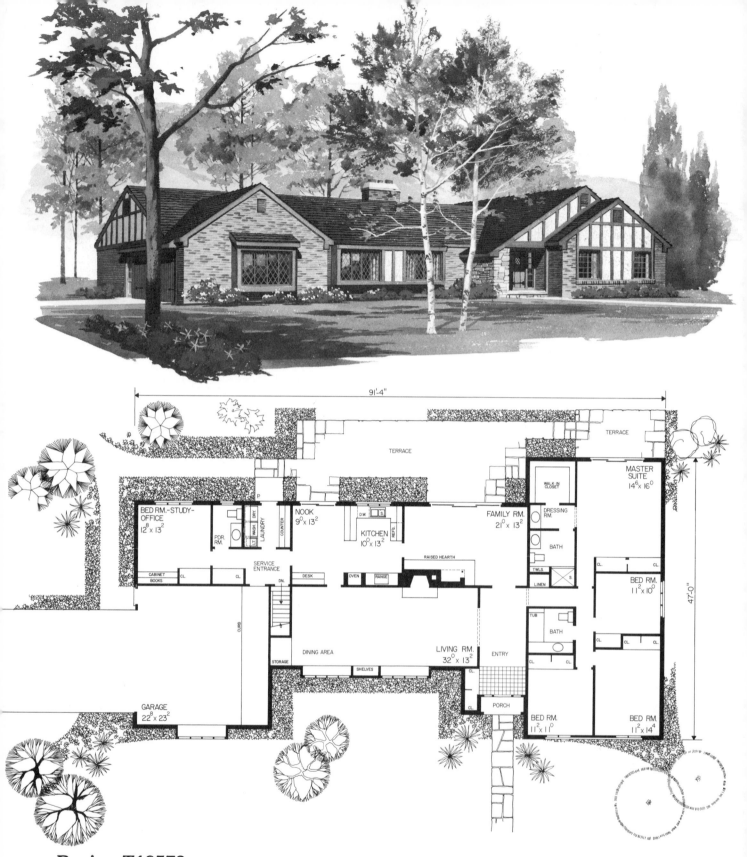

## Design T12573 2,747 Sq. Ft.; 48,755 Cu. Ft.

● A Tudor ranch! Combining brick and wood for an elegant look. With a living/dining room measuring 32' by 13' (large indeed) fully appointed with a traditional fireplace and built-in shelves flanked by diagonally paned windows. There's much more! A family room with a raised hearth fireplace and sliding glass doors that open onto the terrace. A U-shaped kitchen with lots of built-ins . . . a range, an oven, a desk. Plus a separate breakfast nook. The sleeping facilities consist of three family bedrooms plus an elegant master bedroom suite. A conveniently located laundry with a folding counter is in the service entrance. Adjacent to the laundry is a wash room and in the corner of the plan is a study or make it a fifth bedroom if you prefer.

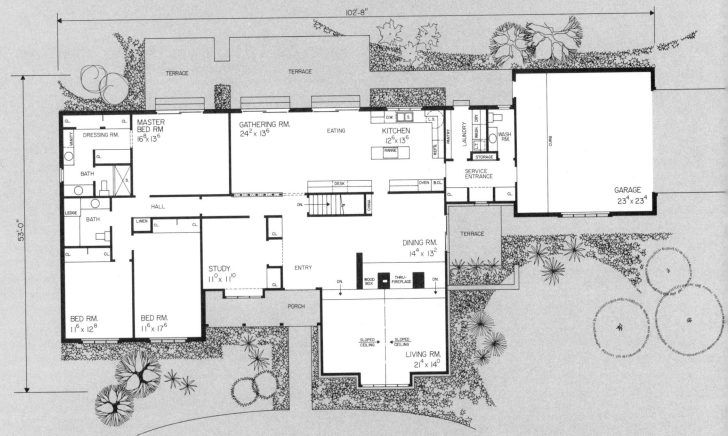

# Design T12746 2,790 Sq. Ft.; 57,590 Cu. Ft.

● This impressive one-story will surely be the talk-of-the-town. And not surprisingly, either. It embodies all the elements to assure a sound investment and years of happy family livability. The projecting living room with its stucco, simulated wood beams, and effective window treatment add a dramatic note. Sunken by two steps, this room will enjoy much privacy. The massive double front doors are sheltered by the covered porch and lead to the spacious entry hall. The interior is particularly well-zoned. The large rear gathering room will cater to the family's gregarious instincts. Outdoor enjoyment can be obtained on the three terraces. Also a study for those extra quiet moments. Be sure to observe the plan closely for all of the other fine features.

175

## Design T12209
**2,659 Sq. Ft.; 45,240 Cu. Ft.**

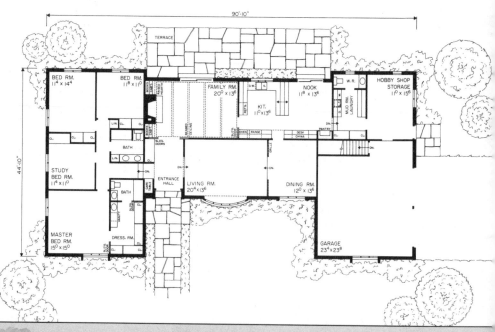

● Such an impressive home would, indeed, be difficult to top. And little wonder when you consider the myriad of features this one-story Colonial possesses. Consider the exquisite detailing, the fine proportions, and the symmetry of the projecting wings. The gracious and inviting double front doors are a prelude to the exceptional interior. Consider the four bedroom, two-bath sleeping wing. Formal entertaining can be enjoyed in the front living and dining rooms. For informal living there is the rear family room.

## Design T12264
**2,352 Sq. Ft.; 33,924 Cu. Ft.**

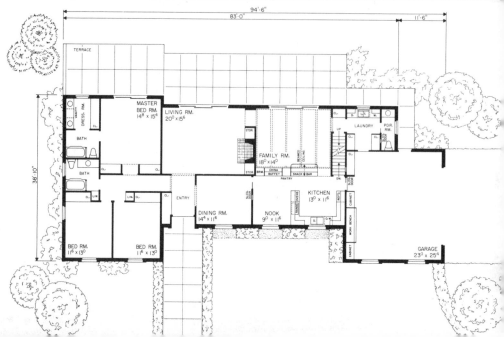

● This U-shaped traditional will be a welcomed addition on any site. It has living facilities which will provide your family with years of delightful livability. The two living areas are located to the rear and function with the outdoor terrace. The outstanding kitchen is strategically located handy to the family room and the eating areas. A separate laundry area with fine storage and nearby powder room is a favorite feature. Note garage size and storage potential. Also notice stairway to attic.

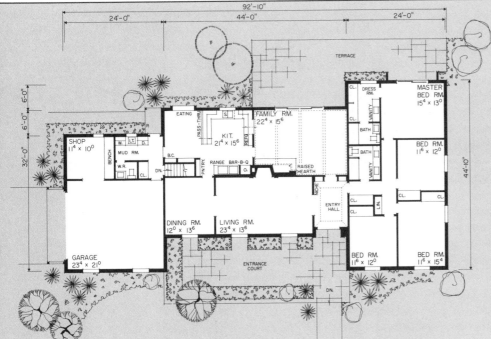

## Design T11761
### 2,548 Sq. Ft.; 43,870 Cu. Ft.

● Low, strong roof lines and solid, enduring qualities of brick give this house a permanent, here-to-stay appearance. Bedroom wing is isolated, and the baths and closets deaden noise from the rest of the house. Center fireplaces in family and living rooms make furniture arrangement easy. There are a number of extras – a workshop, an unusually large garage, and an indoor barbecue. Garage has easy access to both basement and kitchen area. There are two eating areas – a formal dining room and a breakfast nook next to the delightful kitchen.

## Design T12134 2,530 Sq. Ft.; 44,458 Cu. Ft.

## Design T11892
2,036 Sq. Ft.; 26,575 Cu. Ft.

● The romance of French Provincial is captured here by the hip-roof masses, the charm of the window detailing, the brick quoins at the corners, the delicate dentil work at the cornices, the massive centered chimney and the recessed double front doors. The slightly raised entry court completes the picture. The basic floor plan is a favorite of many. And little wonder, for all areas work well together, while still maintaining a fine degree of separation of functions. The highlight of the interior, perhaps, will be the sunken living room.

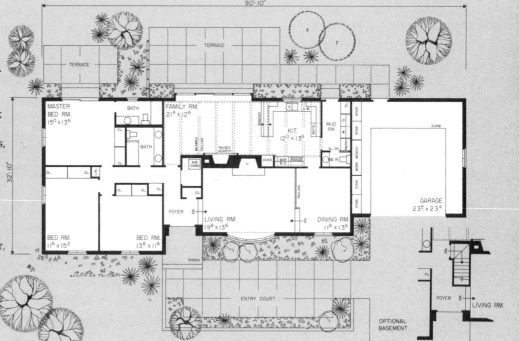

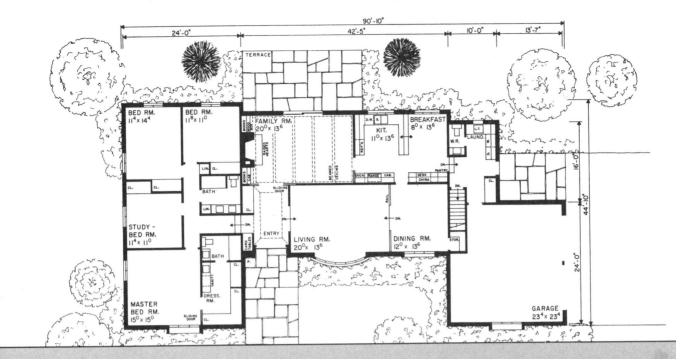

BED RM. 11⁴ x 14⁴

BED RM. 11⁸ x 11⁰

TERRACE

FAMILY RM. 20⁰ x 13⁶

KIT. 11⁰ x 13⁶

BREAKFAST 8⁰ x 13⁶

W.R.

LAUND.

LT.

BOOKS

LIN. CL.

BATH

CL. CL.

BOOKS CAB.

BEAMED CEILING

OVEN RANGE CAB.

DESK CHINA

PANTRY

STOR.

STUDY - BED RM. 11⁴ x 11⁰

LIN.

CL.

SLIDING DOOR

CARD TABLES

ENTRY

LIVING RM. 20⁰ x 13⁶

DINING RM. 12⁰ x 13⁶

RAIL

DN.

DN.

BATH

VANITY

CL.

F.

MASTER BED RM. 15⁰ x 15⁰

DRESS. RM.

SLIDING DOOR

CL.

GARAGE 23⁴ x 23⁴

90'-10"
24'-0"  42'-5"  10'-0"  13'-7"
16'-0"
44'-10"
24'-0"

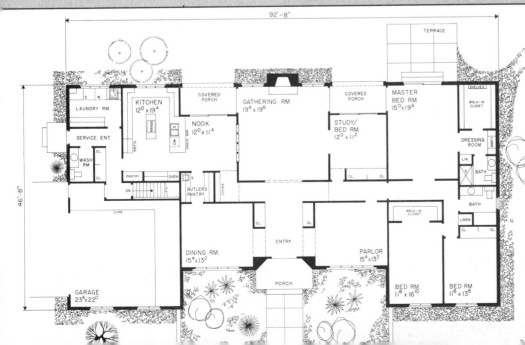

92'-8"

46'-8"

LAUNDRY RM.

KITCHEN 12⁰ x 19⁴

COVERED PORCH

GATHERING RM. 19⁴ x 19⁶

COVERED PORCH

MASTER BED RM. 15⁰ x 19⁶

SHELVES

WALK-IN CLOSET

SERVICE ENT.

NOOK 12⁰ x 11⁴

SNACK BAR

RANGE

REF'G

WASH RM.

CL.

STUDY/ BED RM. 12⁰ x 11²

DRESSING ROOM

VANITY

LIN.

BATH

CURB

PANTRY

BUTLERS PANTRY

OVEN

CHINA

DN.

CL.

CL.

WALK-IN CLOSET

BATH

LINEN

CL.

CL.

GARAGE 23⁴ x 22⁰

DINING RM. 15⁴ x 13²

ENTRY

PORCH

PARLOR 15⁴ x 13²

BED RM 11⁶ x 16¹⁰

BED RM 11⁶ x 13⁶

## Design T12779
**3,225 Sq. Ft.; 70,715 Cu. Ft.**

● This French design is surely impressive. The exterior appearance will brighten any area. The inside is just as appealing. Note the unique placement of rooms and features. The entry hall is large and leads to each of the areas in this plan. To the right of the entry is a sizable parlor. Then there is the gathering room with fireplace, sliding glass doors and adjacent study. The work center is also outstanding. It includes a U-shaped kitchen, large laundry and wash room.

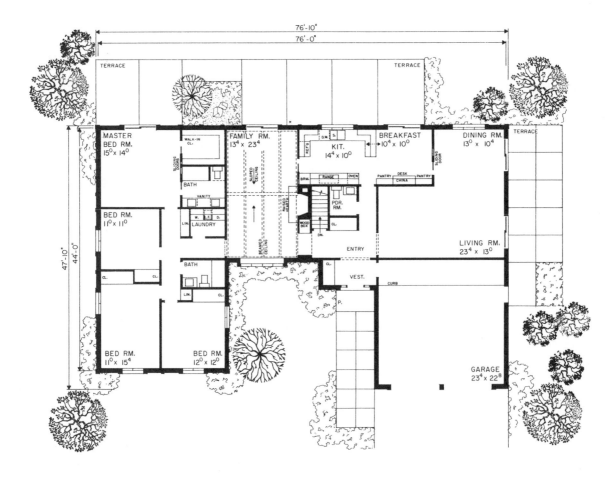

# Design T12142 2,450 Sq. Ft.; 43,418 Cu. Ft.

● Adaptations of Old England have become increasingly popular in today's building scene. And little wonder; for many of these homes when well-designed have a very distinctive charm. Here is certainly a home which will be like no other in its neighborhood. Its very shape adds an extra measure of uniqueness. And inside, there is all the livability the exterior seems to fortell. The sleeping wing has four bedrooms, two full baths and the laundry room — just where the soiled linen originates. The location of the family room is an excellent one. It is convenient for children because their traffic usually flows between family room and bedrooms. The spacious formal living and dining area will enjoy its privacy and be great fun to furnish.

# Design T12181   2,612 Sq. Ft.; 45,230 Cu. Ft.

● It is hard to imagine a home with any more eye-appeal than this one. It is the complete picture of charm. The interior is no less outstanding. Sliding glass doors permit the large master bedroom, the quiet living room, and the all-purpose family room to function directly with the outdoors. The two fireplaces, the built-in china cabinets, the book shelves, the complete laundry and kitchen pass-thru to breakfast room are extra features. Count the closets. There are all kinds of storage facilities. Don't miss those in the beamed ceilinged family room. The oversized garage with its raised curb offers further storage possibilities. Although the illustration of this home shows natural quarried stone, you may wish to substitute brick or even siding. Note location of basement stairs.

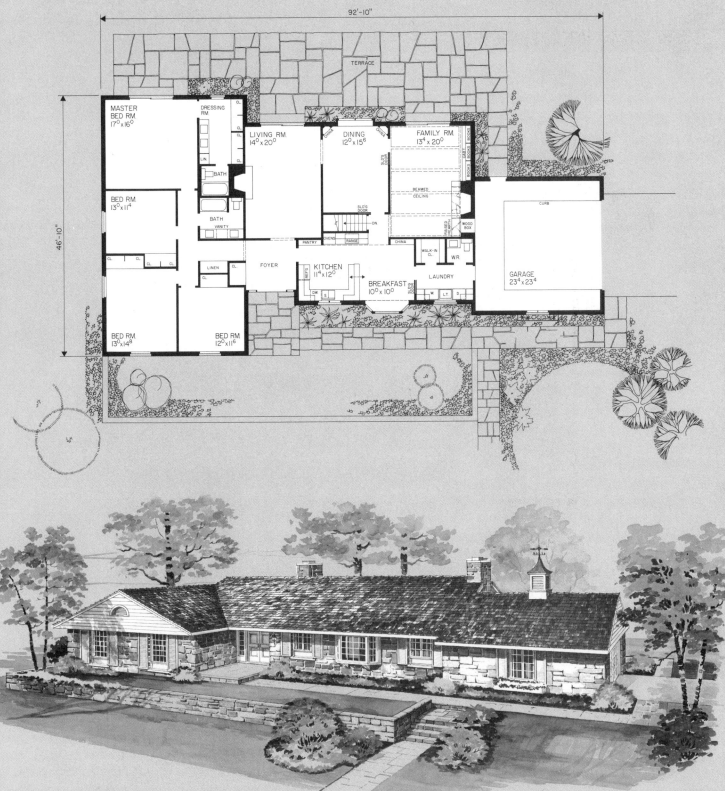

## Design T11989
**2,282 Sq. Ft.; 41,831 Cu. Ft.**

● High style with a plan as contemporary as today and tomorrow. There is, indeed, a feeling of coziness that emanates from the ground-hugging qualities of this picturesque home. Inside, there is livability galore. There's the sunken living room and the separate dining room to function as the family's formal living area. Then, overlooking the rear yard, there's the informal living area with its beamed ceiling family room, kitchen and adjacent breakfast room.

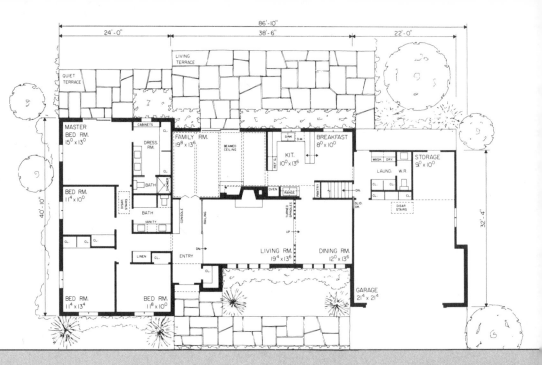

## Design T12378
**2,580 Sq. Ft.; 49,792 Cu. Ft.**

● If yours is a preference for an exterior that exudes both warmth and formality, the styling of English Tudor may suit your fancy. A host of architectural features blend together to produce this delightfully appealing exterior. Notice the interesting use of contrasting exterior materials. Don't overlook the two stylish chimneys. The manner in which the interior functions to provide the fine living patterns is outstanding. Each of four main rooms — look out on the rear terrace.

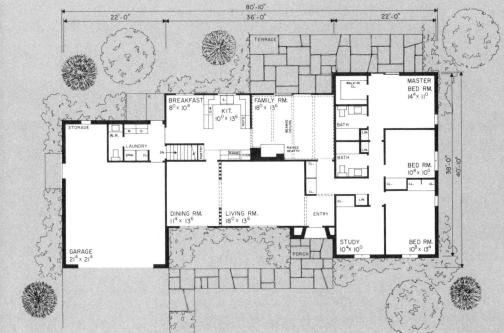

## Design T12129
**2,057 Sq. Ft.; 36,970 Cu. Ft.**

● This four bedroom home is zoned for convenient living. The sleeping area, with its two full baths and plenty of closets, will have a lot of privacy. The formal living and dining rooms function together and may be completely by-passed when desired. The informal living areas are grouped together and overlook the rear yard. The family room with its beamed ceiling is but a step from the kitchen. The U-shaped kitchen is handy to both the breakfast and dining rooms.

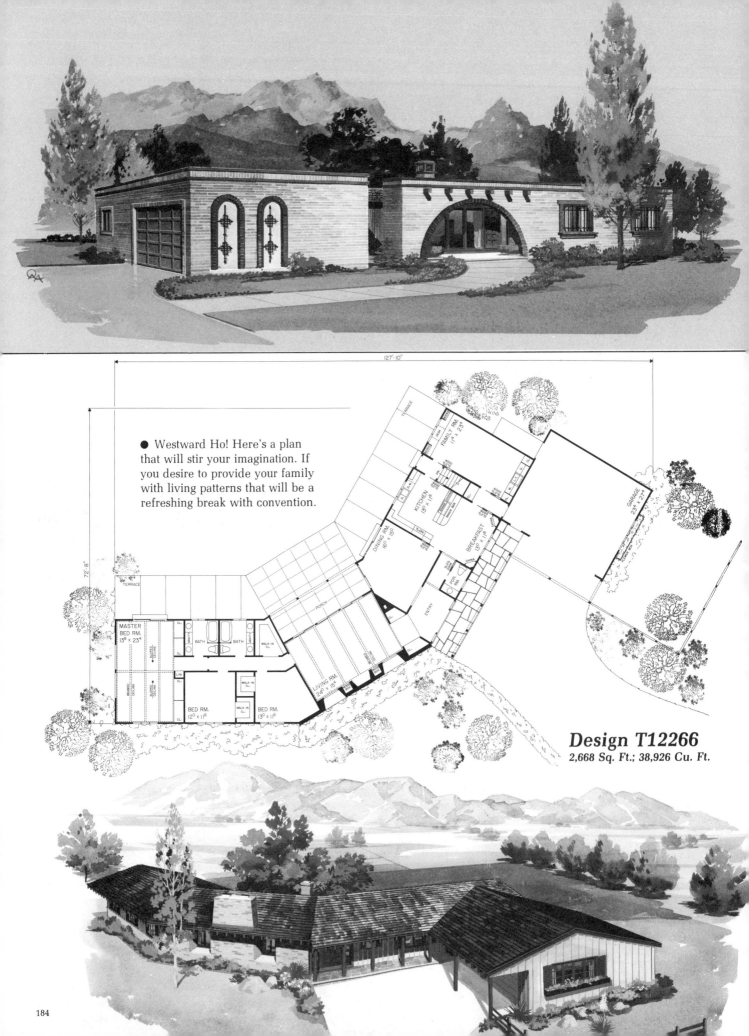

● Westward Ho! Here's a plan that will stir your imagination. If you desire to provide your family with living patterns that will be a refreshing break with convention.

## Design T12266
2,668 Sq. Ft.; 38,926 Cu. Ft.

## Design T12231
### 2,740 Sq. Ft.; 31,670 Cu. Ft.

● The features that will appeal to you about this flat-roofed Spanish hacienda are almost endless. Of course, the captivating qualities of the exterior speak for themselves. The extension of the front bedroom wall to form the inviting arch is distinctive. Once inside, any list of features will continue to grow rapidly. Both the family and living rooms are sunken. Private patio adjacent to the master suite.

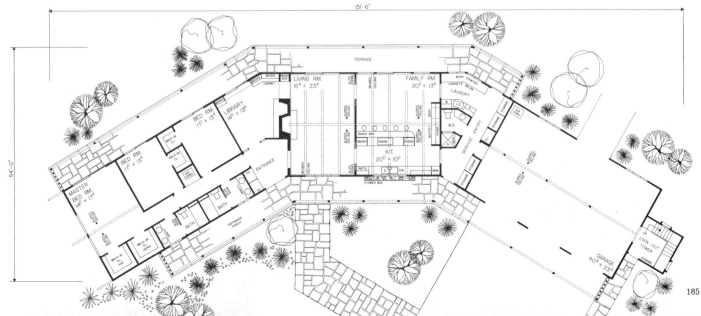

## Design T12258   2,504 Sq. Ft.; 26,292 Cu. Ft.

● Here's a real Western Ranch House with all the appeal of its forebears. As for the livability offered by this angular design, the old days of the rugged west never had anything like this.

# Design T12335
**2,674 Sq. Ft.; 41,957 Cu. Ft.**

● Surely a winner for those who have a liking for the architecture of the Far West. With or without the enclosure of the front court, this home with its stucco exterior, brightly colored roof tiles and exposed rafter tails will be impressive, indeed. The floor plan reflects a wonderfully zoned interior. This results in a separation of functions which helps assure convenient living. The traffic patterns which flow from the spacious foyer are most efficient. While the sleeping wing is angled to the front line of the house, the sunken living room projects at an angle to the rear.

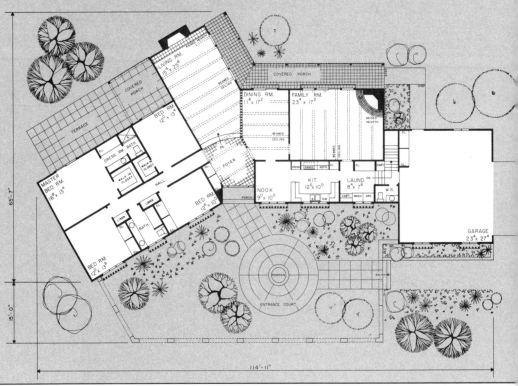

# Design T12236
**2,307 Sq. Ft.; 28,800 Cu. Ft.**

● Living in this Spanish adaptation will truly be fun for the whole family. It will matter very little whether the backdrop matches the mountains below, becomes the endless prairie, turns out to be the rolling farmland, or is the backdrop of a suburban area. A family's flair for distinction will be satisfied by this picturesque exterior, while its requirements for everyday living will be gloriously catered to. The hub of the plan will be the kitchen-family room area. The beamed ceiling and raised hearth fireplace will contribute to the cozy, informal atmosphere. The separate dining room and the sunken living room function together formally.

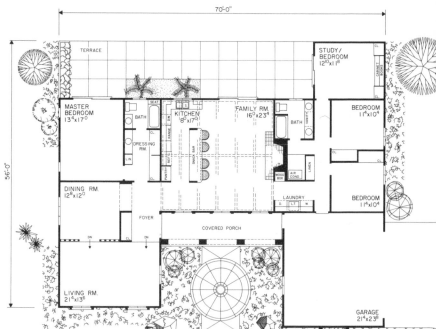

# Design T12820
**2,261 Sq. Ft.; 46,830 Cu. Ft.**

● A privacy wall around the courtyard with pool and trellised planter area is a gracious area by which to enter this one-story design. The Spanish flavor is accented by the grillework and the tiled roof. Interior livability has a great deal to offer. The front living room has sliding glass doors which open to the entrance court; the adjacent dining room features a bay window. Informal activities will be enjoyed in the rear family room. Its many features include a sloped, beamed ceiling, raised hearth fireplace, sliding glass doors to the terrace and a snack bar for those very informal meals. Four bedrooms are in the private, sleeping wing of the house.

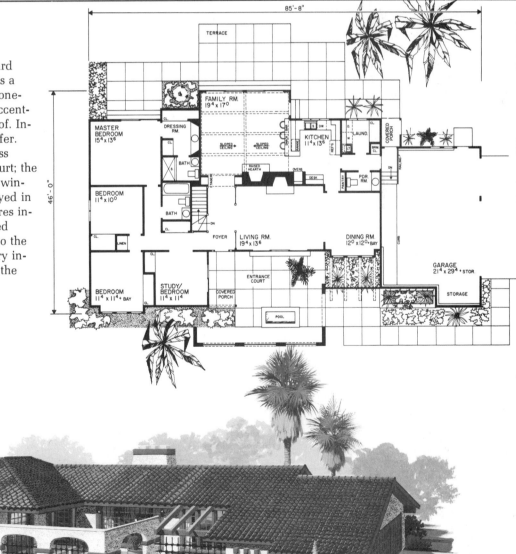

# Design T12756 2,652 Sq. Ft.; 51,540 Cu. Ft.

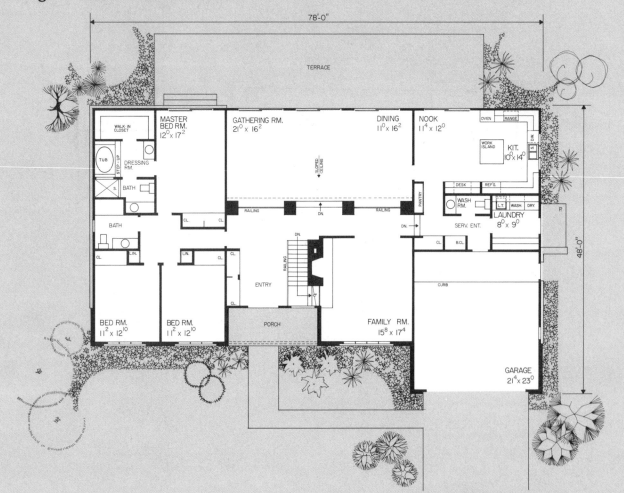

● This one-story contemporary is bound to serve your family well. With its many fine features it will assure the best in contemporary living. Notice the bath with tub and stall shower, dressing room and walk-in closet featured with the master bedroom. Two more family bedrooms. The sunken gathering room/dining room is highlighted by the sloped ceiling and sliding glass doors to the large rear terrace. This formal area is a full 32' x 16'. Imagine the great furniture placement that can be done in this area. In addition to the gathering room, there is an informal family room with fireplace. You will enjoy the efficient kitchen and get much use out of the work island, pantry and built-in desk. Note the service entrance with bath and laundry.

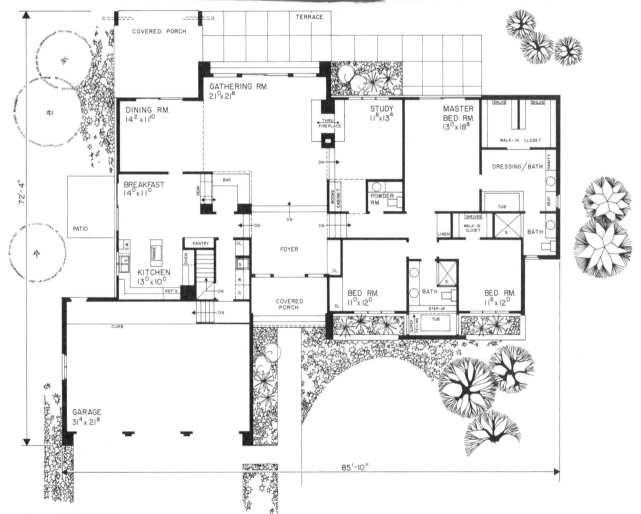

## Design T12789 2,732 Sq. Ft.; 54,935 Cu. Ft.

● An attached three car garage! What a fantastic feature of this three bedroom contemporary design. And there's more. As one walks up the steps to the covered porch and through the double front doors the charm of this design will be overwhelming. Inside, a large foyer greets all visitors and leads them to each of the three areas, each down a few steps. The living area has a large gathering room with fireplace and a study adjacent on one side and the formal dining room on the other. The work center has an efficient kitchen with island range, breakfast room, laundry and built-in desk and bar. Then there is the sleeping area. Note the raised tub with sloped ceiling.

● A spectacular foyer! Fully 21' long, it offers double entry to the heart of this home . . . a 21' by 21' gathering room complete with sloped ceiling, raised hearth fireplace and sliding glass doors onto the terrace. There's a formal dining room, too. Plus a well-located study . . . insuring space for solitude or undisturbed work. The kitchen features a snack bar and a breakfast nook with sliding doors onto the terrace. An arrangement that's sure to make every meal easy and pleasant. For more convenience, a pantry and first-floor laundry. In the master suite, a dressing room with entry to the bath, four closets and sliding doors onto the terrace! Two more bedrooms if you wish to convert the study or one easily large enough for two children with a dressing area and private entry to the second bath.

## Design T12229
**2,728 Sq. Ft.; 29,482 Cu. Ft.**

● Rustic in character, this ranch home offers all of the amenities that carefree living should be heir to. The irregular shape results in an enclosed front entrance court. Twin gates open to the coverd walk which looks out upon the delightful private court on its way to the front door. Traffic patterns are interesting. This house is zoned so as to provide maximum privacy to the living room and master bedroom. At the other end of the house are the children's rooms and the informal, multi-purpose family room. The kitchen is strategically located between these two areas. The projecting, sunken dining room with its abundance of glass will permit the fullest enjoyment of the outdoors at mealtime. Sloped ceilings are in almost every room.

## Design T12594 2,294 Sq. Ft.; 42,120 Cu. Ft.

## Design T11754
**2,080 Sq. Ft.; 21,426 Cu. Ft.**

● Boasting a traditional Western flavor, this rugged U-shaped ranch home has all the features to assure grand living. The low-pitched, wide-overhanging roof with exposed rafters, the masses of brick, and the panelled doors with their carriage lamps above are among the exterior highlights which create this design's unique character. The private front flower court, inside the high brick wall, fosters a delightfully dramatic atmosphere which carries inside. The floor plan is positively unique and exceptionally livable. Wonderfully zoned, the three bedrooms enjoy their full measure of privacy. Observe the dressing room, walk-in closet and linen storage. The formal living and dining rooms function together in a most pleasing fashion. An attractive open railing separates the dining room from the sunken living room.

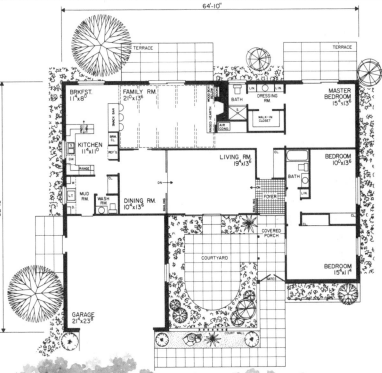

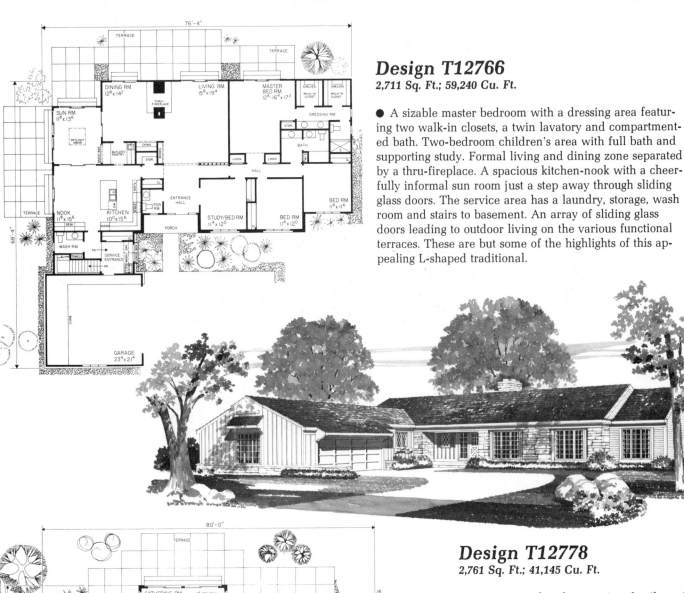

## Design T12766
**2,711 Sq. Ft.; 59,240 Cu. Ft.**

● A sizable master bedroom with a dressing area featuring two walk-in closets, a twin lavatory and compartmented bath. Two-bedroom children's area with full bath and supporting study. Formal living and dining zone separated by a thru-fireplace. A spacious kitchen-nook with a cheerfully informal sun room just a step away through sliding glass doors. The service area has a laundry, storage, wash room and stairs to basement. An array of sliding glass doors leading to outdoor living on the various functional terraces. These are but some of the highlights of this appealing L-shaped traditional.

## Design T12778
**2,761 Sq. Ft.; 41,145 Cu. Ft.**

● No matter what the occasion, family and friends alike will enjoy the sizable gathering room. A spacious 20' x 23', this room has a thru fireplace to the study and two sets of sliding glass doors to the large rear terrace. Indoor-outdoor living can also be enjoyed from the dining room, study and master bedroom. There is also a covered porch accessible through sliding glass doors in the dining room and breakfast nook.

# TWO-STORY HOMES . . . .

*Your two-story home can contain as many as 3671 square feet (below) or as few as 1216 (page 214). And, of course, it can be anywhere in between. However, regardless of size, if you build a two-story, you can be assured of an economical use of your construction dollar. This is because less roof structure and foundation are required for a two-story than for the same size one-story. Going upstairs to bed provides the two-story with its own stamp of distinction. This selection offers a myraid of examples of how the two-story home can vary in its size, style and variety of living features.*

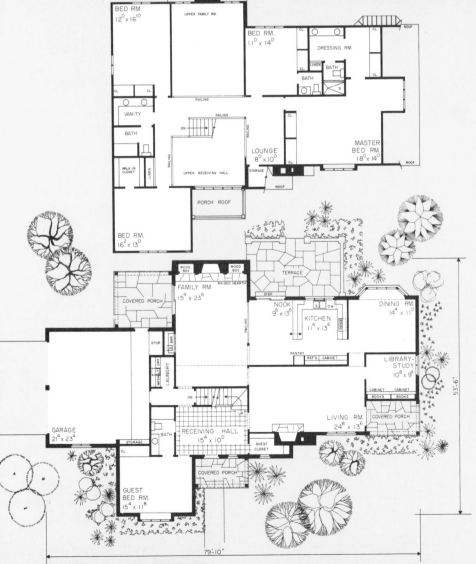

## Design T12356

**1,969 Sq. Ft. - First Floor**
**1,702 Sq. Ft. - Second Floor**
**55,105 Cu. Ft.**

● Here is truly an exquisite Tudor adaptation. The exterior with its interesting roof lines, window treatment, stately chimney and its appealing use of brick and stucco, could hardly be more dramatic. Inside, the drama really begins to unfold as one envisions his family's living patterns. The delightfully large receiving hall has a two story ceiling and controls the flexible traffic patterns. The living and dining rooms with the library nearby will cater to the formal living pursuits. The guest room offers another haven for the enjoyment of peace and quiet. Observe the adjacent full bath. Just inside the entrance from the garage is the laundry room. For the family's informal activities there are the interactions of the family room - covered porch - nook - kitchen zone. Notice the raised hearth fireplace, the wood boxes, the sliding glass doors, built-in bar and the kitchen pass-thru.

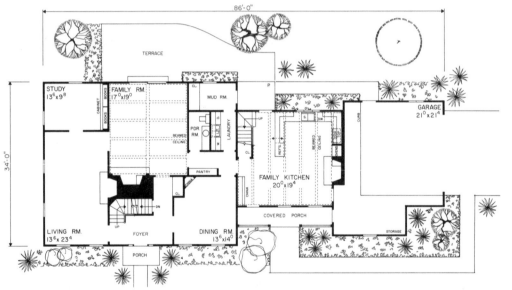

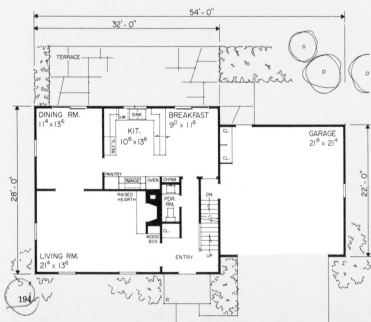

## Design T11986 896 Sq. Ft. - First Floor
### 1,148 Sq. Ft. - Second Floor; 28,840 Cu. Ft.

● This design with its distinctive Gambrel roof will spell charm wherever it may be situated - far out in the country, or on a busy thoroughfare. Compact and economical to build, it will be easy on the budget. Note the location of the family room. It is over the garage on the second floor.

# Design T12320 *1,856 Sq. Ft. - First Floor; 1,171 Sq. Ft. - Second Floor; 46,699 Cu. Ft.*

● A charming Colonial adaptation with a Gambrel roof front exterior and a Salt Box rear. The focal point of family activities will be the spacious family kitchen with its beamed ceiling and fireplace. Blueprints include details for both three and four bedroom options. In addition to the family kitchen, note beamed ceiling family room with fireplace. Don't miss the study with built-in book shelves and cabinets. Gracious living will be enjoyed throughout this design.

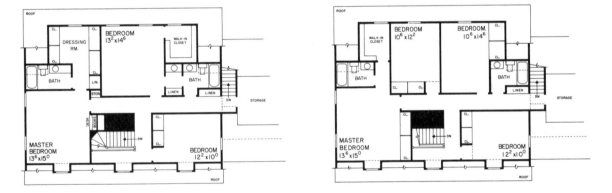

## Design T12535

**986 Sq. Ft. - First Floor**
**1,436 Sq. Ft. - Second Floor; 35,835 Cu. Ft.**

● What a great package this is! An enchanting Colonial exterior and an exceptional amount of interior livability. Utilizing the space over the garage results in a fifth bedroom with bath.

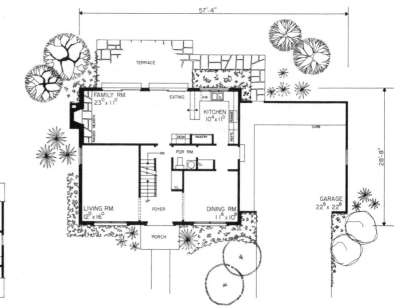

## Design T12558

**1,030 Sq. Ft. - First Floor**
**840 Sq. Ft. - Second Floor; 27,120 Cu. Ft.**

● This relatively low-budget house is long on exterior appeal and interior livability. It has all the features to assure years of convenient living. Make a list of your favorite features.

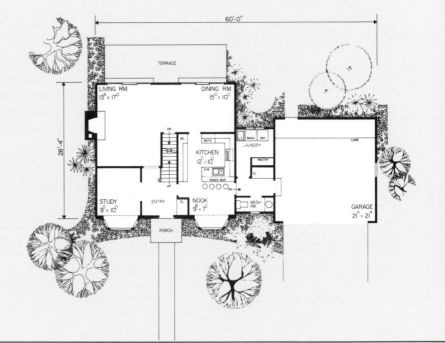

## Design T12540

**1,306 Sq. Ft. - First Floor**
**1,360 Sq. Ft. - Second Floor; 40,890 Cu. Ft.**

● This efficient Colonial abounds in features. A spacious entry flanked by living areas. A kitchen flanked by eating areas. Upstairs, four bedrooms including a sitting room in the master suite.

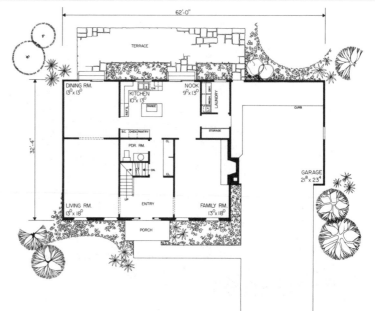

## Design T12646
**1,274 Sq. Ft. - First Floor**
**1,322 Sq. Ft. - Second Floor; 42,425 Cu. Ft.**

● What a stylish departure from today's usual architecture. This refreshing exterior may be referred to as Neo-Victorian. Its vertical lines, steep roofs and variety of gables remind one of the old Victorian houses of yesteryear. Inside, there is an efficiently working floor plan that is delightfully spacious.

## Design T12647 2,104 Sq. Ft. - First Floor; 1,230 Sq. Ft. - Second Floor; 56,395 Cu. Ft.

● Another Neo-Victorian, and what an impressive and unique design it is. Observe the roof lines, the window treatment, the use of contrasting exterior materials and the arched, covered front entrance.

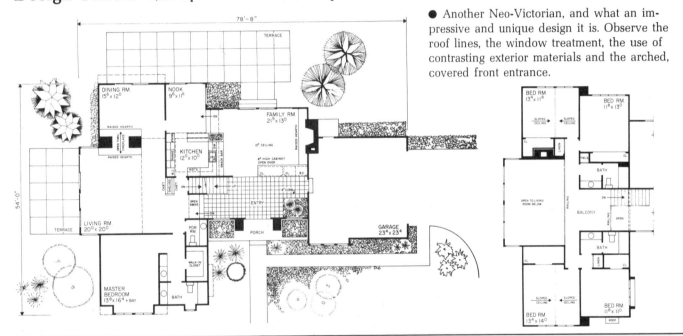

## Design T12645 1,600 Sq. Ft. - First Floor; 1,305 Sq. Ft. - Second Floor
### 925 Sq. Ft. - Third Floor; 58,355 Cu. Ft.

● Reminiscent of the Gothic Victorian style of the mid-19th Century, this delightfully detailed, three-story house has a wrap-around veranda for summertime relaxing. The parlor and family room, each with fireplaces, provide excellent formal and informal living facilities. The third floor houses two more great areas plus bath.

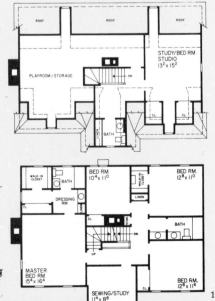

# Design T12518
**1,630 Sq. Ft. - First Floor**
**1,260 Sq. Ft. - Second Floor**
**43,968 Cu. Ft.**

● For those who have a predilection for the Spanish influence in their architecture. Outdoor oriented, each of the major living areas on the first floor have direct access to the terraces. Traffic patterns are excellent.

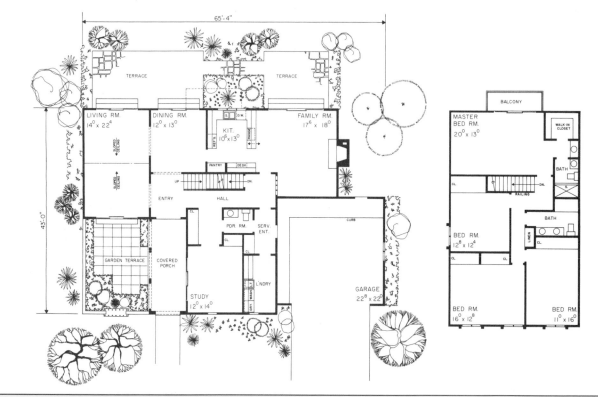

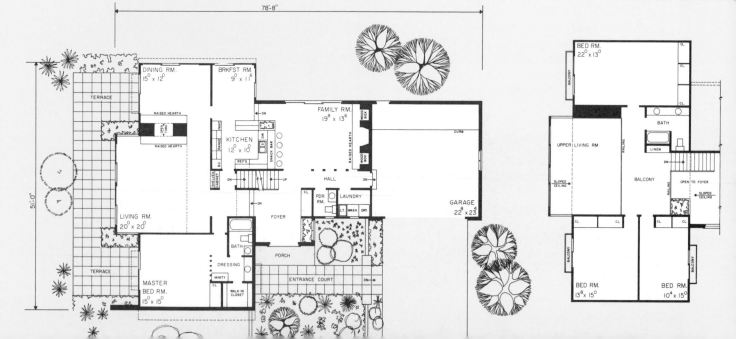

## Design T12517
**1,767 Sq. Ft. - First Floor**
**1,094 Sq. Ft. - Second Floor**
**50,256 Cu. Ft.**

● Wherever built - north, east, south, or west - this home will surely command all the attention it deserves. And little wonder with such a well-designed exterior and such an outstanding interior. List your favorite features.

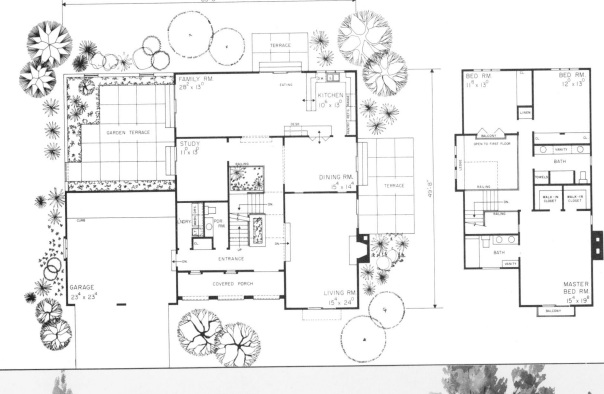

## Design T12512
**2,074 Sq. Ft. - First Floor**
**1,116 Sq. Ft. - Second Floor**
**41,500 Cu. Ft.**

● A Georgian Colonial adaptation on the grand scale. The authentic front entrance is delightfully detailed. Two massive end chimneys, housing four fireplaces, are in keeping with the architecture of its day.

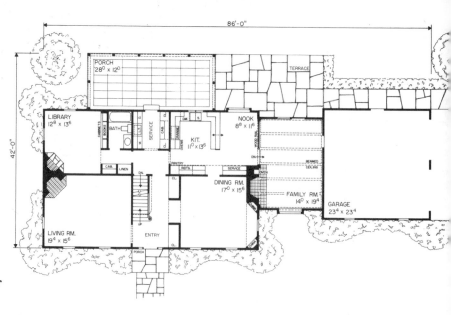

## Design T12221 1,726 Sq. Ft. - First Floor
1,440 Sq. Ft. - Second Floor; 50,204 Cu. Ft.

## Design T12610 1,505 Sq. Ft. - First Floor
1,344 Sq. Ft. - Second Floor; 45,028 Cu. Ft.

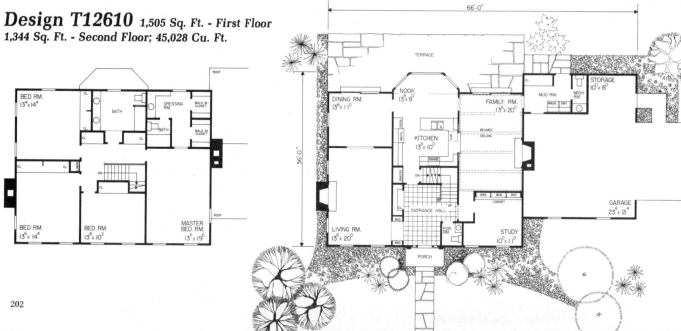

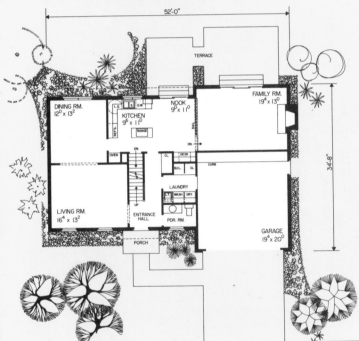

TERRACE

DINING RM.
12⁰ x 13²

KITCHEN
9⁶ x 11⁰

NOOK
9⁶ x 11⁰

FAMILY RM.
19⁴ x 13⁰

RANGE

OVEN

DESK

LAUNDRY
WASH. DRY.

LIVING RM.
16⁴ x 13²

UP

ENTRANCE
HALL

PDR. RM.

GARAGE
19⁴ x 20⁰

PORCH

52'-0"

34'-8"

# Design T12733
**1,177 Sq. Ft. - First Floor**
**1,003 Sq. Ft. - Second Floor; 32,040 Cu. Ft.**

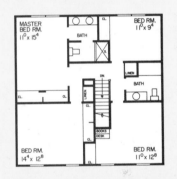

MASTER
BED RM.
11⁰ x 15⁴

BATH

BED RM.
11⁰ x 9⁴

LINEN

BATH

DN

BED RM.
14⁴ x 12⁸

BED RM.
11⁰ x 12⁸

BOOKS
DESK

● This is definitely a four bedroom Colonial with charm galore. The kitchen features an island range and other built-ins. All will enjoy the sunken family room with fireplace, which has sliding glass doors leading to the terrace. Also a basement for recreational activities with laundry remaining on first floor for extra convenience.

203

# Design T12148
**1,656 Sq. Ft. - First Floor**
**1,565 Sq. Ft. - Second Floor; 48,292 Cu. Ft.**

● The charm of this Tudor adaptation could hardly be improved upon. Its fine proportion and exquisite use of materials result in a most distinctive home.

# Design T12855
**1,372 Sq. Ft. - First Floor**
**1,245 Sq. Ft. - Second Floor; 44,495 Cu. Ft.**

● This elegant Tudor house is perfect for the family who wants to move up in living area, style and luxury. As you enter this home you will find a large living room with a fireplace. Adjacent, the formal dining room has easy access to the kitchen. Sunken a few steps, the spacious family room is highlighted by a fireplace and access to the rear, covered porch. Note the optional planning of the garage storage area. Plan this area according to the needs of your family.

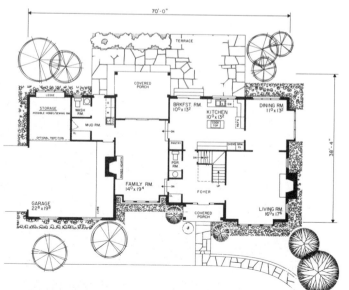

# Design T12794 1,680 Sq. Ft. - First Floor; 1,165 Sq. Ft. - Second Floor; 867 Sq. Ft. - Apartment; 55,900 Cu. Ft.

● A private apartment is over the garage of this exceptionally pleasing Tudor design. Use the main entrance, enter into the foyer and begin your journey throughout this design.

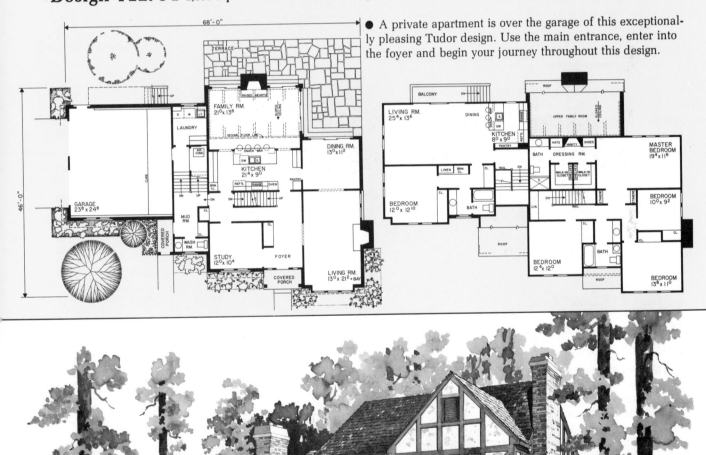

# Design T11858

**1,794 Sq. Ft. - First Floor**
**1,474 Sq. Ft. - Second Floor**
**424 Sq. Ft. - Studio; 54,878 Cu. Ft.**

● You'll never regret your choice of this Georgian design. Its stately facade seems to foretell all of the exceptional features to be found inside. From the delightful spacious front entry hall, to the studio or maid's room over the garage, this home is unique all along the way. Imagine four fireplaces, three full baths, two extra wash rooms, a family room, plus a quiet library. Don't miss the first floor laundry. Note the separate set of stairs to the studio, or maid's room. The center entrance leads to the vestibule and the wonderfully spacious entry hall. All the major areas are but a step or two from this formal hall. The kitchen is well-planned and strategically located between the separate dining room and the breakfast room. Sliding glass doors permit easy access to the functional rear terraces.

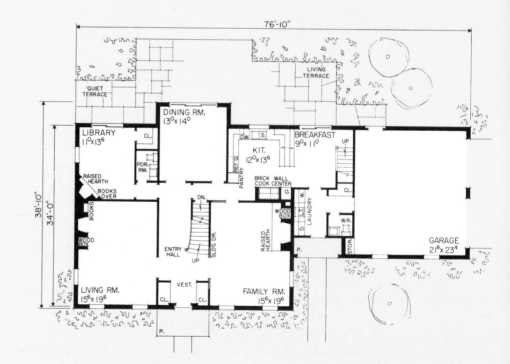

206

# Design T12543

*2,345 Sq. Ft. - First Floor*
*1,687 Sq. Ft. - Second Floor; 76,000 Cu. Ft.*

● Certainly a dramatic French adaptation highlighted by effective window treatment, delicate cornice detailing, appealing brick quoins and excellent proportion. Stepping through the double front doors the drama is heightened by the spacious entry hall with its two curving staircases to the second floor. The upper hall is open and looks down to the hall below. There is a study and a big gathering room which look out on the raised terrace. The work center is outstanding. The garage will accommodate three cars.

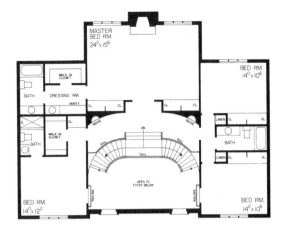

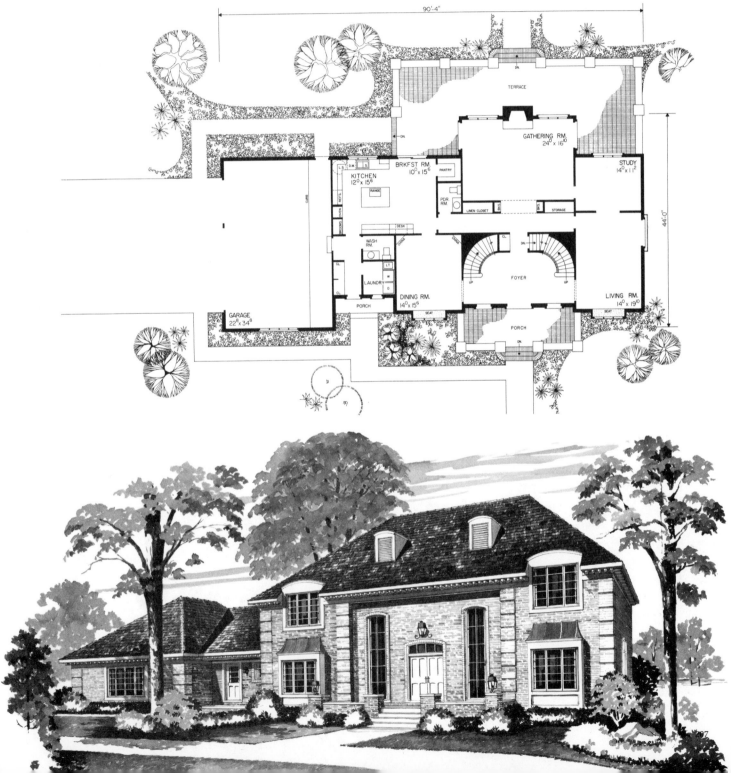

## Design T12107

**1,020 Sq. Ft. - First Floor**
**720 Sq. Ft. - Second Floor**
**25,245 Cu. Ft.**

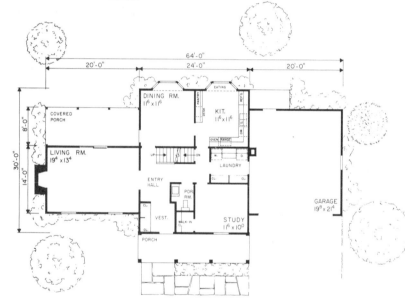

## Design T11773

**1,546 Sq. Ft. - First Floor**
**1,040 Sq. Ft. - Second Floor**
**33,755 Cu. Ft.**

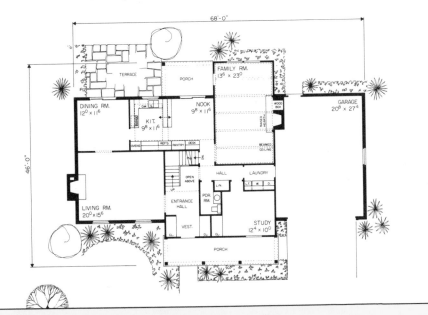

## Design T11208

**1,170 Sq. Ft. - First Floor**
**768 Sq. Ft. - Second Floor**
**26,451 Cu. Ft.**

## Design T12539
**1,450 Sq. Ft. - First Floor**
**1,167 Sq. Ft. - Second Floor; 46,738 Cu. Ft.**

● This appealingly proportioned Gambrel exudes an aura of coziness. The beauty of the main part of the house is delightfully symmetrical and is enhanced by the attached garage and laundry room. The center entrance routes traffic directly to all major zones of the house.

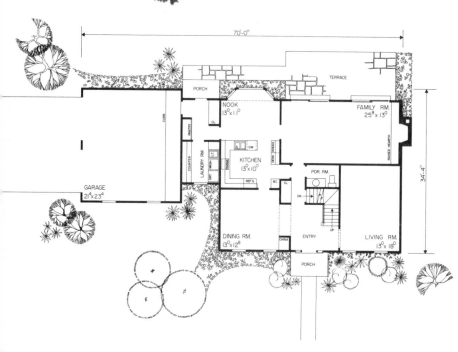

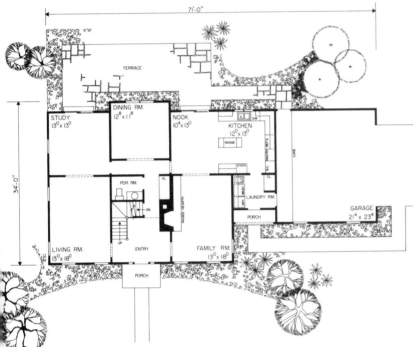

## Design T12538

**1,503 Sq. Ft. - First Floor**
**1,095 Sq. Ft. - Second Floor; 44,321 Cu. Ft.**

● This Salt Box is charming, indeed. The livability it has to offer to the large and growing family is great. The entry is spacious and is open to the second floor balcony. For living areas, there is the study in addition to the living and family rooms.

## Design T12731

**1,039 Sq. Ft. - First Floor**
**973 Sq. Ft. - Second Floor; 29,740 Cu. Ft.**

● The multi-paned windows with shutters of this two-story highlight the exterior delightfully. Inside the livability is ideal. Formal and informal areas are sure to serve your family with ease. Note efficient U-shaped kitchen with handy first-floor laundry. Sleeping facilities on second floor.

211

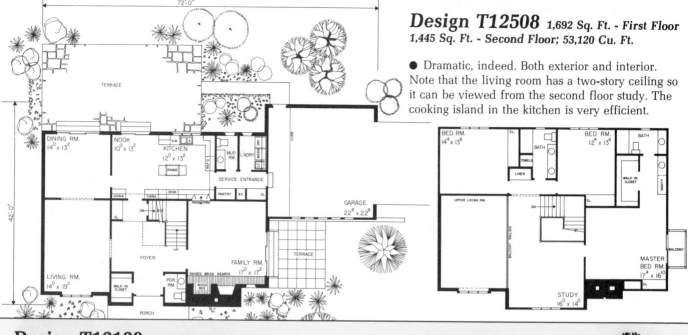

## Design T12508 1,692 Sq. Ft. - First Floor
1,445 Sq. Ft. - Second Floor; 53,120 Cu. Ft.

● Dramatic, indeed. Both exterior and interior. Note that the living room has a two-story ceiling so it can be viewed from the second floor study. The cooking island in the kitchen is very efficient.

## Design T12128 1,152 Sq. Ft. - First Floor
896 Sq. Ft. - Second Floor; 30,707 Cu. Ft.

● Here is proof that your restricted building budget can return to you wonderfully pleasing design and loads of livability. This is an English Tudor adaptation that will surely become your subdivision's favorite facade. Its mark of individuality is obvious to all.

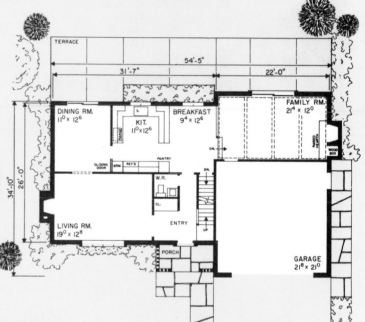

## Design T12800
**999 Sq. Ft. - First Floor**
**997 Sq. Ft. - Second Floor; 31,390 Cu. Ft.**

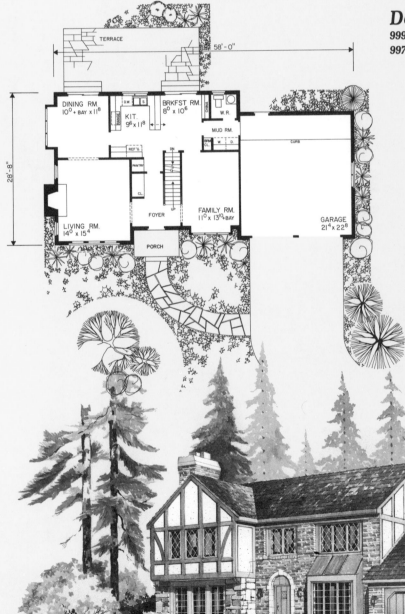

● This Tudor design has many fine features. The exterior is enhanced by front and side bay windows in the family and dining rooms. Along with an outstanding exterior, it also contains a modern and efficient floor plan within its modest proportions. Flanking the entrance foyer is a comfortable living room. The U-shaped kitchen is conveniently located between the dining and breakfast rooms.

## Design T12798
### 1,149 Sq. Ft. - First Floor
### 850 Sq. Ft. - Second Floor; 28,450 Cu. Ft.

● This compact two-story design has an island range in the kitchen which is a great feature of the work center. The breakfast room has an open railing to the family room so it can enjoy the view of the family room's fireplace. Sliding glass doors in each of the major rear rooms lead to the terrace.

## Design T12801   1,172 Sq. Ft. - First Floor
### 884 Sq. Ft. - Second Floor; 32,510 Cu. Ft.

● The great room in this design will be just that. It is sunken two steps, has a beamed ceiling, the beauty of a fireplace and two sets of sliding glass doors to a front and rear courtyard. Family room features include a built-in wet bar and fireplace. Built-ins are located throughout the plan. Four bedrooms are on the second floor.

## Design T12131
**1,214 Sq. Ft. - First Floor**
**1,097 Sq. Ft. - Second Floor**
**30,743 Cu. Ft.**

● The Gambrel-roof home is often the very embodiment of charm from the Early Colonial Period in American architechtural history. Fine proportion and excellent detailing were the hallmarks of the era.

Design T12211
**1,214 Sq. Ft. - First Floor**
**1,146 Sq. Ft. - Second Floor**
**32,752 Cu. Ft.**

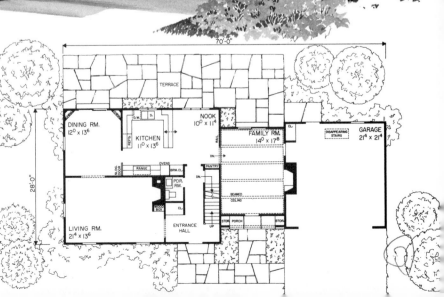

● The appeal of this Colonial home will be virtually everlasting. It will improve with age and service the growing family well. Imagine your family living here. There are four bedrooms, 2½ baths, plus plenty of first floor living space.

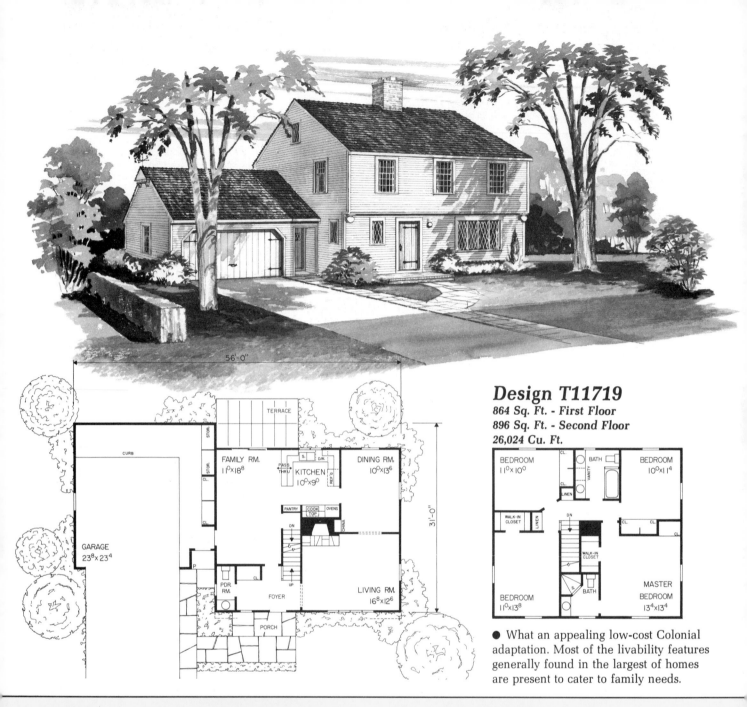

## Design T11719
**864 Sq. Ft. - First Floor**
**896 Sq. Ft. - Second Floor**
**26,024 Cu. Ft.**

● What an appealing low-cost Colonial adaptation. Most of the livability features generally found in the largest of homes are present to cater to family needs.

OPTIONAL 3 BEDROOM PLAN -

## Design T11956
**990 Sq. Ft. - First Floor**
**728 Sq. Ft. - Second Floor**
**23,703 Cu. Ft.**

● The blueprints for this home include details for both the three bedroom and four bedroom options. The first floor livability does not change.

## Design T12774 1,370 Sq. Ft. - First Floor
969 Sq. Ft. - Second Floor; 38,305 Cu. Ft.

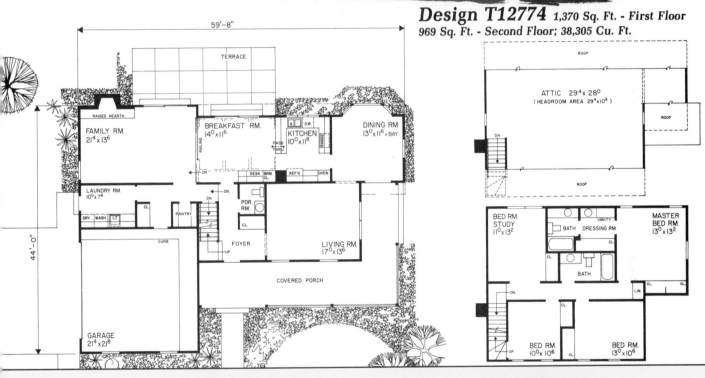

FAMILY RM. 21⁴ x 13⁶

RAISED HEARTH

BREAKFAST RM. 14⁰ x 11⁶

KITCHEN 10⁰ x 11⁸

DINING RM. 13⁰ x 11⁶ + BAY

TERRACE

59'-8"

44'-0"

LAUNDRY RM. 10⁰ x 7⁶

DRY. WASH. LT.

PANTRY

CL.

PDR. RM.

CL.

FOYER

DESK BRM. CL. REF'G OVEN

LIVING RM. 17⁰ x 13⁶

COVERED PORCH

CURB

GARAGE 21⁴ x 21⁸

ATTIC 29⁴ x 28⁰ (HEADROOM AREA 29⁴ x 10⁶)

ROOF

BED RM. STUDY 11⁰ x 13²

BATH

DRESSING RM.

VANITY

MASTER BED RM. 13⁰ x 13²

BATH

BED RM. 10⁰ x 10⁶

BED RM. 13⁰ x 10⁶

LIN.

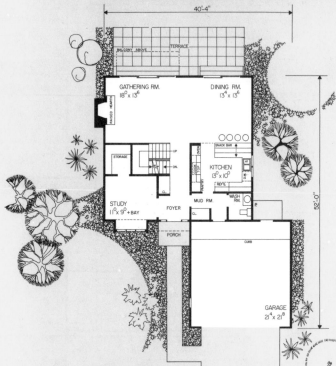

## Design T12711 975 Sq. Ft. - First Floor
**1,024 Sq. Ft. - Second Floor; 31,380 Cu. Ft.**

● Special features! A complete master suite with a private balcony plus two more bedrooms and a bath upstairs. The first floor has a study with a storage closet. A convenient snack bar between kitchen and dining room. The kitchen offers many built-in appliances. Plus a gathering room and dining room that measures 31 feet wide. Note the curb area in the garage and fireplace in gathering room.

## Design T12748
**1,232 Sq. Ft. - First Floor**
**720 Sq. Ft. - Second Floor**
**27,550 Cu. Ft.**

● This four bedroom contemporary will definitely have appeal for the entire family. The U-shaped kitchen-nook area with its built-in desk, adjacent laundry/wash room and service entrance will be very efficient for the busy kitchen activities. The living and family rooms areboth sunken one step.

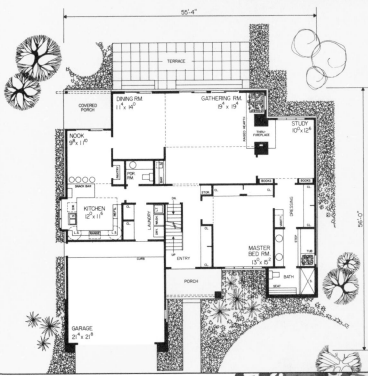

## Design T12701 *1,909 Sq. Ft. - First Floor*
### *891 Sq. Ft. - Second Floor; 50,830 Cu. Ft.*

● A snack bar in the kitchen! Plus a breakfast nook and formal dining room. Whether it's an elegant dinner party or a quick lunch, this home provides the right spot. There's a wet bar in the gathering room. Built-in bookcases in the study. And between these two rooms, a gracious fireplace. Three large bedrooms. Including a luxury master suite. Plus a balcony lounge overlooking gathering room below.

## Design T12729

**1,590 Sq. Ft. - First Floor**
**756 Sq. Ft. - Second Floor**
**39,310 Cu. Ft.**

● Entering this home will surely be a pleasure through the sheltered walk-way to the double front doors. And the pleasure and beauty does not stop there. The entry hall and sunken gathering room are open to the upstairs for added dimension.

There's even a built-in seat in the entry area. The kitchen-nook area is very efficient with its many built-ins and the adjacent laundry room. There is fine indoor-outdoor living relationship in this design. Note the private terrace off the luxurious

master bedroom suite, a living terrace accessible from the gathering room, dining room and nook plus the balcony off the upstairs bedroom. Upstairs there is a total of two bedrooms, each having its own private bath and plenty of closets.

# Design T12379  *1,525 Sq. Ft. - First Floor; 748 Sq. Ft. - Second Floor; 26,000 Cu. Ft.*

● A house that has "everything" may very well look just like this design. Its exterior is well-proportioned and impressive. Inside the inviting double front doors there are features galore. The living room and family room level are sunken. Separating these two rooms is a dramatic thru fireplace. A built-in bar, planter and beamed ceiling highlight the family room. Nearby is a full bath and a study which could be utilized as a fourth bedroom. The fine functioning kitchen has a pass-thru to the snack bar in the breakfast nook. The adjacent dining room overlooks the living room and has sliding doors to the covered porch. Upstairs three bedrooms, two baths and an outdoor balcony. Blueprints for this design include optional basement details.

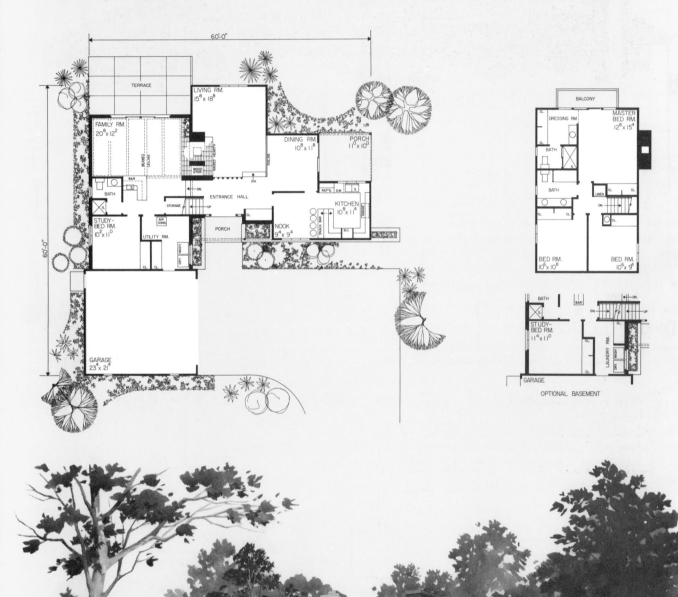

## Design T12530 1,616 Sq. Ft. - First Floor
### 997 Sq. Ft. - Second Floor; 41,925 Cu. Ft.

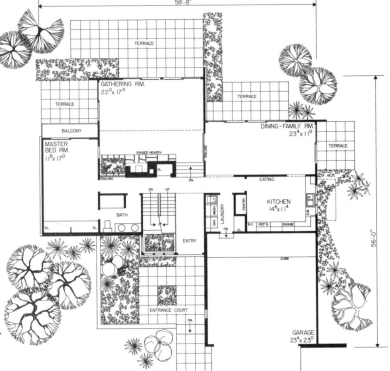

● This exciting contemporary has dramatic roof lines and appealing glass areas. The sunken gathering room is a delightful area with its dramatic raised hearth fireplace and planter, and access to two terraces. The second floor lounge looks down into this area.

## Design T12390 1,368 Sq. Ft. - First Floor
1,428 Sq. Ft. - Second Floor; 37,734 Cu. Ft.

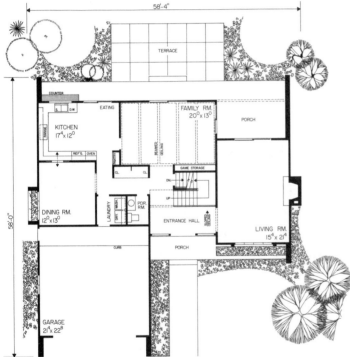

● If yours is a large family and you like the architecture of the Far West, don't look further. Particularly if you envision building on a modest sized lot. Projecting the garage to the front contributes to the drama of this two-story. Its stucco exterior is beautifully enchance by the clay tiles of the roof.

## Design T12781 2,132 Sq. Ft. - First Floor
1,156 Sq. Ft. - Second Floor; 47,365 Cu. Ft.

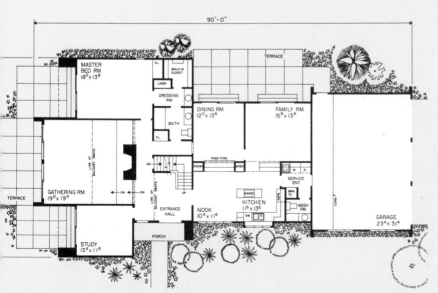

## Design T11354 644 Sq. Ft. - First Floor
**572 Sq. Ft. - Second Floor; 11,490 Cu. Ft.**

● Livability galore for the 50 foot building site. The homemaker will enjoy the U-shaped work center with the extra washroom and laundry equipment nearby. Three bedrooms are housed on the second floor. This compact design offers a lot of livability.

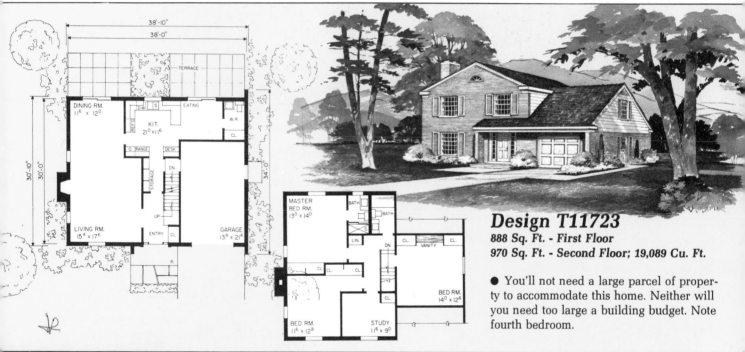

## Design T11723
**888 Sq. Ft. - First Floor**
**970 Sq. Ft. - Second Floor; 19,089 Cu. Ft.**

● You'll not need a large parcel of property to accommodate this home. Neither will you need too large a building budget. Note fourth bedroom.

## Design T12622 624 Sq. Ft. - First Floor
**624 Sq. Ft. - Second Floor; 19,864 Cu. Ft.**

● Appealing design can envelope little packages, too. Here is a charming, Early Colonial adaptation with an attached two-car garage to serve the young family with a modest building budget.

# Multi-Level Homes

For new dimensions in living, the multi-level home can be just what the active family is looking for. Grouped into this section are hillside designs, split-levels and bi-levels. Each type of design offers a distinctive set of living patterns. The hillside home may be two or three levels. However, the bottom level is generally exposed, thus providing an extra full level of cheerful livability. The split-level can have several configurations with each level generally performing a separate function. These levels may be for sleeping, living and recreation. The bi-level, sometimes called a raised one-story, usually has a foyer from which one short flight of stairs leads up to a level, while a second flight leads down to a level. Study the variations of multi-levels on the following pages.

UPPER GATHERING RM.

BALCONY | BALCONY

BED RM.
11⁸ x 13⁸

BUNK RM.
11⁸ x 19⁰

BALCONY | RAILING

CL | CL

BATH

RAILING | UPPER FOYER | DN.

CL | CL

40'-4"

DECK

GATHERING RM.
15⁴ x 18⁴

BALCONY

STUDY-
BED RM.
11⁸ x 13⁸

DINING RM.
11⁸ x 11⁸

52'-0"

LINEN | CL

SNACK BAR

BATH

KITCHEN
11⁸ x 9⁸

FOYER | DN. | UP

PANTRY REF. RANGE

PORCH

ENTRANCE COURT

TERRACE

ACTIVITIES RM.
15⁴ x 18⁴

BASEMENT

BUNK RM. OPTIONAL
11⁴ x 15⁸

STORAGE

RAISED HEARTH

AIR COND.

CARPORT
11⁸ x 20⁰

BATH

UP

STORAGE CABINETS

CL | LT. | WASH. DRY.

## Design T12511
**1,043 Sq. Ft. - Main Level
703 Sq. Ft. - Upper Level
794 Sq. Ft. - Lower Level
30,528 Cu. Ft.**

● Study this outstanding multi-level with its dramatic outdoor deck and balconies. This home is ideal if you are looking for a home that is new and exciting. The livability that it offers will efficiently serve your family.

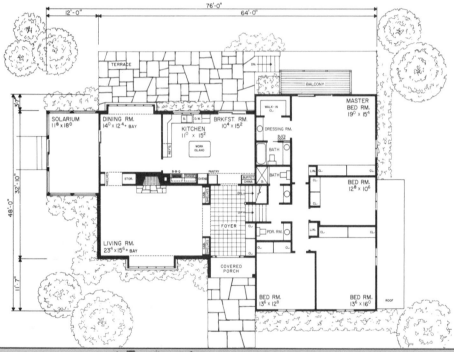

## Design T12254

**1,220 Sq. Ft. - Main Level**
**1,344 Sq. Ft. - Upper Level**
**659 Sq. Ft. - Lower Level**
**56,706 Cu. Ft.**

● Tudor charm is deftly exemplified by this outstanding four level design. The window treatment, the heavy timber work and the chimney pots help set the character of this home. Contributing an extra measure of appeal is the detailing of the delightful solarium. The garden view of this home is equally appealing. The upper level balcony looks down onto the two terraces. The covered front entry leads to the spacious formal entrance hall with its slate floor. . .

## Design T12243

**1,274 Sq. Ft. - Main Level; 960 Sq. Ft. - Upper Level**
**936 Sq. Ft. - Lower Level; 42,478 Cu. Ft.**

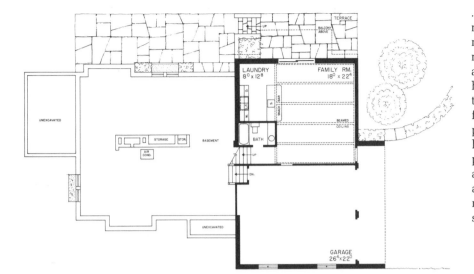

. . . Straight ahead is the kitchen and nook. The open planning of this area results in a fine feeling of spaciousness. Both living and dining rooms are wonderfully large. Each room highlights a big bay window. Notice the built-in units. Upstairs there are four bedrooms, two full baths and a powder room. Count the closets. The lower level is reserved for the all-purpose room, the separate laundry and a third full bath. The garage is adjacent. A fourth level is a basement with an abundance of space for storage and hobbies.

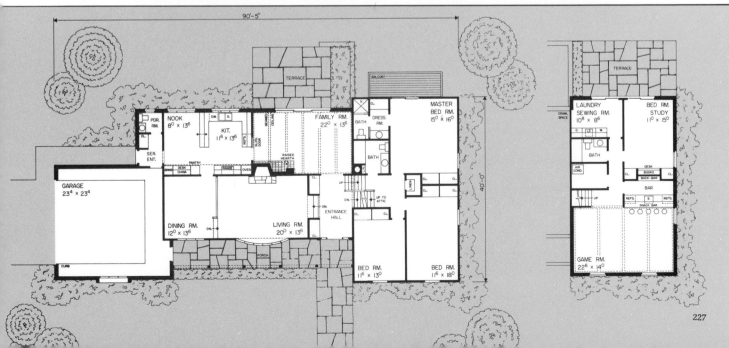

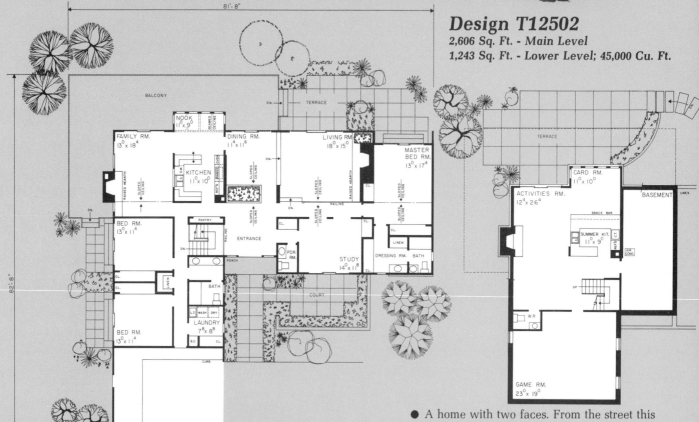

## Design T12502

**2,606 Sq. Ft. - Main Level**
**1,243 Sq. Ft. - Lower Level; 45,000 Cu. Ft.**

● A home with two faces. From the street this design gives all the appearances of being a one-story, L-shaped home. One can only guess at the character of the rear elevation as dictated by the sloping terrain. A study of the interior reveals tremendous convenient living potential.

# Design T12504
**1,918 Sq. Ft. - Main Level**
**1,910 Sq. Ft. - Lower Level; 39,800 Cu. Ft.**

● A front court area welcomes guests on their way to the double front doors. These doors, flanked by floor-to-ceiling glass panels, are sheltered by the porch. Adjacent to this area is the sliding glass doors of the breakfast nook which can enjoy to the fullest the beauty of the front yard. This design has taken the advantage of the sloping site to open up the lower level. In this case, the lower level has virtually the same glass treatment as its corresponding room above.

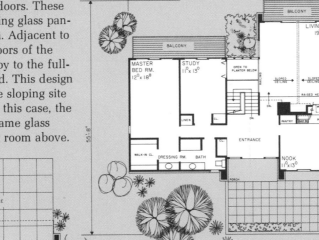

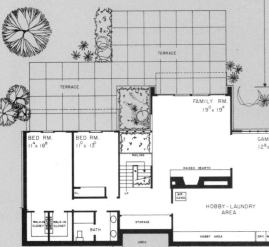

● Projecting over the lower level in Garrison Colonial style is the upper level containing three bedrooms a compartmented bath with twin lavatories and two handy linen closets. The main level consists of an L-shaped kitchen with convenient eating space, a formal dining room with sliding glass doors to the terrace and a sizable living room. On the lower level there is access to the outdoors, a spacious family room and a laundry-wash room area.

● Here are four levels just waiting for the opportunity to serve the living requirements of the active family. The traditional appeal of the exterior will be difficult to beat. Observe the window treatment, the double front doors, the covered front porch and the wrought iron work.

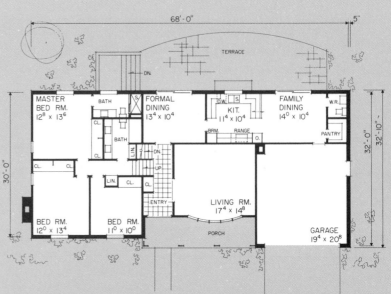

**Design T11308** 496 Sq. Ft. - Main Level; 572 Sq. Ft. - Upper Level; 537 Sq. Ft. - Lower Level; 16,024 Cu. Ft.

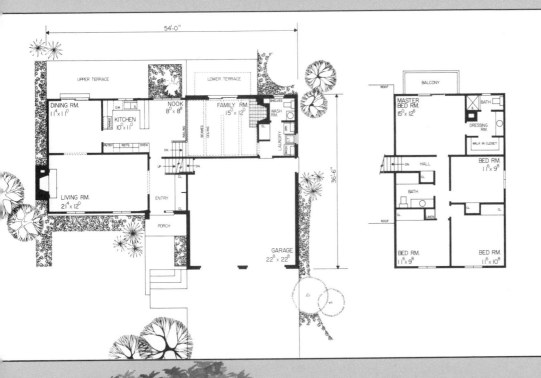

# Design T12608
**728 Sq. Ft. - Main Level**
**874 Sq. Ft. - Upper Level**
**310 Sq. Ft. - Lower Level**
**27,705 Cu. Ft.**

● Here is tri-level livability with a fourth basement level for bulk storage and, perhaps, a shop area. There are four bedrooms, a handy laundry, two eating areas, formal and informal living areas and two fireplaces. Sliding glass doors in the formal dining room and the family room open to a terrace. The U-shaped kitchen has a built-in range/oven and pantry.

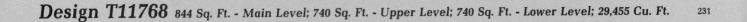

**Design T11768** 844 Sq. Ft. - Main Level; 740 Sq. Ft. - Upper Level; 740 Sq. Ft. - Lower Level; 29,455 Cu. Ft.

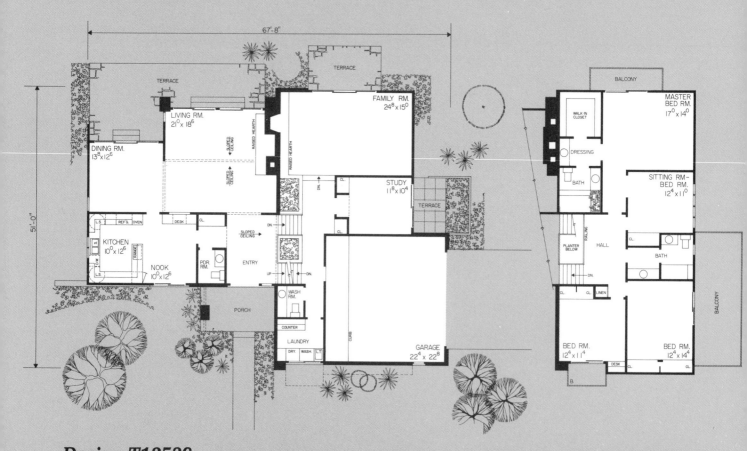

# Design T12536 1,077 Sq. Ft. - Main Level; 1,319 Sq. Ft. - Upper Level; 914 Sq. Ft. - Lower Level; 31,266 Cu. Ft.

● Here are three levels of outstanding livability all packed in a delightfully contemporary exterior. The low pitched roof has a wide overhang with exposed rafter tails. The stone masses contrast effectively with the vertical siding and the glass areas. The extension of the sloping roof provides the recessed feature of the front entrance with the patterned double doors. The homemaker's favorite highlight will be the layout of the kitchen. No crossroom traffic here. Only a few steps from the formal and informal eating areas, it is the epitome of efficiency. A sloping beamed ceiling, sliding glass doors and a raised hearth fireplace enhance the appeal of the living room. The upper level offers the option of a fourth bedroom or a sitting room functioning with the master bedroom. Note the three balconies. On the lower level, the big family room, quiet study, laundry and extra washroom are present.

● The rustic nature of this split-level design is captured by the rough-textured stone, natural-toned wood siding and wide, overhanging roof with exposed beams. Indoor-outdoor living relationships are outstanding. The foyer will be dramatic, indeed.

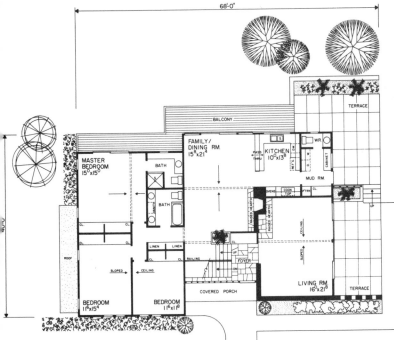

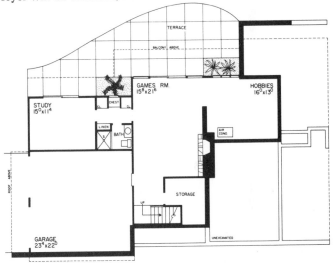

# Design T12248

**1,501 Sq. Ft. - Upper Level; 511 Sq. Ft. - Living Room Level**
**1,095 Sq. Ft. - Lower Level; 30,486 Cu. Ft.**

# Design T11981

784 Sq. Ft. - Main Level
912 Sq. Ft. - Upper Level
336 Sq. Ft. - Lower Level
26,618 Cu. Ft.

● This traditional split-level design is ideal for those who have a restricted building budget. All three levels, plus a basement, are housed in a 52 foot wide structure so it can fit on a relatively narrow building site. Two fireplaces; one in the formal living room, the other in the family room. Four bedrooms are on the upper level. The master bedroom even has its own outdoor balcony. Study the two Tudor split-levels also featured on this page.

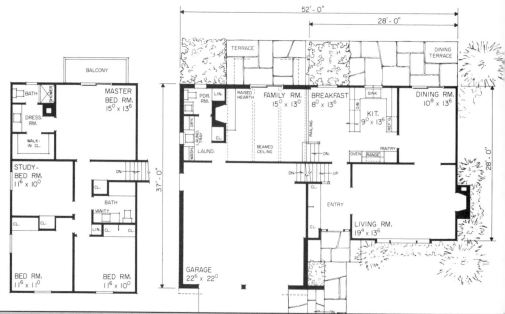

# Design T12137

987 Sq. Ft. - Main Level
1,043 Sq. Ft. - Upper Level; 463 Sq. Ft. - Lower Level
29,382 Cu. Ft.

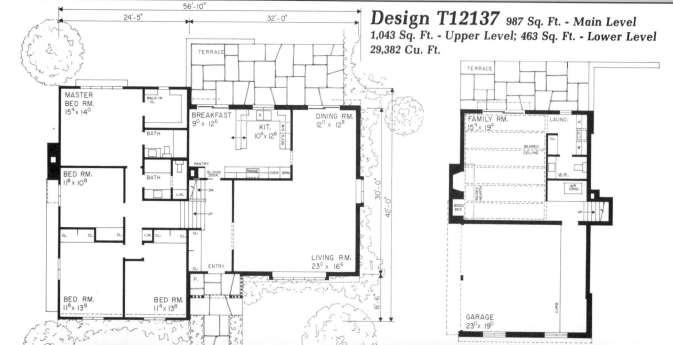

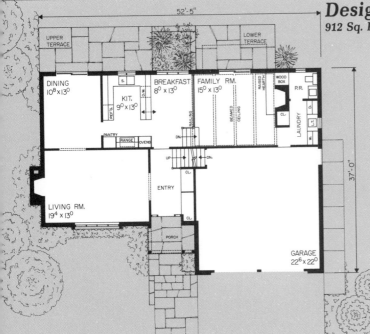

## Design T12171 795 Sq. Ft. - Main Level
### 912 Sq. Ft. - Upper Level; 335 Sq. Ft. - Lower Level; 33,243 Cu. Ft.

UPPER TERRACE

LOWER TERRACE

DINING 10⁸ x 13⁰

KIT. 9⁰ x 13⁰

BREAKFAST 8⁰ x 13⁰

FAMILY RM. 15⁰ x 13⁰

BEAMED CEILING

RAISED HEARTH

WOOD BOX

P.R.

LAUNDRY

PANTRY

RANGE

OVENS

52'-5"

UP

DN

CL.

LIVING RM. 19⁴ x 13⁰

ENTRY

CL.

PORCH

CL.

GARAGE 22⁶ x 22⁰

37'-0"

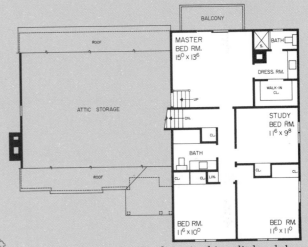

BALCONY

ROOF

ATTIC STORAGE

ROOF

MASTER BED RM. 15⁰ x 13⁶

BATH

DRESS. RM.

WALK-IN CL.

UP

DN

CL.

BATH

CL.

LIN.

STUDY BED RM. 11⁶ x 9⁸

CL.

CL.

BED RM. 11⁶ x 10⁰

BED RM. 11⁶ x 11⁰

● There are many fine qualities in this split-level design. Note the living room fireplace in addition to that in the family room with a wood box. A large attic storage area is over the living and dining rooms.

## Design T12716 1,013 Sq. Ft. - Main Level
### 885 Sq. Ft. - Upper Level; 1,074 Sq. Ft. - Lower Level; 32,100 Cu. Ft.

● A genuine master suite! It overlooks the gathering room through shuttered windows and includes a private balcony, a 9' by 9' sitting/dressing room and a full bath. There's more, a two-story gathering room with a raised hearth fireplace, sloped ceiling and sliding glass doors onto the main balcony. Plus, a family room and a study both having a fireplace. A kitchen with lots of built-ins and a separate dining nook.

**BALCONY**

**MASTER BED RM.** 15⁴ x 12⁰

**DECK**

**LIVING RM.** 15⁴ x 17⁶

**DINING RM.** 12⁴ x 14⁰

WALK-IN CLOSET

LINEN

DRESSING RM.

VANITY

BATH

CL

**NOOK** 10⁰ x 10⁰

BALCONY

UP

DN

**BED RM. - STUDY** 15⁴ x 11⁴

PDR. RM.

ENTRY

CL

REFG. OVENS

SNACK BAR

**KITCHEN** 12⁰ x 11⁰

RANGE

DW

L.S.

PORCH

**TERRACE**

**TERRACE**

**BED RM.** 15⁴ x 11⁰

CL

RAISED HEARTH

**ACTIVITIES RM.** 26¹⁰ x 17⁶

BATH

DRY. WASH. LT. LINEN

**LAUNDRY**

DN

UP

AIR COND.

CURB

CL

CL

CL

**BED RM.** 15² x 11²

STORAGE

MECH. RM.

**GARAGE** 23⁴ x 24⁰

UNEX.

68'-0"

48'-0"

# Design T12763
947 Sq. Ft. - Main Level; 640 Sq. Ft. - Upper Level
640 Sq. Ft. - Lower Level; 844 Sq. Ft. - Activities Level; 34,090 Cu. Ft.

## Design T12788
**1,795 Sq. Ft. - Upper Level**
**866 Sq. Ft. - Lower Level**
**34,230 Cu. Ft.**

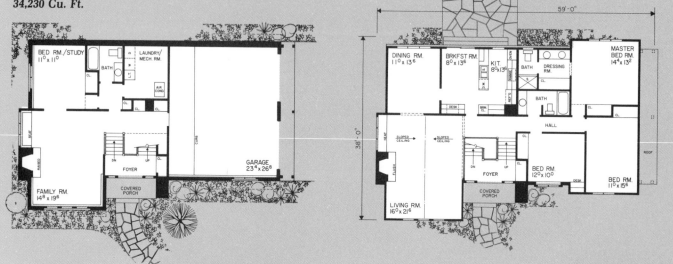

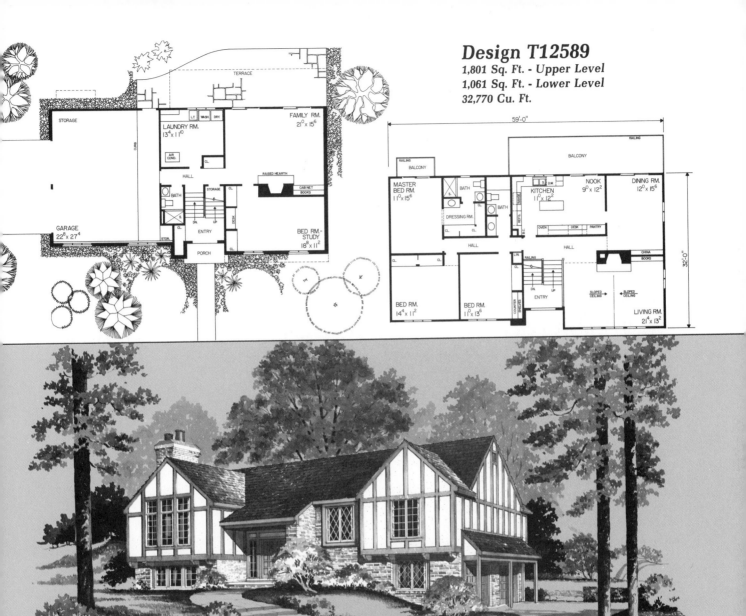

## Design T12589
1,801 Sq. Ft. - Upper Level
1,061 Sq. Ft. - Lower Level
32,770 Cu. Ft.

**Lower Level Floor Plan:**
- STORAGE
- LAUNDRY RM. 13⁴ x 11⁶
- FAMILY RM. 21⁰ x 15⁶
- AIR COND.
- LT. WASH. DRY.
- CL.
- HALL
- RAISED HEARTH
- CABINET BOOKS
- BATH
- STORAGE
- CL.
- DN. UP
- DESK
- ENTRY
- STOR.
- GARAGE 22⁸ x 27⁴
- PORCH
- CL.
- BED RM.-STUDY 18⁸ x 11²
- TERRACE
- CURB

**Upper Level Floor Plan:** 59'-0" / 32'-0"
- RAILING
- BALCONY
- MASTER BED RM. 11⁰ x 15⁶
- BATH
- DRESSING RM.
- CL.
- KITCHEN 11⁰ x 12²
- NOOK 9⁰ x 12²
- DINING RM. 12⁰ x 15⁶
- BATH
- OVEN DESK PANTRY
- HALL
- CL. CL.
- BED RM. 14⁴ x 11²
- BED RM. 11⁰ x 13⁵
- LIN. RAILING
- CL.
- DN. UP
- ENTRY
- COUNTER SHELVES
- CHINA BOOKS
- SLOPED CEILING
- LIVING RM. 21⁰ x 13²

## Design T11267
1,114 Sq. Ft. - Upper Level
1,194 Sq. Ft. - Lower Level
23,351 Cu. Ft.

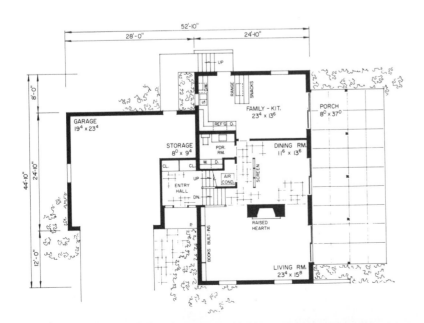

**Lower Level:** 52'-10" / 28'-0" / 24'-10" / 44'-10" / 24'-0" / 8'-0" / 12'-0"
- GARAGE 19⁴ x 23⁴
- UP
- RANGE
- SNACKS
- FAMILY - KIT. 23⁴ x 13⁶
- PORCH 8⁰ x 37⁰
- REF'G. O.
- STORAGE 8⁰ x 9⁴
- PDR. RM.
- DINING RM. 11⁶ x 13⁶
- CL.
- W. D.
- UP
- AIR COND.
- SCREEN
- ENTRY HALL
- DN.
- BOOKS BUILT-INS
- RAISED HEARTH
- LIVING RM. 23⁴ x 15⁸

**Upper Level:**
- CL.
- DRESS. RM.
- MASTER BED RM. 15⁰ x 13⁶
- CL.
- BATH
- LIN. CL. CHEST CL.
- BATH VANITY
- DN.
- BED RM. 11⁶ x 11⁰
- WALK IN CL.
- STOR.
- ROOF
- BED RM. 11⁶ x 10⁰
- BED RM. 11⁶ x 13⁴
- ROOF

# Design T12761 1,242 Sq. Ft. - Main Level
## 1,242 Sq. Ft. - Lower Level; 25,045 Cu. Ft.

● Here is another one-story that doubles its livability by exposing the lowest level at the rear. Formal living on the main level and informal living, the activity room and study, on the lower level. Observe the wonderful outdoor living facilities. The deck acts as a cover for the terrace.

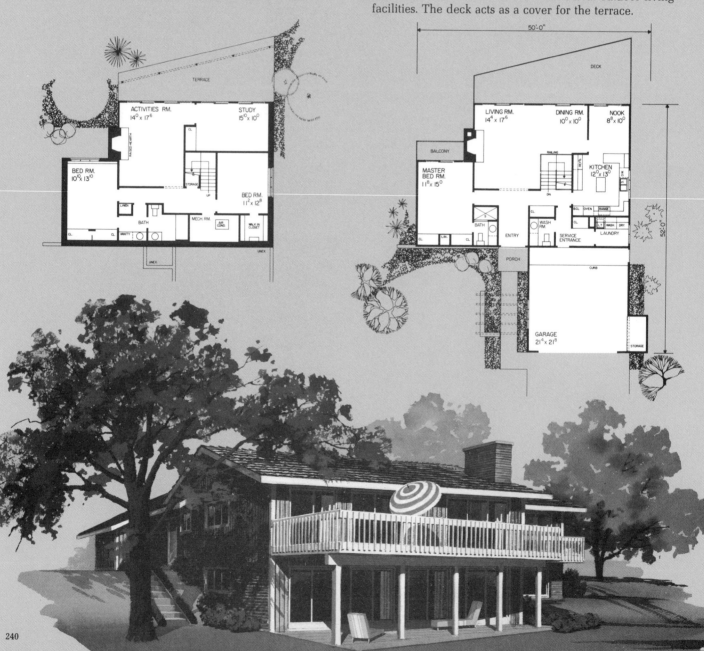

# Design T12842
**156 Sq. Ft. - Entrance Level; 1,040 Sq. Ft. - Upper Level**
**1,022 Sq. Ft. - Lower Level; 25,630 Cu. Ft.**

● This narrow, 42 foot width, house can be built on a narrow lot to cut down overall costs. Yet its dramatic appeal surely is worth a million. The projecting front garage creates a pleasing curved drive. One enters this house through the covered porch to the entrance level foyer. At this point the stairs lead down to the living area consisting of formal living room, family room, kitchen and dining area then up the stairs to the four bedroom-two bath sleeping area. The indoor-outdoor living relationship at the rear is outstanding.

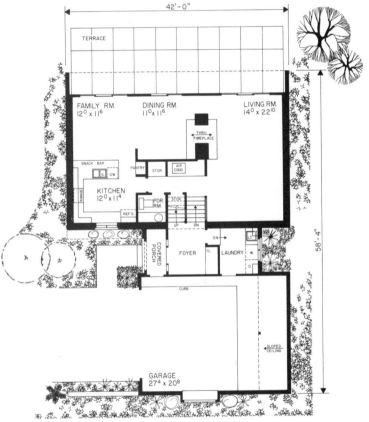

# Design T11850

**1,456 Sq. Ft. - Upper Level**
**728 Sq. Ft. - Lower Level**
**23,850 Cu. Ft.**

● This attractive, traditional bi-level house will surely prove to be an outstanding investment. While it is a perfect rectangle - which leads to economical construction - it has a full measure of eye-appeal. Setting the character of the exterior is the effective window treatment, plus the unique design of the recessed front entrance.

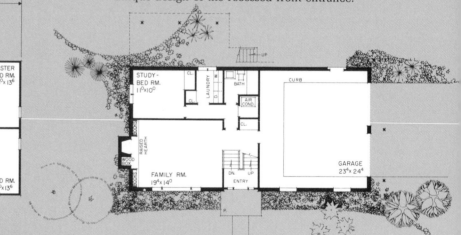

# Design T11219

1,456 Sq. Ft. - Upper Level
670 Sq. Ft. - Lower Level
22,772 Cu. Ft.

● This bi-level home has large glass areas to enhance the exterior appeal. They will also enable you to have an exciting and commanding view of your natural surroundings. Two terraces and a balcony to serve the family outdoors. Interior livability will take place on the upper level with the exception of the family room on the lower level.

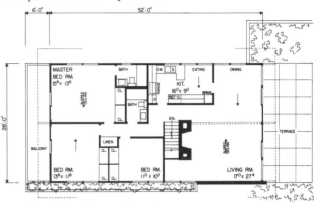

# Design T11220

1,456 Sq. Ft. - Upper Level
862 Sq. Ft. - Lower Level
22,563 Cu. Ft.

● This fresh, contemporary exterior sets the stage for exceptional livability. Measuring only 52 across the front, this bi-level home offers the large family outstanding features. Whether called upon to function as a four or five bedroom home, there is plenty of space in which to move around.

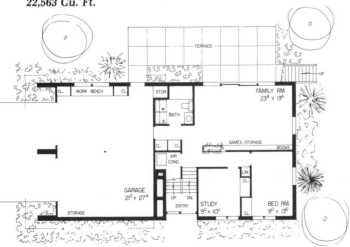

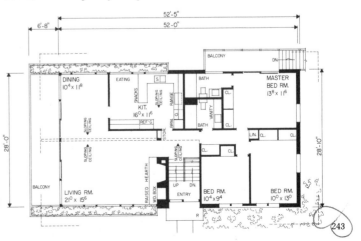

# Design T12847
**1,874 Sq. Ft. - Main Level**
**1,131 Sq. Ft. - Lower Level; 44,305 Cu. Ft.**

● This is an exquisitely styled Tudor, hillside design, ready to serve its happy occupants for many years. The contrasting use of material surely makes the exterior eye-catching.

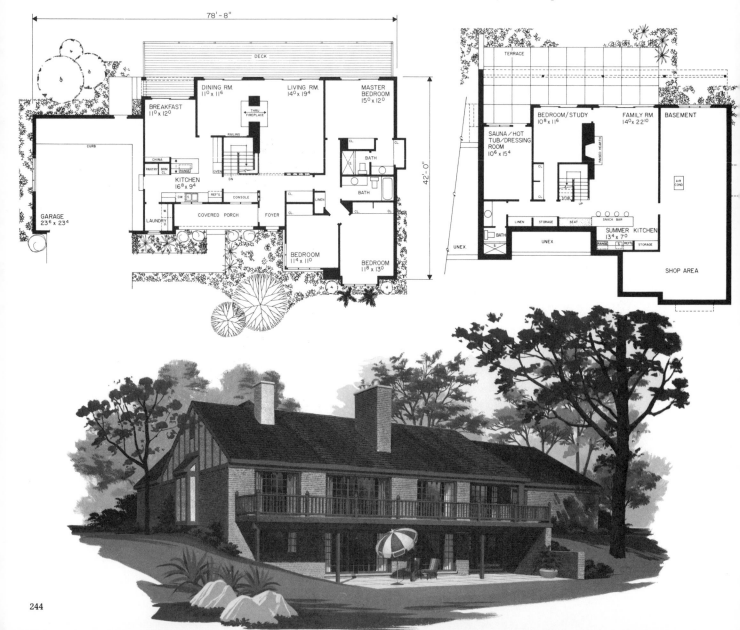

**Main Level Floor Plan**

78'-8"
42'-0"

DECK

DINING RM. 11⁰ x 11⁶
LIVING RM. 14⁰ x 19⁴
MASTER BEDROOM 15⁰ x 12⁰
BREAKFAST 11⁰ x 12⁰
THRU FIREPLACE
RAILING
CHINA
PANTRY BRM CL RANGE
KITCHEN 16⁸ x 9⁴
OVEN
BATH
BATH
DW REF'S CONSOLE
LINEN
LAUNDRY
COVERED PORCH
FOYER
GARAGE 23⁶ x 23⁴
CURB
BEDROOM 11⁴ x 11⁰
BEDROOM 11⁸ x 13⁰

**Lower Level Floor Plan**

TERRACE
BEDROOM/STUDY 10⁸ x 11⁶
FAMILY RM. 14⁰ x 22¹⁰
BASEMENT
SAUNA/HOT TUB/DRESSING ROOM 10⁶ x 15⁴
RAISED HEARTH
AIR COND.
UNEX.
BATH
UNEX.
LINEN STORAGE SEAT
SNACK BAR
SUMMER KITCHEN 13⁴ x 7⁰
RANGE REF'G
STORAGE
SHOP AREA

244

## Design T12844 1,882 Sq. Ft. - Upper Level
### 1,168 Sq. Ft. - Lower Level; 37,860 Cu. Ft.

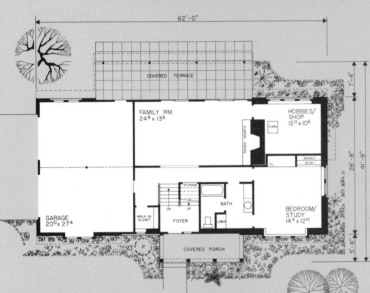

● Bi-level living will be enjoyed to the fullest in this Tudor design. The split-foyer type design will be very efficient for the active family. Three bedrooms are on the upper level, a fourth on the lower level.

# Design T12393 392 Sq. Ft. - Entry Level; 841 Sq. Ft. - Upper Level; 848 Sq. Ft. - Lower Level; 24,980 Cu. Ft.

● For those with a flair for something refreshingly contemporary both inside and out. This modest sized multi-level has a unique exterior and an equally interesting interior. The low-pitched, wide-overhanging roof protects the inviting double front doors and the large picture window. The raised planter and the side balcony add an extra measure of appeal. Inside, the living patterns will be delightful! The formal living room will look down into the dining room. Like the front entry, the living room has direct access to the lower level. The kitchen is efficient and spacious enough to accommodate an informal breakfast eating area. The laundry room is nearby. The all-purpose family room has beamed ceiling, fireplace and sliding glass doors to rear terrace. The angular, open stairwell to the upper level is dramatic, indeed. Notice how each bedroom has direct access to an outdoor balcony.

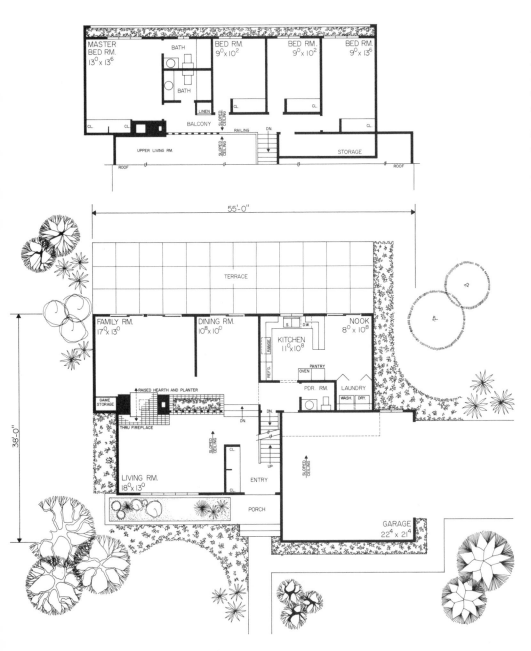

MASTER BED RM. 13⁰ x 13⁶
BATH
BATH
BED RM. 9⁰ x 10²
BED RM. 9⁰ x 10²
BED RM. 9⁰ x 13⁶
LINEN
CL.
CL.
CL.
CL.
BALCONY
SLOPED CEILING
RAILING
DN.
UPPER LIVING RM.
SLOPED CEILING
STORAGE
ROOF
ROOF

55'-0"

38'-0"

TERRACE

FAMILY RM. 17⁰ x 13⁰
DINING RM. 10⁸ x 10⁰
S
D.W.
NOOK 8⁰ x 10⁸
RANGE
KITCHEN 11⁰ x 10⁸
REF'G.
PANTRY
OVEN
PDR. RM.
LAUNDRY
WASH. DRY.
RAISED HEARTH AND PLANTER
GAME STORAGE
THRU FIREPLACE
SLOPED CEILING
CL.
DN.
DN.
UP
SLOPED CEILING
LIVING RM. 18⁰ x 13⁰
CL.
ENTRY
PORCH
GARAGE 22⁴ x 21⁴

## Design T12377
**388 Sq. Ft. - Living Room Level**
**782 Sq. Ft. - Main Level**
**815 Sq. Ft. - Upper Level**
**22,477 Cu. Ft.**

● What an impressive up-to-date multi-level home this is. Its refreshing configuration will command a full measure of attention. Separating the living and slightly lower levels is a thru-fireplace which has a raised hearth in the family room. An adjacent planter with vertical members provides additional interest and beauty. The rear terrace is accessible from nook, family and dining rooms. Notice the powder room, the convenient laundry area and the basement stairs. Four bedrooms serviced by two full baths comprise the upper level which looks down into the living room. A large walk-in storage closet will be ideal for those seasonal items. An attractive outdoor planter extends across the rear just outside the bedroom windows. This will surely be a house that will be fun in which to live.

## Design T12843

**1,861 Sq. Ft. - Upper Level**
**1,181 Sq. Ft. - Lower Level; 32,485 Cu. Ft.**

● Bi-level living will be enjoyed to its fullest in this Spanish styled design. There is a lot of room for the various family activities. Informal living will take place on the lower level in the family room and lounge. The formal living and dining rooms, sharing a thru-fire-place, are located on the upper level.

# Design T12846
**2,341 Sq. Ft. - Main Level; 1,380 Sq. Ft. - Lower Level; 51,290 Cu. Ft.**

● The street view of this Spanish design shows a beautifully designed one-story home, but now take a look at the rear elevation. This home has been designed to be built into a hill so the lower level can be opened to the sun. By so doing, the total livability is almost doubled. A unique feature of the lower level is the summer kitchen.

## Design T12758

**1,143 Sq. Ft. - Main Level**
**792 Sq. Ft. - Upper Level**
**770 Sq. Ft. - Lower Level**
**43,085 Cu. Ft.**

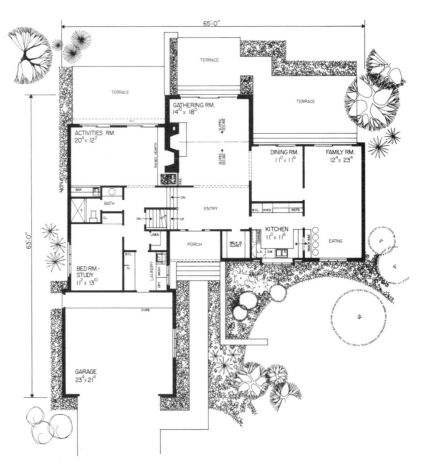

● An outstanding Tudor with three levels of exceptional livability, plus a basement. A careful study of the exterior reveals many delightful architectural details which give this home a character of its own. Notice the appealing recessed front entrance. Observe the overhanging roof with the exposed rafters. Don't miss the window treatment, the use of stucco and simulated beams, the masses of brick and the stylish chimney. Inside, the living potential is unsurpassed. Imagine, there are three living areas - the gathering, family and activities rooms. Having a snack bar, informal eating area and dining room, eating patterns can be flexible. In addition to the three bedrooms, two-bath upper level, there is a fourth bedroom with adjacent bath on the lower level.

# Design T12624

**904 Sq. Ft. - Main Level**
**1,120 Sq. Ft. - Upper Level**
**404 Sq. Ft. - Lower Level; 39,885 Cu. Ft.**

60'-6"

39'-6"

LOWER TERRACE

UPPER TERRACE

FAMILY RM. 19⁰ x 13⁶

WASH RM.

LAUNDRY

WOOD BOX

NOOK 8⁶ x 9¹⁰

KITCHEN 10⁰ x 13

RANGE

BEAMED CEILING

RAILING

DN.

DN.    UP

OVEN    DESK    PANTRY    B.CL.

WOOD BOX

ENTRY

DINING RM. 12⁰ x 13⁶

D.W.

REFG.

LIVING RM. 20⁶ x 13⁶

PORCH

GARAGE 26⁸ x 24²

BALCONY

BATH

DRESSING RM.

WALK-IN CLOSET

MASTER BED RM. 18⁸ x 13⁶

CL.

DN.

CL.

BED RM. 11² x 10¹⁰

CL.    CL.

BATH

VANITY

LINEN    CL.    CL.

BED RM. 13⁶ x 12⁰

BED RM. 13⁶ x 11⁰

● This is tri-level living at its best. The exterior is that of the most popular Tudor styling. A facade which will hold its own for many a year to come. Livability will be achieved to its maximum on the four (including basement) levels. The occupants of the master bedroom can enjoy the outdoors on their private balcony. Additional outdoor enjoyment can be gained on the two terraces. That family room is more than 19' x 13' and includes a beamed ceiling and fireplace with wood box. Its formal companion, the living room, is similar in size and also will have the added warmth of a fireplace.

## Design T12786 *871 Sq. Ft. - Main Level*
### *1,132 Sq. Ft. - Upper Level; 528 Sq. Ft. - Lower Level; 44,000 Cu. Ft.*

● A bay window in each the formal living room and dining room. A great interior and exterior design feature to attract attention to this four-bedroom, tri-level home. The exterior also is enhanced by a covered front porch to further the Colonial charm. The interior livability is outstanding, too. An abundance of built-ins in the kitchen create an efficient work center. Features include an island range, pantry, broom closet, desk and breakfast room with sliding glass doors to the rear terrace. The lower level houses the informal family room, wash room and laundry. Further access is available to the outdoors by the family room to the terrace and laundry room to the side yard.

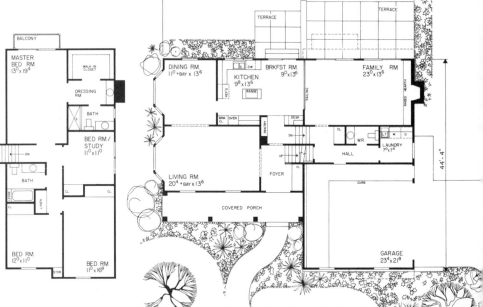

## Design T12787 976 Sq. Ft. - Main Level
### 1,118 Sq. Ft. - Upper Level; 524 Sq. Ft. - Lower Level
### 36,110 Cu. Ft.

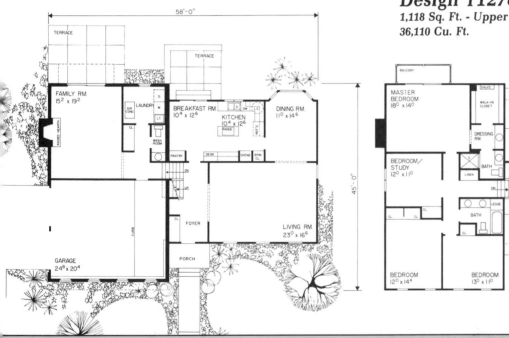

● Three level living! Main, upper and lower levels to serve you and your family with great ease. Start from the bottom and work your way up. Family room with raised hearth fireplace, laundry and wash room on the lower level. Formal living and dining rooms, kitchen and breakfast room on the main level. The upper level houses the three bedrooms, study (or fourth bedroom if you prefer) and two baths. This design has really stacked up its livability to serve its occupants to their best advantage.

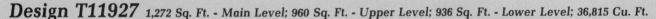

## Design T11927 1,272 Sq. Ft. - Main Level; 960 Sq. Ft. - Upper Level; 936 Sq. Ft. - Lower Level; 36,815 Cu. Ft.

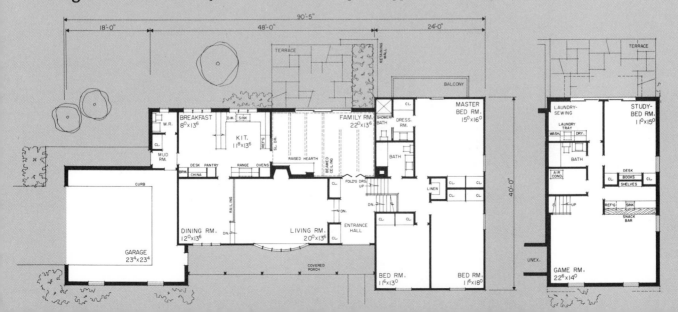

## Design T12354
**936 Sq. Ft. - Main Level; 971 Sq. Ft. - Upper Level**
**971 Sq. Ft. - Lower Level; 34,561 Cu. Ft.**

● This English flavored tri-level design may be built on a flat site. Its configuration permits a flexible orientation on the site with either the garage doors or the front door facing the street. The interior offers a unique and practical floor plan layout. Flanking the spacious entrance hall is the cozy, sunken living room and the formal dining room. Looking out upon the front porch is the kitchen with its adjacent nook. A mud room is strategically located just inside the door from the garage. Opposite the front door are two flights of stairs. One leads to the upper level with its three bedrooms and two baths. The other leads to the lower level. Here is the fourth bedroom, third bathroom, a big beamed ceiling family room, a hobby room and a laundry. A real winner for family living.

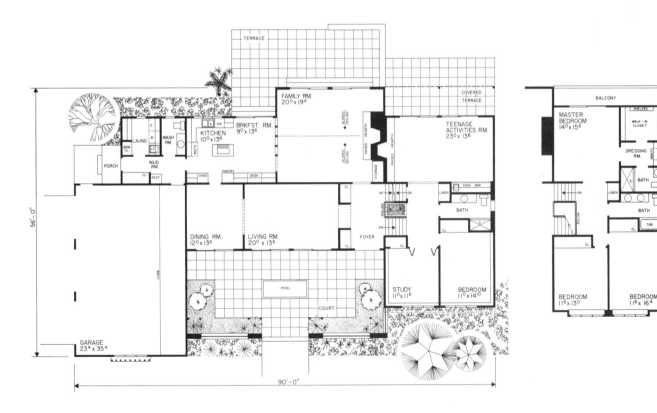

# Design T12850

*1,530 Sq. Ft. - Main Level; 984 Sq. Ft. - Upper Level; 951 Sq. Ft. - Lower Level; 53,780 Cu. Ft.*

● Entering through the entry court of this Spanish design is very impressive. Partially shielded from the street, this court features planting areas and a small pool. Enter into the foyer and this split-level interior will begin to unfold. Down six steps from the foyer is the lower level housing a bedroom and full bath, study and teenage activities room. Adults, along with teenagers, will enjoy the activities room which has a raised hearth fireplace, soda bar and sliding glass doors leading to a covered terrace. Six steps up from the foyer is the upper level bedroom area. The main level has the majority of the living areas. Formal living and dining rooms, informal family room, kitchen with accompanying breakfast room and mud room consisting of laundry and wash room. This home even has a three-car garage. Livability will be achieved with the greatest amount of comfort in this home.

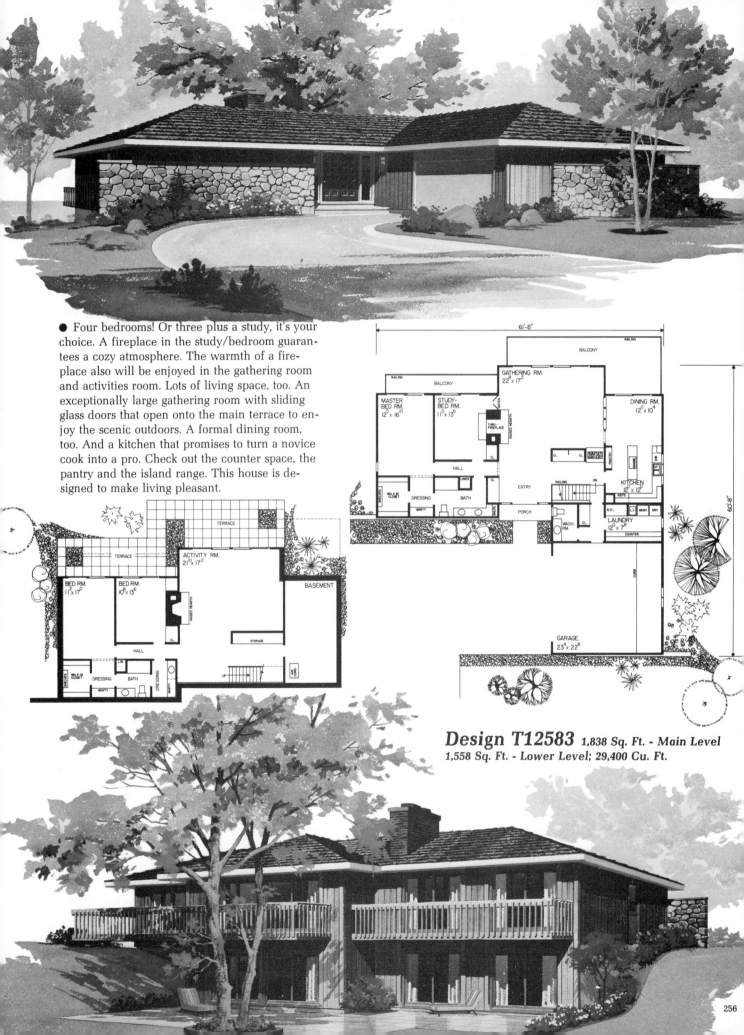

● Four bedrooms! Or three plus a study, it's your choice. A fireplace in the study/bedroom guarantees a cozy atmosphere. The warmth of a fireplace also will be enjoyed in the gathering room and activities room. Lots of living space, too. An exceptionally large gathering room with sliding glass doors that open onto the main terrace to enjoy the scenic outdoors. A formal dining room, too. And a kitchen that promises to turn a novice cook into a pro. Check out the counter space, the pantry and the island range. This house is designed to make living pleasant.

**Design T12583** 1,838 Sq. Ft. - Main Level
1,558 Sq. Ft. - Lower Level; 29,400 Cu. Ft.

# COUNTRY-ESTATE HOMES . . . .

*Whether situated in the lowlands, in suburbia, or the countryside; in the north, or the south, the estate home is characterized by the gracious formality that seems to foretell of the good life. Space there is in abundance - indoors as well as out. Construction cost factors are but a secondary consideration. There is room for everybody and everybody has a room. The plan affords space for large or small gatherings on any occasion. Yet there will always be a room for privacy, when desired or needed. As shown on the following pages, the country-estate home can be traditional or contemporary in its styling. It can be one, 1½ or two-story, a bi-level or a split-level.*

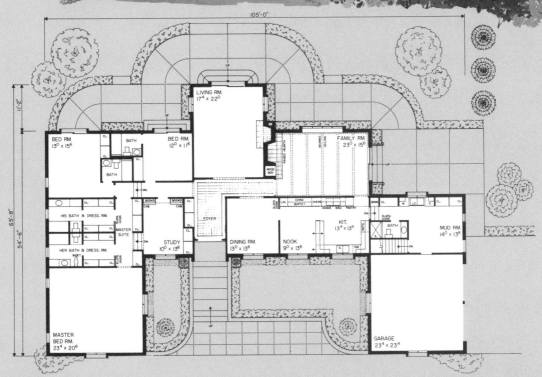

● From the graceful, curving drive court to the formal living room, this expansive, hospitable French country house welcomes the visitor. Truely a house for gracious living.

## Design T12212
3,577 Sq. Ft.; 76,208 Cu. Ft.

# Exquisite Good Taste - French Provincial

● The elegance of pleasing proportion and delightful detailing has seldom been better exemplified than by this classic French country manor adaptation. Approaching the house across the drive court, the majesty of this multi-roofed structure is breathtaking, indeed.

While there is an aura of old world formality, there is also an accompanying feeling of contemporary livability. The graciousness with which it will unfold, will be awaiting only the arrival of the occupants; for all the elements are present to guarantee

complete livability both indoors and out. A trip through the house reveals a fine arrangement of large, spacious rooms. If necessary, the library may be called upon to become the fourth bedroom or guest room. Observe the work center of kitchen area.

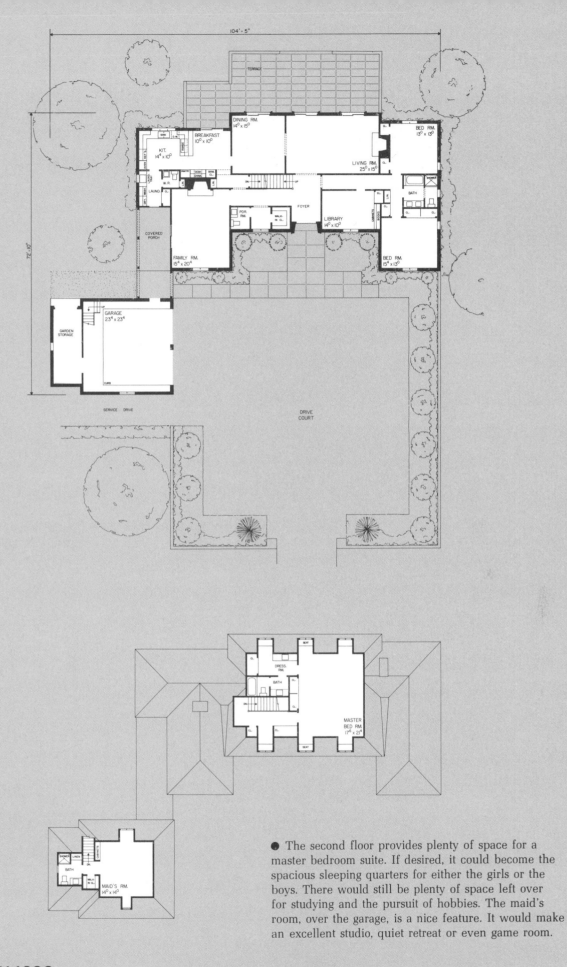

104'-5"

72'-10"

TERRACE

DINING RM.
14⁰ x 15⁰

BREAKFAST
10⁰ x 10⁰

KIT.
14⁴ x 10⁰

BED RM.
13⁰ x 13⁰

LIVING RM.
25⁰ x 15⁰

LAUND.

W.R.

BATH

SHOWER

FOYER

POR. RM.

WALK-IN CL.

LIBRARY
14⁰ x 10⁰

BOOKS

COVERED PORCH

FAMILY RM.
15⁴ x 20⁴

BED RM.
15⁴ x 13⁰

GARDEN STORAGE

GARAGE
23⁴ x 23⁴

CURB

SERVICE DRIVE

DRIVE COURT

DRESS. RM.

SEAT

BATH

MASTER BED RM.
17⁶ x 21⁴

SEAT

SHOWER

LINEN

CABINETS

BATH

MAID'S RM.
14⁰ x 14⁰

WALK-IN CL.

● The second floor provides plenty of space for a master bedroom suite. If desired, it could become the spacious sleeping quarters for either the girls or the boys. There would still be plenty of space left over for studying and the pursuit of hobbies. The maid's room, over the garage, is a nice feature. It would make an excellent studio, quiet retreat or even game room.

**Design T11993** 2,658 Sq. Ft. - First Floor; 840 Sq. Ft. - Master Suite; 376 Sq. Ft. - Maid's Suite; 57,057 Cu. Ft.

## Design T12245
**2,855 Sq. Ft. - First Floor**
**955 Sq. Ft. - Second Floor**
**57,645 Cu. Ft.**

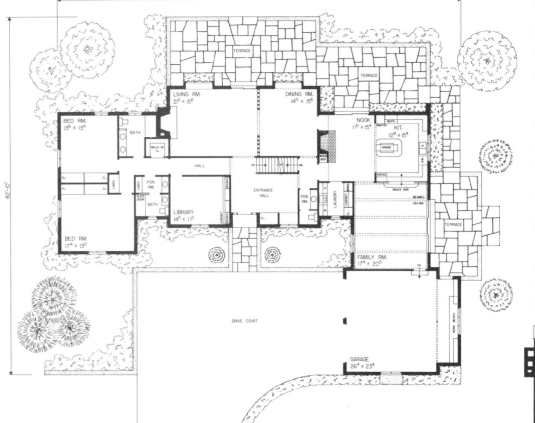

● The graciousness of this impressive English country house will endure for generations. The fine proportions, the exquisite architectural detailing and the interesting configuration are among the elements that create such an overwhelming measure of true character. The interior of this home will be as dramatic as the exterior. The recessed front entrance opens into a spacious, formal entrance hall. From here traffic patterns flow efficiently to all areas of the house. The garden view shows the three spacious outdoor terrace areas.

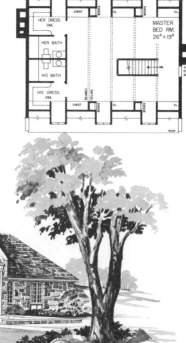

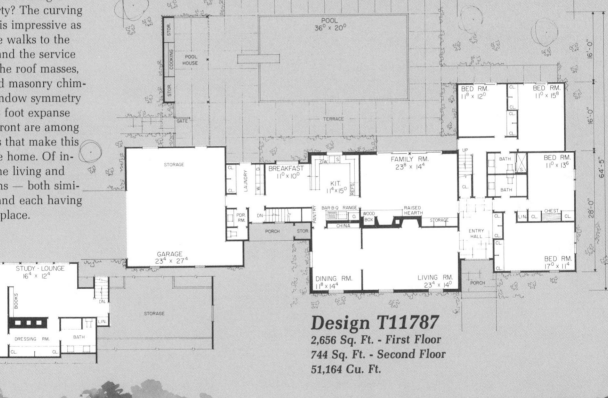

● Can't you picture this dramatic home sitting on your property? The curving front drive is impressive as it passes the walks to the front door and the service entrance. The roof masses, the centered masonry chimney, the window symmetry and the 108 foot expanse across the front are among the features that make this a distinctive home. Of interest are the living and family rooms — both similar in size and each having its own fireplace.

## Design T11787
**2,656 Sq. Ft. - First Floor**
**744 Sq. Ft. - Second Floor**
**51,164 Cu. Ft.**

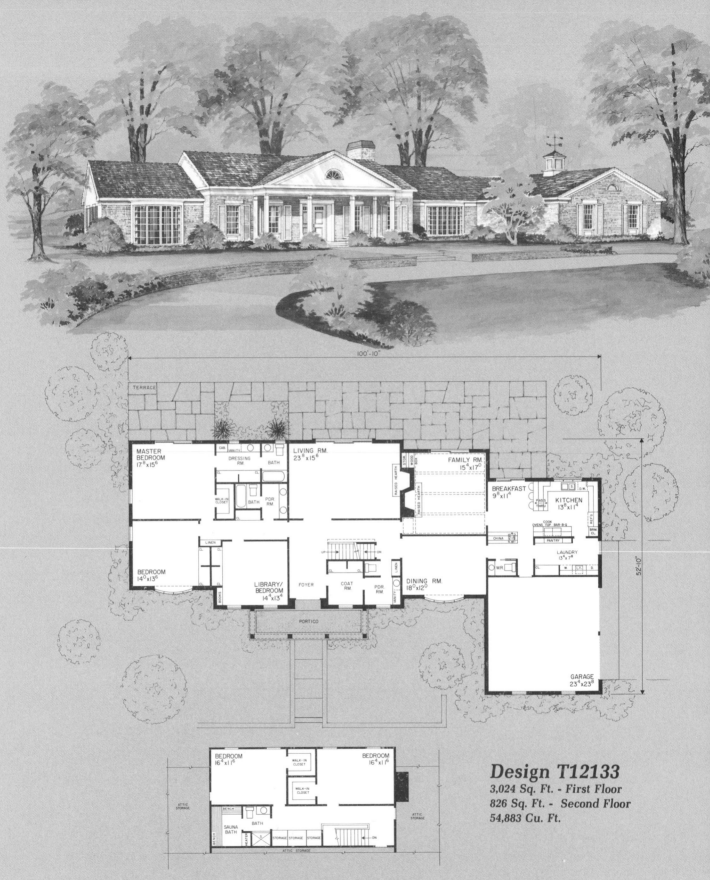

**Design T12133**
3,024 Sq. Ft. - First Floor
826 Sq. Ft. - Second Floor
54,883 Cu. Ft.

● A country-estate home which will command all the attention it truly deserves. The projecting pediment gable supported by the finely proportioned columns lends an aura of elegance. The window treatment, the front door detailing, the massive, capped, chimney, the cupola, the brick veneer exterior and the varying roof planes complete the characterization of this impressive home. Inside, there are 3,024 square feet on the first floor. In addition, there is a two bedroom second floor should its development be necessary. However, whether called upon to function as a one, or 1½ story home it will provide a lifetime of gracious living. Don't overlook the compartment baths, the laundry and the many built-ins available.

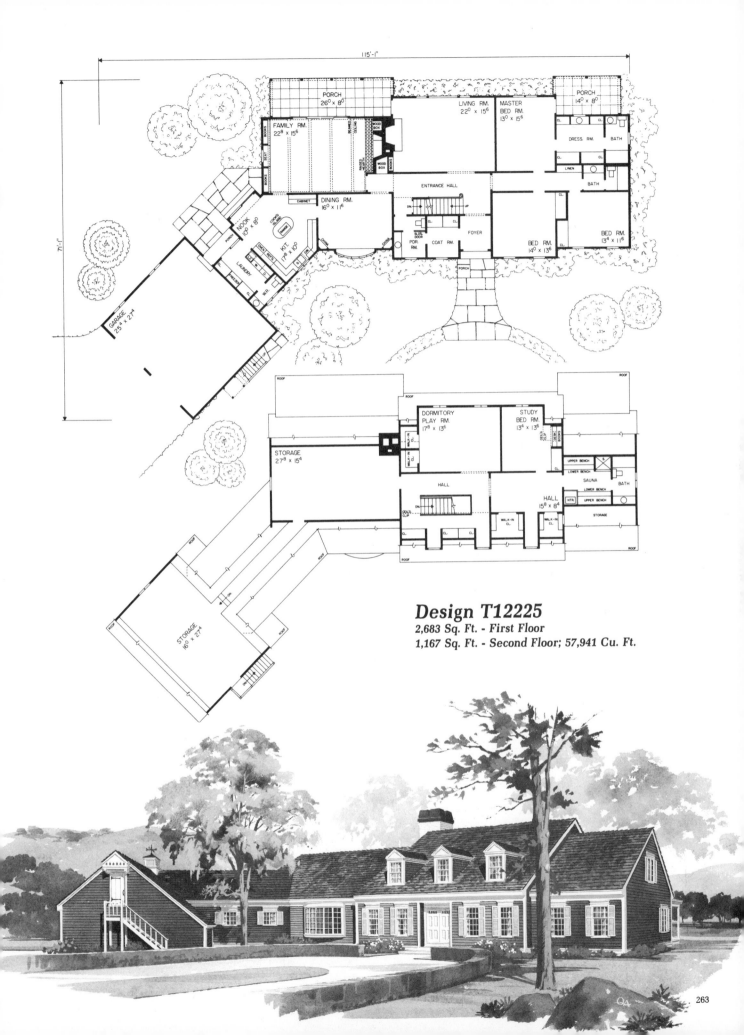

**First Floor**

115'-1"

71'-1"

PORCH 26⁰ x 8⁰

LIVING RM. 22⁰ x 15⁶

MASTER BED RM. 13⁰ x 15⁶

PORCH 14⁰ x 8⁰

FAMILY RM. 22⁸ x 15⁶

WOOD BOX

BEAMED CEILING

RAISED HEARTH

WOOD BOX

DRESS. RM.

BATH

CABINET

DINING RM. 16⁰ x 11⁶

ENTRANCE HALL

LINEN

BATH

NOOK 10⁰ x 9⁰

RANGE

DN UP

CL CL

FOYER

CL

BED RM. 13⁴ x 11⁶

KIT. 17⁸ x 10⁰

LAUNDRY

W.R.

PDR. RM.

COAT RM.

BED RM. 14⁰ x 13⁶

PORCH

GARAGE 25⁴ x 27⁴

**Second Floor**

ROOF

DORMITORY PLAY RM. 17⁸ x 13⁶

STUDY BED RM. 13⁴ x 13⁶

STORAGE 27⁸ x 15⁴

WALK-IN

UPPER BENCH

LOWER BENCH

SAUNA

BATH

HALL

LOWER BENCH

HALL 15⁸ x 8⁴

HTR.

UPPER BENCH

STORAGE

DN

DBL'S CLIP

CL

CL CL

WALK-IN CL.

WALK-IN CL.

ROOF

STORAGE 16⁰ x 27⁴

ROOF

## Design T12225
2,683 Sq. Ft. - First Floor
1,167 Sq. Ft. - Second Floor; 57,941 Cu. Ft.

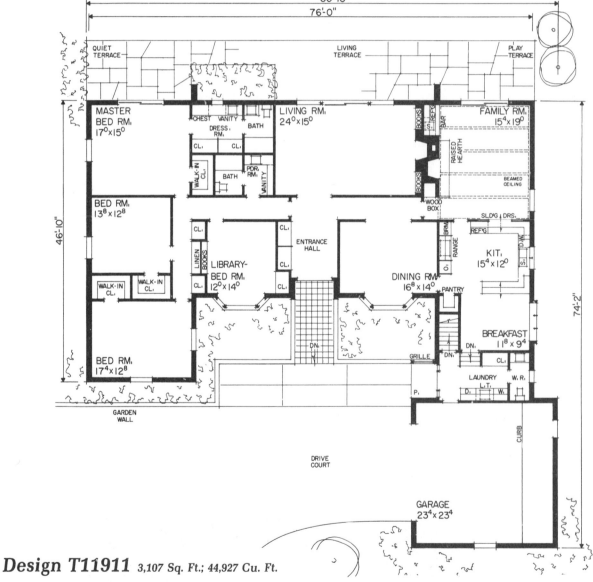

Floor plan labels:

- 80'-10"
- 76'-0"
- 46'-10"
- 74'-2"

QUIET TERRACE

LIVING TERRACE

PLAY TERRACE

MASTER BED RM. 17⁰x15⁰

CHEST · VANITY

DRESS RM.

CL. · CL.

WALK-IN CL.

BATH

BATH

PDR. RM.

VANITY

LIVING RM. 24⁰x15⁰

BOOKS

BAR

S.

REF'G

FAMILY RM. 15⁴x19⁰

RAISED HEARTH

BEAMED CEILING

BED RM. 13⁸x12⁸

CL.

LINEN BOOKS

CL.

LIBRARY-BED RM. 12⁰x14⁰

CL.

CL.

CL.

ENTRANCE HALL

BOOKS

WOOD BOX

SLD'G. DRS.

REF'G.

B.RM.

RANGE

KIT. 15⁴x12⁰

S.

D.W.

WALK-IN CL.

WALK-IN CL.

BED RM. 17⁴x12⁸

DN.

DINING RM. 16⁸x14⁰

PANTRY

GRILLE

DN.

DN.

BREAKFAST 11⁸x9⁴

CL.

LAUNDRY

L.T.

D. · W.

W.R.

P.

CURB

GARDEN WALL

DRIVE COURT

GARAGE 23⁴x23⁴

# Design T11911  3,107 Sq. Ft.; 44,927 Cu. Ft.

● For luxurious, country-estate living it would be difficult to beat the livability offered ·by these two impressive traditional designs. To begin with, their exterior appeal is, indeed, gracious. Their floor plans highlight plenty of space, excellent room arrangements, fine traffic circulation, and an abundance of convenient living features. It is interesting to note that each design features similar livability facilities. Both may function as four bedroom homes . . .

## Design T12615
2,563 Sq. Ft. - First Floor
552 Sq. Ft. - Second Floor; 59,513 Cu. Ft.

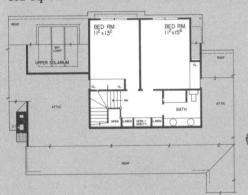

● The exterior detailing of this design recalls 18th-Century New England architecture. Enter by way of the centered front door and you are greeted into the foyer. Directly to the right is the study or optional bedroom or to the left is the living room. This large formal room features sliding glass doors to the sun-drenched solarium. The beauty of the solarium will be appreciated from the master bedroom and the dining room along with the living room.

# Design T12317 3,161 Sq. Ft.; 57,900 Cu. Ft.

● Here's a rambling English manor with its full measure of individuality. Its fine proportions and irregular shape offer even the most casual of passersby delightful views of fine architecture. The exterior boasts an interesting use of varying materials. In addition to the brick work, there is vertical siding, wavy-edged horizontal siding and stucco. Three massive chimneys provide each of the three major wings with a fireplace. The overhanging roof provides the cover for the long front porch. Note the access to both the foyer as well as the service hall. The formal living room, with its sloping beamed ceiling, and fireplace flanked by book shelves and cabinets, will be cozy, indeed. Study rest of plan. It's outstanding. Don't miss the three fireplaces and three full baths.

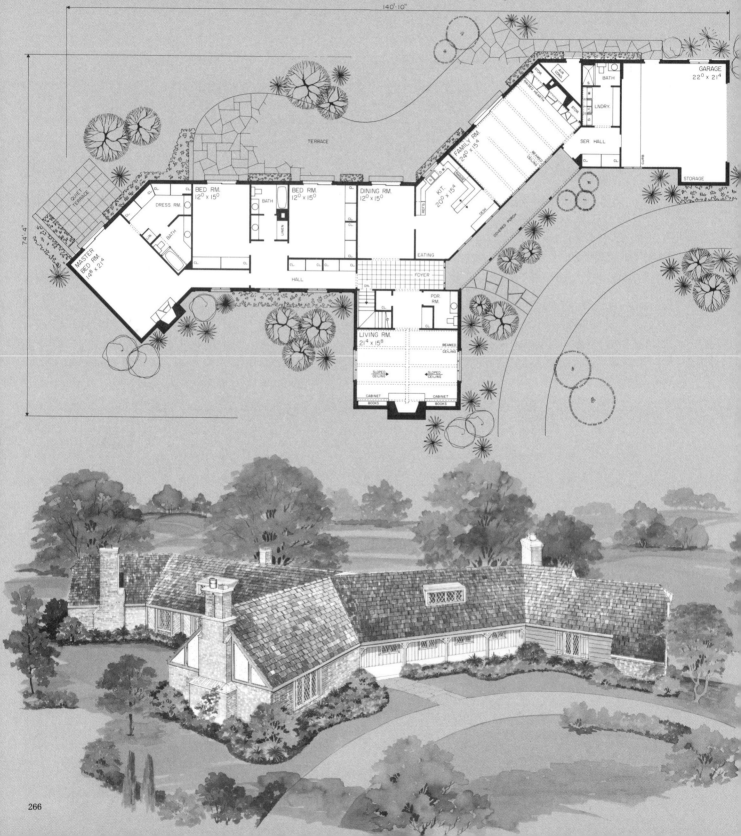

● Echoing design themes of old Spain, this history house distills the essence of country houses built by rancheros in Early California. Yet its floor plan provides all the comfort and convenience essential to our contemporary living.

Among its charming features is a secluded court, or patio; a greenhouse tucked in behind the garage; a covered rear porch; a low-pitched wide overhanging roof with exposed rafter tails; sloping beamed ceilings. Contri-

buting to the authenticity of the design are the two sets of panelled doors. The covered walk to the front doors provides a sheltered area adjacent to the court. Once inside, the feeling of space continues to impress.

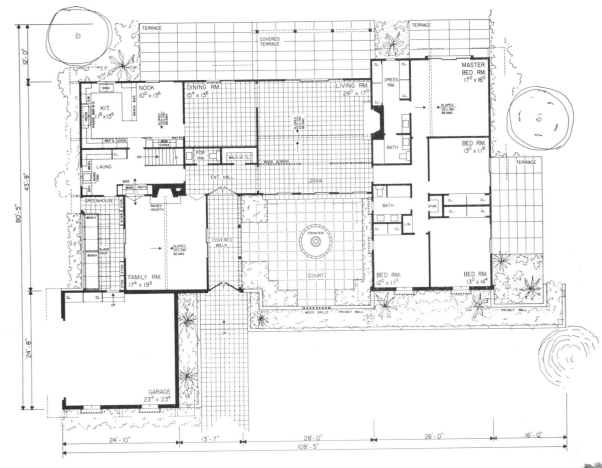

### Design T11997
3,348 Sq. Ft.; 48,933 Cu. Ft.

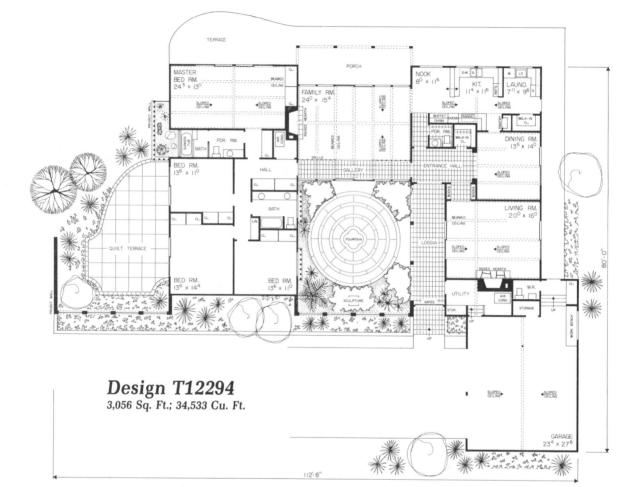

## Design T12294
3,056 Sq. Ft.; 34,533 Cu. Ft.

● Here is a western ranch with an authentic Spanish flavor. Striking a note of distinction, the arched privacy walls provide a fine backdrop for the long, raised planter. The low-pitched roof features tile and has a wide overhang with exposed rafter tails. The interior is wonderfully zoned. The all-purpose family room is flanked by the sleeping wing and the living wing. Study each area carefully for the planning is excellent and the features are many. Indoor-outdoor integration is outstanding. At left — the spacious interior court. The covered passage to the double front doors is dramatic, indeed.

# Design T12534 3,262 Sq. Ft.; 58,640 Cu. Ft.

● The angular wings of this ranch home surely contribute to the unique character of the exterior. These wings effectively balance what is truly a dramatic and inviting front entrance. Massive masonry walls support the wide overhanging roof with its exposed wood beams. The patterned double front doors are surrounded by delightful expanses of glass. The raised planters and the masses of quarried stone (make it brick if you prefer) enhance the exterior appeal. Inside, a distinctive and practical floor plan stands ready to shape and serve the living patterns of the active family. The spacious entrance hall highlights sloped ceiling and an attractive open stairway to the lower level recreation area. An impressive fireplace and an abundance of glass are features of the big gathering room. Interestingly shaped dining room and study flank this main living area. The large kitchen offers many of the charming aspects of the family-kitchen of yesteryear. The bedroom wing has a sunken master suite.

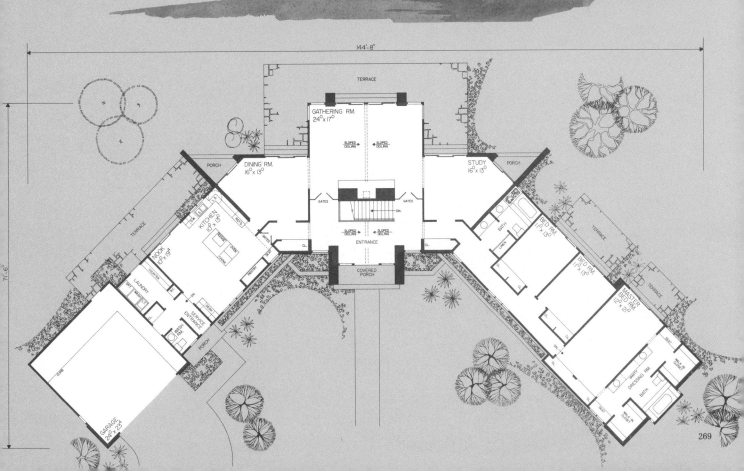

# Design T12251
**3,112 Sq. Ft.; 36,453 Cu. Ft.**

● It will not matter at all where this distinctive ranch home is built. Whether located in the south, east, north or west the exterior design appeal will be breathtakingly distinctive and the interior livability will be delightfully different. The irregular shape is enhanced by the low-pitched, wide overhanging roof. From the main living area of the house two wings project to help form an appealing entrance court. Variations in grade result in the garage being on a lower level. The plan reflects an interesting study in zoning and a fine indoor-outdoor relationship of the various areas.

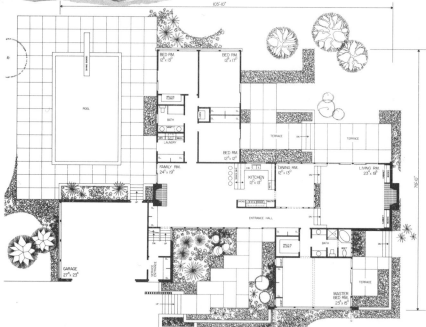

## Design T12747   3,211 Sq. Ft.; 50,930 Cu. Ft.

● This home will surely provide its occupants with a glorious adventure in contemporary living. Its impressive exterior seems to foretell that great things are in store for even most casual visitor. A study of the plan reveals a careful zoning for both the younger and older family members. The quiet area consists of the exceptional master bedroom suite with private terrace, the study and the isolated living room. For the younger generation, there is a zone with two bedrooms, family room and nearby pool. The kitchen is handy also and serves the nook and family rooms well. Be sure not to miss the sloping ceilings, the dramatic planter and the functional terrace.

# Design T12391 *2,496 Sq. Ft. - First Floor; 958 Sq. Ft. - Second Floor; 59,461 Cu. Ft.*

● Here is a stately English adaptation that is impressive, indeed. The two-story octagonal foyer strikes a delightfully authentic design note. The entrance hall with open staircase and two-story ceiling is spacious. Clustered around the efficient kitchen are the formal living areas and those catering to informal activities. The family room with its beamed ceiling and raised hearth fireplace functions, like the formal living/dining zone, with the partially enclosed outdoor terrace. Three bedrooms with two baths comprise the first floor sleeping zone. Each room will enjoy its access to the terrace. Upstairs there are two more bedrooms and a study. Notice the sliding glass doors to the balcony and how the study looks down into the entrance hall. The three-car garage is great. Your own list of favorite features will surely be lengthy.

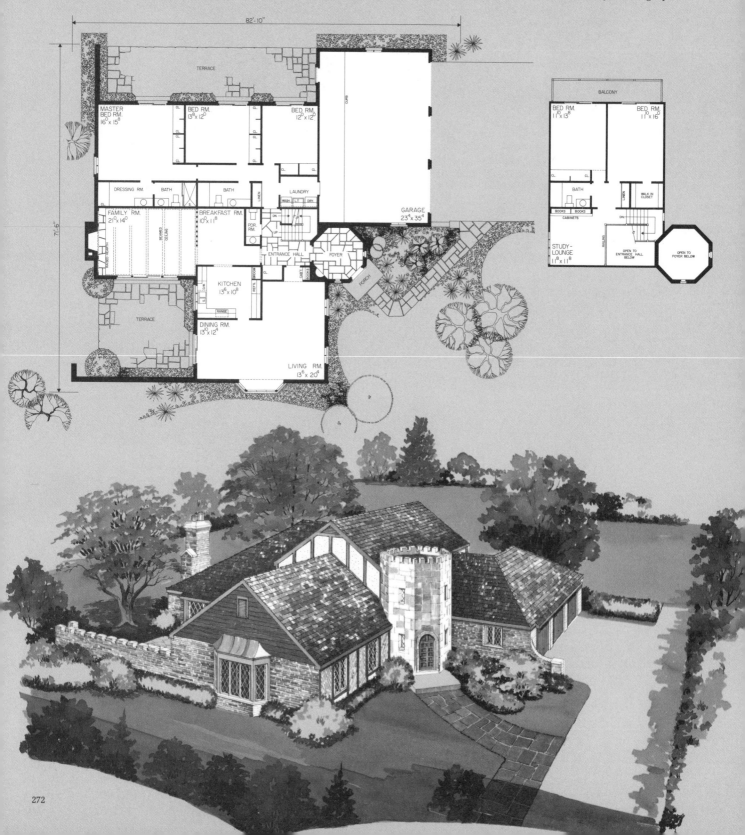

## Design T12889

**2,529 Sq. Ft. - First Floor**
**1,872 Sq. Ft. - Second Floor**
**80,670 Cu. Ft.**

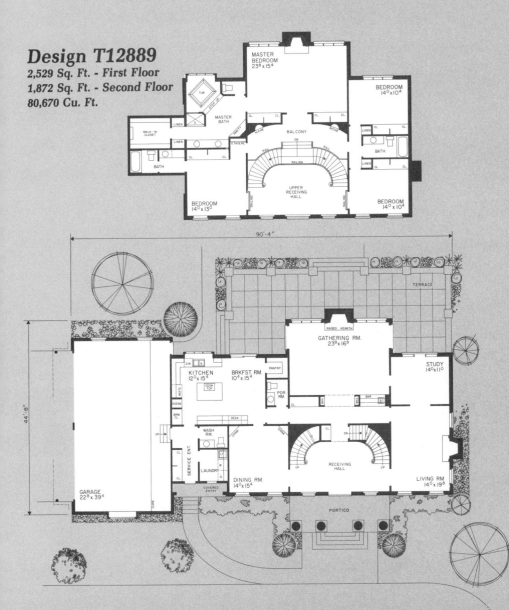

● This is truly classical, Georgian design at its best. Some of the exterior highlights of this two-story include the pediment gable with cornice work and dentils, the beautifully proportioned columns, the front door detailing and the window treatment. These are just some of the features which make this design so unique and appealing. Behind the facade of this design is an equally elegant interior. Imagine greeting your guests in the large receiving hall. It is graced by two curving staircases and opens to the formal living and dining rooms. Beyond the living room is the study. It has access to the rear terrace. Those large, informal occasions for family get-togethers or entertaining will be enjoyed in the spacious gathering room. It has a centered fireplace flanked by windows on each side, access to the terrace and a wet bar. Your appreciation for this room will be never-ending. The work center is efficient: the kitchen with island cook top, breakfast room, washroom, laundry and service entrance. The second floor also is outstanding. Three family bedrooms and two full baths are joined by the feature-filled master bedroom suite. Study this area carefully. If you like this basic floor plan but would prefer a French exterior, see Design T12543 on page 207.

# Design T12783
**3,210 Sq. Ft.; 57,595 Cu. Ft.**

● The configuration of this traditional design is outstanding indeed. The garage-bedroom wing on one side and the master bedroom on the other create an inviting U-shaped entry court. This area is raised two steps from the driveway and has a 6 foot high masonry wall with coach lamps for an added attraction. Upon entrance through the double front doors one will begin to enjoy the livability that this design has to offer. Each room is well planned and deserves praise. The sizeable master bedroom has a fireplace and sliding glass doors to the entry court. Another sizeable room, the gathering room, has access to the rear terrace along with the dining room, family room and rear bedroom. Note interior kitchen which is adjacent to each of the major rooms.

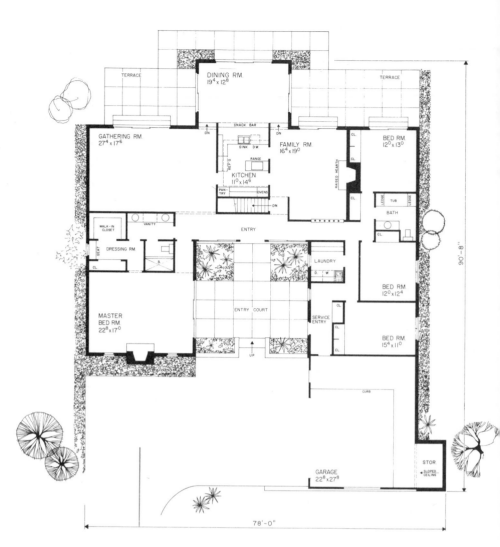

# Design T12183 3,074 Sq. Ft.; 33,587 Cu. Ft.

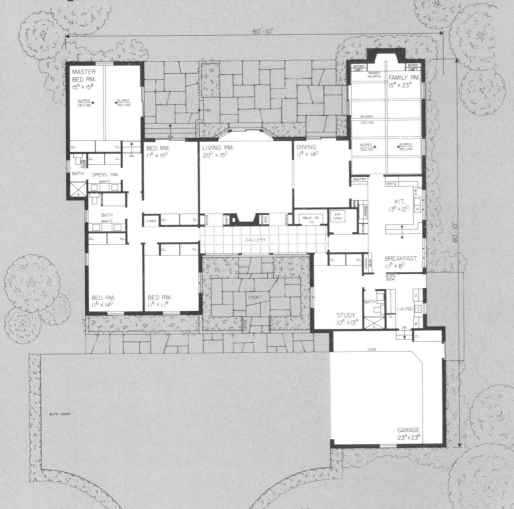

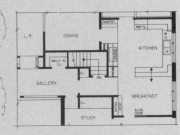

OPTIONAL BASEMENT PLAN

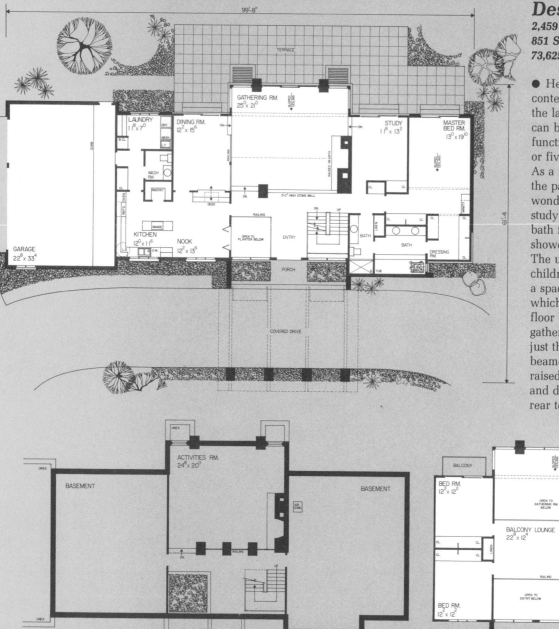

## Design T12562

**2,459 Sq. Ft. - First Floor**
**851 Sq. Ft. - Second Floor**
**73,625 Cu. Ft.**

● Here is an exciting contemporary design for the large, active family. It can be called upon to function as either a four or five bedroom home. As a four bedroom home the parents will enjoy a wonderful suite with study and exceptional bath facilities. Note stall shower, plus sunken tub. The upstairs features the children's bedrooms and a spacious balcony lounge which looks down to the floor below. The sunken gathering room will be just that with its sloped beamed ceiling, dramatic raised hearth fireplace and direct access to the rear terrace.

276

## Design T12579
**2,383 Sq. Ft. - Upper level**
**1,716 Sq. Ft. - Lower Level**
**43,842 Cu. Ft.**

● A huge gathering room, almost 27' with a raised hearth fireplace in the center, sloped ceilings and separate areas for dining and games. Plus balconies on two sides and a deck on the third. A family room on the lower level of equal size to the gathering room with its own center fireplace and adjoining terrace. An activities room to enjoy more living space. A room both youngsters along with adults can utilize. There is an efficient kitchen and dining nook with a built-in desk. Four bedrooms, including a master suite with private bath, two walk-in closets and a private balcony. In fact, every room in the house opens onto a terrace, a deck or a balcony. Sometimes more than one! Indoor-outdoor living will be enjoyed to the maximum. With a total of over 4,000 square feet, there are truly years of gracious living ahead.

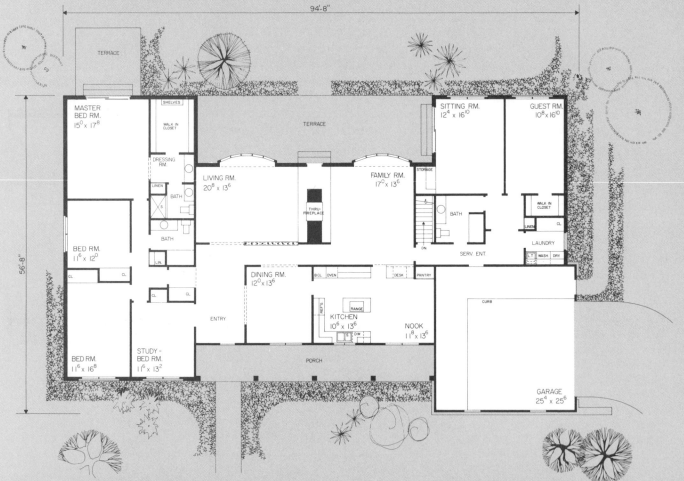

# Design T12768 3,436 Sq. Ft.; 65,450 Cu. Ft.

● Besides its elegant traditionally styled exterior with its delightfully long covered front porch, this home has an exceptionally livable interior. There is the outstanding four bedroom and two-bath sleeping wing. Then, the efficient front kitchen with island range flanked by the formal dining room and the informal breakfast nook. Separated by the two-way, thru fireplace are the living and family rooms which look out on the rear yard. Worthy of particular note is the development of a potential live-in relative facility. These two rooms would also serve the large family well as a hobby room and library or additional bedrooms. A full bath is adjacent as well as the laundry. Note curb area in the garage for the storage of outdoor equipment.

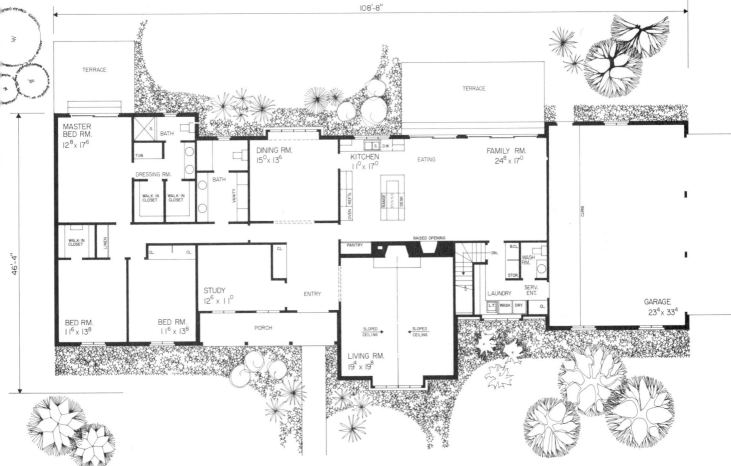

# Design T12767 *3,000 Sq. Ft.; 58,460 Cu. Ft.*

● What a sound investment this impressive home will be. And while its value withstands the inflationary pressures of ensuing years, it will serve your family well. It has all the amenities to assure truly pleasurable living. The charming exterior will lend itself to treatment other than the appealing fieldstone, brick and frame shown. Inside, the plan will impress you with large, spacious living areas, formal and informal dining areas, three large bedrooms, two full baths with twin lavatories, walk-in closets and a fine study. The kitchen features an island work center with range and desk. The two fireplaces will warm their surroundings in both areas. Two separate terraces for a variety of uses. Note laundry, wash room and three-car garage with extra curb area.

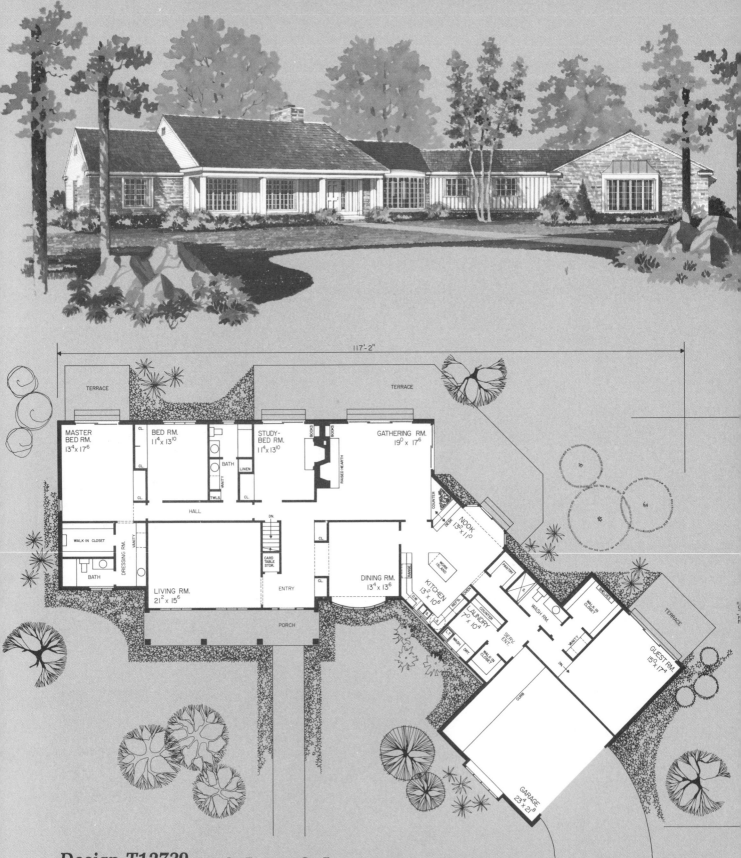

# Design T12739 *3,313 Sq. Ft.; 65,230 Cu. Ft.*

● If you and your family are looking for new living patterns, try to envision your days spent in this traditionally styled home. Its Early American flavor is captured by the effective window and door treatment, the cornice work and the stolid porch pillars. Its zoning is interesting. The interior leaves nothing to be desired. There are three bedrooms and two full baths in the sleeping area. A quiet, formal living room separate from other living areas. The gathering and dining rooms are adjacent to each other and function with the excellent kitchen and its breakfast eating area. Then, there is an extra guest room sunken one step. A live-in relative would enjoy the privacy of this room. Full bath is nearby. This is definitely a home for all to enjoy.

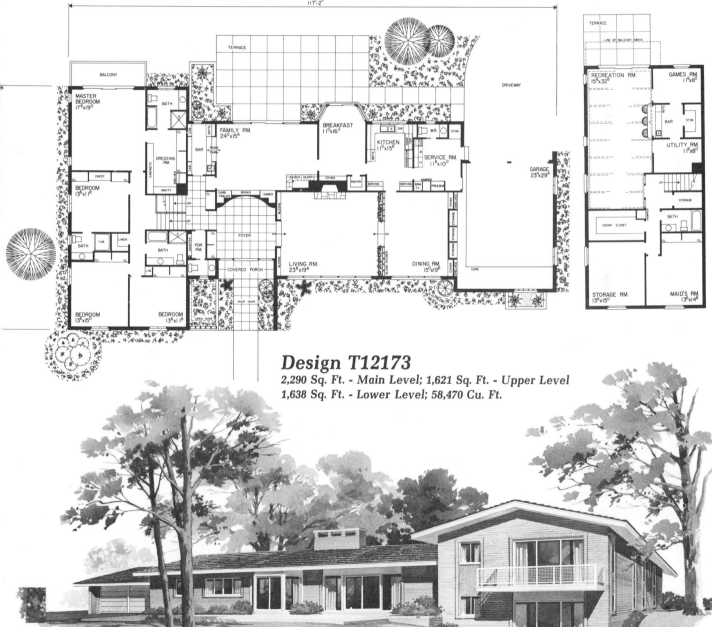

## Design T12173
**2,290 Sq. Ft. - Main Level; 1,621 Sq. Ft. - Upper Level**
**1,638 Sq. Ft. - Lower Level; 58,470 Cu. Ft.**

Floor plan labels:

117'-2"

BALCONY

MASTER BEDROOM 17'6"x19'0"

BATH

DRESSING RM.

BAR

CABINETS

VANITY

SHELVES

BEDROOM 13'6"x11'8"

CHEST

CL

BATH

TUB

LINEN

BEDROOM 13'6"x15'0"

BEDROOM 13'6"x11'8"

OPEN OVER

ROOF OVER

PDR. RM.

BATH

FOYER

COVERED PORCH

CARD TABLES

BOOKS

GAMES

TERRACE

FAMILY RM. 24'0"x15'6"

BREAKFAST 11'6"x16'2"

KITCHEN 11'0"x15'6"

W.R.

STOR.

SERVICE RM. 11'6"x10'0"

SERVING

HAMPER

FREEZER

RAISED HEARTH

CHINA

PANTRY

LIVING RM. 23'6"x19'6"

DINING RM. 15'0"x19'0"

CHINA

GLASS DIVIDER

STORAGE

CURB

GARAGE 23'6"x29'4"

DRIVEWAY

TERRACE

LINE OF BALCONY ABOVE

RECREATION RM. 15'6"x32'0"

GAMES RM. 11'6"x8'0"

BAR

STOR.

UTILITY RM. 11'6"x8'0"

STORAGE

UP

CEDAR CLOSET

BATH

STORAGE RM. 13'6"x15'0"

MAID'S RM. 13'6"x14'8"

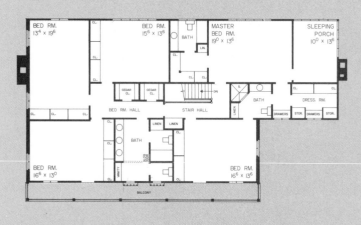

## Design T12214 3,011 Sq. Ft. - First Floor
### 2,297 Sq. Ft. - Second Floor; 78,585 Cu. Ft.

● A Spanish hacienda with all the appeal and all the comforts one would want in a new home. This is a house that looks big and really is big. Measuring 100 feet across the front with various appendages and roof planes, this design gives the appearance of a cluster of units. The house represents over 5,000 square feet of livability, excluding the garage. There are five bedrooms on the second floor plus a sixth bedroom and a study on the first floor. The master bedroom features two full baths and a sleeping porch. The living room is 27 feet long and if you wanted more space you could do away with the plant area. Or, maybe you'd prefer to make this a music area. A full house can be seated in the 18 foot dining room. Kitchen is nearby for ease in serving. Certainly a great house for the large, active family.

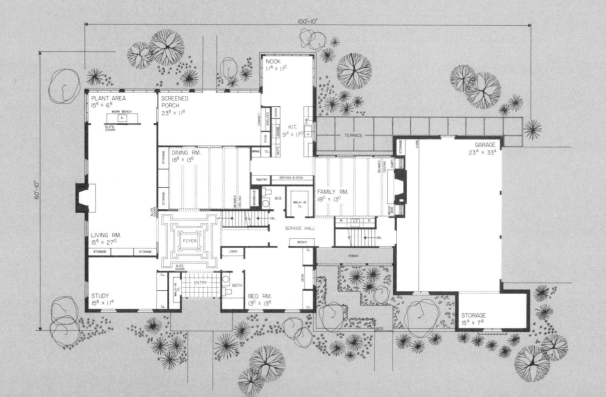

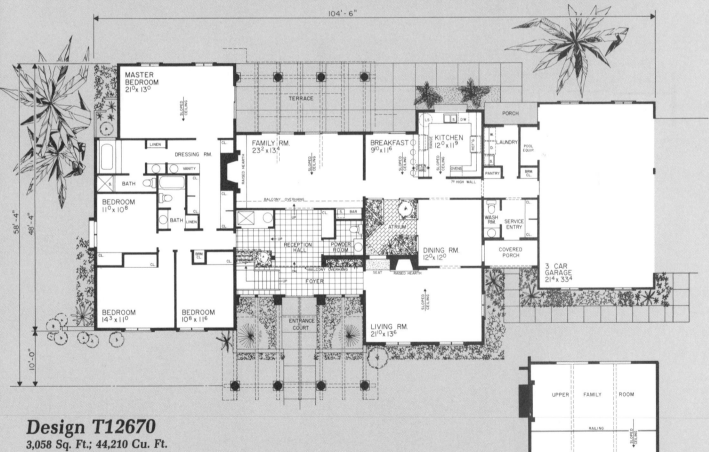

# Design T12670
**3,058 Sq. Ft.; 44,210 Cu. Ft.**

● A centrally located interior atrium is one of the most interesting features of this Spanish design. The atrium has a built-in seat and will bring light to its adjacent rooms; living, dining and breakfast. Beyond the foyer, sunken one step, is a tiled reception hall that includes a powder room. This area leads to the sleeping wing and up one step to the family room. Overlooking the family room is a railed lounge, 279 square feet, which can be used for various activities. The work center area will be convenient to work in.

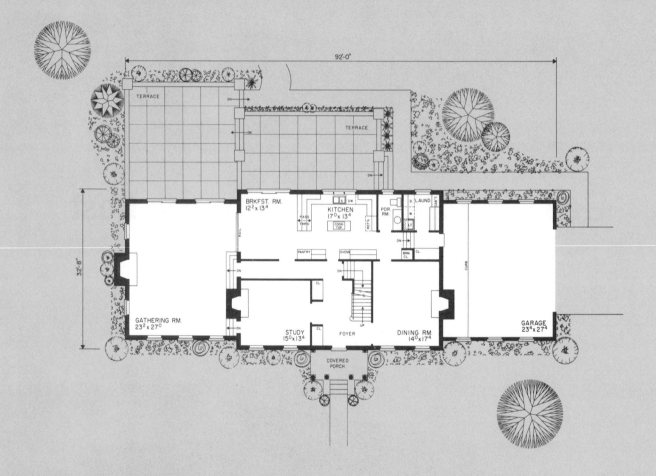

# Design T12683 *2,126 Sq. Ft. - First Floor; 1,882 Sq. Ft. - Second Floor; 78,828 Cu.Ft.*

● This historical Georgian home has its roots in the 18th-Century. Dignified symmetry is a hallmark of both front and rear elevations. The full two-story center section is delightfully complimented by the 1½-story wings. Interior livability has been planned to serve today's active family. The elegant gathering room, three steps down from the rest of the house, has ample space for entertaining on a grand scale. It fills an entire wing and is dead-ended so that traffic does not pass through it. Guests and family alike will enjoy the two rooms flanking the foyer, the study and formal dining room. Each of these rooms will have a fireplace as its highlight. The breakfast room, kitchen, powder room and laundry are arranged for maximum efficiency. This area will always have that desired light and airy atmosphere with the sliding glass door and the triple window over the kitchen sink. The second floor houses the family bedrooms. Take special note of the spacious master bedroom suite. It has a deluxe bath, fireplace and sunken lounge with dressing room and walk-in closet. Surely an area to be appreciated.

# Georgian Elegance from the Past

# A Lifetime of Exciting, Contemporary Living Patterns

● Here is a home for those with a bold, contemporary living bent. The exciting exteriors give notice of an admirable flair for something delightfully different. The varying roof planes and textured blank wall masses are distinctive. Two sets of panelled front doors permit access to either level. The inclined ramp to the upper main level is dramatic, indeed. The rear exterior highlights a veritable battery of projecting balconies. This affords direct access to outdoor living for each of the major rooms in the house. Certainly an invaluable feature should your view be particularly noteworthy. Notice two covered outdoor balconies plus a covered terrace. Indoor-outdoor living at its greatest.

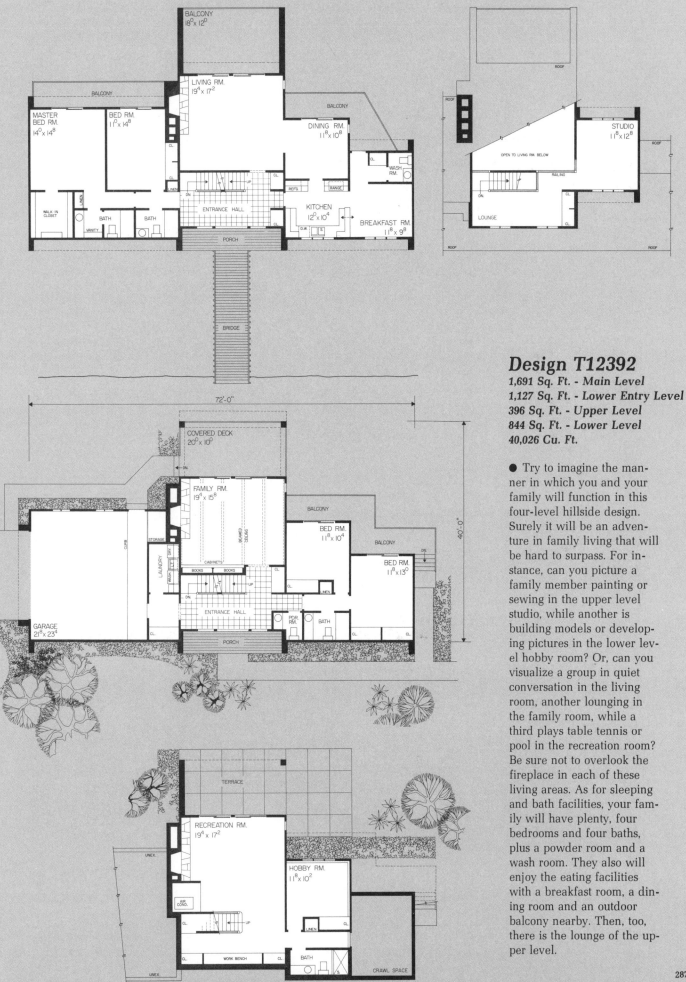

**Design T12392**

*1,691 Sq. Ft. - Main Level*
*1,127 Sq. Ft. - Lower Entry Level*
*396 Sq. Ft. - Upper Level*
*844 Sq. Ft. - Lower Level*
*40,026 Cu. Ft.*

● Try to imagine the manner in which you and your family will function in this four-level hillside design. Surely it will be an adventure in family living that will be hard to surpass. For instance, can you picture a family member painting or sewing in the upper level studio, while another is building models or developing pictures in the lower level hobby room? Or, can you visualize a group in quiet conversation in the living room, another lounging in the family room, while a third plays table tennis or pool in the recreation room? Be sure not to overlook the fireplace in each of these living areas. As for sleeping and bath facilities, your family will have plenty, four bedrooms and four baths, plus a powder room and a wash room. They also will enjoy the eating facilities with a breakfast room, a dining room and an outdoor balcony nearby. Then, too, there is the lounge of the upper level.

287

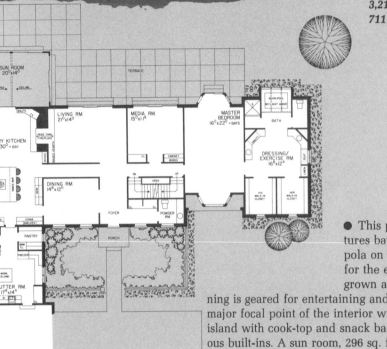

## Design T12921
**3,215 Sq. Ft - First Floor**
**711 Sq. Ft - Second Floor; 69,991 Cu. Ft.**

● This popular traditionally styled house features bay windows, shutters, a fanlight and a cupola on the roof. Interior planning was designed for the empty-nester; those whose children are grown and moved out on their own. Open planning is geared for entertaining and relaxing rather than child-rearing. The major focal point of the interior will be the country kitchen. It has a work island with cook-top and snack bar and a spacious dining area with numerous built-ins. A sun room, 296 sq. ft. and 3,789 cu. ft. not included in the totals above, is in the rear corner of the house, adjacent to the kitchen. Its sloped ceiling and glass walls open this room to the outdoors. Also adjacent to the kitchen, there is a "clutter room". It includes a workshop, laundry, pantry and washroom.

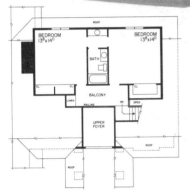

## Design T12920
**3,067 Sq. Ft. - First Floor**
**648 Sq. Ft. - Second Floor; 67,881 Cu. Ft.**

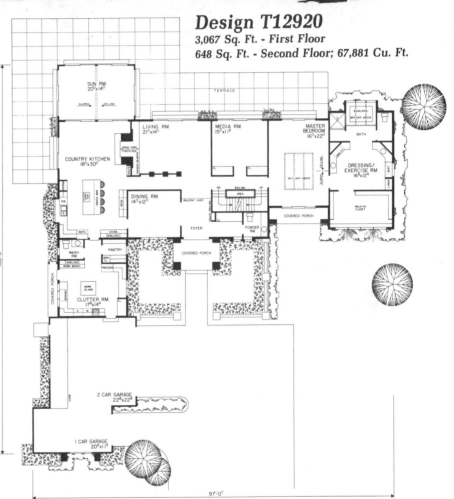

● Utilizing the same floor plan as Design T12921, This contemporary design also has a great deal to offer. Study the living areas. A fireplace opens up to both the living room and country kitchen. Privacy is the key word when describing the sleeping areas. The first floor master bedroom is away from the traffic of the house and features a dressing/exercise room, whirlpool tub and shower and a spacious walk-in closet. Two more bedrooms and a full bath are on the second floor. The three-car garage is arranged so that the owners have use of a double-garage with an attached single on reserve for guests.

# All The "TOOLS" You And Your Builder Need...

## 1. THE PLAN BOOKS

Home Planners' unique Design Category Series makes it easy to look at and study only the types of designs for which you and your family have an interest. Each of six plan books features a specific type of home, namely: Two-Story, 1½ Story, One-Story Over 2000 Sq. Ft., One-Story Under 2000 Sq. Ft., Multi-Levels and Vacation Homes. In addition to the convenient Design Category Series, there is an impressive selection of other current titles. While the home plans featured in these books are also to be found in the Design Category Series, they, too, are edited for those with special tastes and requirements. Your family will spend many enjoyable hours reviewing the delightfully designed exteriors and the practical floor plans. Surely your home or office library should include a selection of these popular plan books. Your complete satisfaction is guaranteed.

## 2. THE CONSTRUCTION BLUEPRINTS

There are blueprints available for each of the designs published in Home Planners' current plan books. Depending upon the size, the style and the type of home, each set of blueprints consists of from five to ten large sheets. Only by studying the blueprints is it possible to give complete and final consideration to the proper selection of a design for your next home. The blueprints provide the opportunity for all family members to familiarize themselves with the features of all exterior elevations, interior elevations and details, all dimensions, special built-in features and effects. They also provide a full understanding of the materials to be used and/or selected. The low-cost of our blueprints makes it possible and indeed, practical, to study in detail a number of different sets of blueprints before deciding upon which design to build.

## 3. THE MATERIALS LIST

A separate list of materials, available for a small fee, is an important part of the plan package. It comprises the last sheet of each set of blueprints and serves as a handy reference during the period of construction. Of course, at the pricing and the material ordering stages, it is indispensable.

## 4. THE SPECIFICATION OUTLINE

Each order for blueprints is accompanied by one Specification Outline. You and your builder will find this a time-saving tool when deciding upon your own individual specifications. An important reference document should you wish to write your own specifications.

## 5. THE PLUMBING & ELECTRICAL PACKAGE

The construction blueprints you order from Home Planners, Inc. include locations for all plumbing fixtures — sinks, lavatories, tubs, showers, water closets, laundry trays, hot water heaters, etc. The blueprints also show the locations of all electrical switches, plugs, and outlets. These plumbing and electrical details are sufficient to present to your local contractor for discussions about your individual specifications and subsequent installations in conformance with local codes. However, for those who wish to acquaint themselves with many of the intricacies of residential plumbing and electrical details and installations, Home Planners, Inc. has made available this package. We do not recommend that the layman attempt to do his own plumbing and electrical work. It is, nevertheless, advisable that owners be as knowledgeable as possible about each of these disciplines. The entire family will appreciate the educational value of these low-cost, easy-to-understand details.

# 1250 HOME DESIGNS
## ONE OF THEM IS YOURS.

You and your family will enjoy browsing through the hundreds of traditional and contemporary home designs, each featuring detailed exterior illustrations and innovative floor plans.

**(1) 315 ONE STORY HOMES UNDER 2,000 Sq. Ft.**
Create a fantastic home on a modest budget. Gathering rooms, formal and informal dining, two to four bedrooms, great indoor/outdoor livability. 192 pages. $4.95

**(2) 210 ONE STORY HOMES OVER 2,000 Sq. Ft.**
Enjoy gracious living in one-story, Spanish, Western, Tudor, French, Contemporary and other styles. Sunken living rooms, master bedroom suites, atriums and courtyards. 192 pages. $4.95

**(3) 150 1-1/2 STORY HOMES**
Explore Cape Cod, Georgian, Tudor and Contemporary homes in low-budget and country-estate sizes. Formal dining rooms, sloped ceilings, country kitchens, covered porches and terraces. 128 pages. $3.95

**(4) 360 TWO STORY HOMES**
Experience two-story living at its finest. English and American Tudors, Farmhouses, Georgians, Southern Colonials, French Mansards and more! Fabulous entryways, gathering rooms, libraries and dining rooms. 288 pages. $6.95

**(5) 215 MULTI-LEVEL HOMES**
Discover new dimensions in family living! Exciting designs for flat and sloping sites. Bi-levels, tri-levels, hillside homes with sloped ceilings, balconies, decks and terraces. 192 pages. $4.95

**(6) 223 VACATION HOMES**
Recreation or year-round homes. A-Frames, Chalets, Hexagons, Ski Lodges, and Cluster Homes. Dual-purpose spaces, decks, balconies, terraces, lofts and fireplaces. 176 pages. (120 in full color). $4.95

**SAVE!** Order our complete collection, all 6 books, a $30.70 value, for only $19.95!

**Credit Card Orders Call
Toll-Free 1-800-322-6797**

**Frontal Sheet**

**Detailed Floor Plans**

**Foundation Plans**

**House Cross-Sections**

**Interior Elevations**

**Exterior Elevations**

**Materials List**

# What Our Plans Include

## The Blueprints

### 1. FRONTAL SHEET.
Artist's landscaped sketch of the exterior and ink-line floor plans are on the frontal sheet of each set of blueprints.

### 2. FOUNDATION PLAN.
¼" Scale basement and foundation plan. All necessary notations and dimensions. Plot plan diagram for locating house on building site.

### 3. DETAILED FLOOR PLAN.
¼" Scale first and second floor plans with complete dimensions. Cross-section detail keys. Diagrammatic layout of electrical outlets and switches.

### 4. HOUSE CROSS-SECTIONS.
Large scale sections of foundation, interior and exterior walls, floors and roof details for design and construction control.

### 5. INTERIOR ELEVATIONS.
Large scale interior details of the complete kitchen cabinet design, bathrooms, powder room, laundry, fireplaces, paneling, beam ceilings, built-in cabinets, etc.

### 6. EXTERIOR ELEVATIONS.
¼" Scale exterior elevation drawings of front, rear, and both sides of the house. All exterior materials and details are shown to indicate the complete design and proportions of the house.

### 7. MATERIALS LIST.
For a small additional fee, complete lists of all materials required for the construction of the house as designed are included in each set of blueprints (one charge for any size order).

### THIS BLUEPRINT PACKAGE
will help you and your family take a major step forward in the final appraisal and planning of your new home. Only by spending many enjoyable and informative hours studying the numerous details included in the complete package will you feel sure of, and comfortable with, your commitment to build your new home. To assure successful and productive consultation with your builder and/or architect, reference to the various elements of the blueprint package is a must. The blueprints, materials list and specification outline will save much consultation time and expense. Don't be without them.

## The Materials List

For a small extra charge, you will receive a materials list with each set of blueprints you order (one fee for any size order). Each list shows you the quantity, type and size of the non-mechanical materials required to build your home. It also tells you where these materials are used. This makes the blueprints easy to understand.

Influencing the mechanical requirements are geographical differences in availability of materials, local codes, methods of installation and individual preferences. Because of these factors, your local heating, plumbing and electrical contractors can supply you with necessary material take-offs for their particular trades.

Materials lists simplify your material ordering and enable you to get quicker price quotations from your builder and material dealer. Because the materials list is an integral part of each set of blueprints, it is not available separately.

Among the materials listed:

• Masonry, Veneer & Fireplace • Framing Lumber • Roofing & Sheet Metal • Windows & Door Frames • Exterior Trim & Insulation • Tile Work, Finish Floors • Interior Trim, Kitchen Cabinets • Rough & Finish Hardware

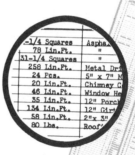

## The Specification Outline

This fill-in type specification lists over 150 phases of home construction from excavating to painting and includes wiring, plumbing, heating and air-conditioning. It consists of 16 pages and will prove invaluable for specifying to your builder the exact materials, equipment and methods of construction you want in your new home. One Specification Outline is included free with each order for blueprints. Additional Specification Outlines are available at $5.00 each.

### CONTENTS
• General Instructions, Suggestions and Information • Excavating and Grading • Masonry and Concrete Work • Sheet Metal Work • Carpentry, Millwork, Roofing, and Miscellaneous Items • Lath and Plaster or Drywall Wallboard • Schedule for Room Finishes • Painting and Finishing • Tile Work • Electrical Work • Plumbing • Heating and Air-Conditioning

# More Products from Home Planners To Help You Plan Your Home

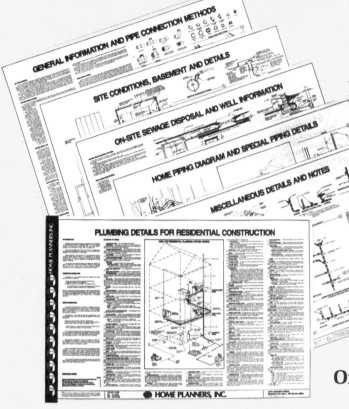

## Comprehensive Plumbing Details for All Types of Residential Construction

If you want to find out more about the intricacies of household plumbing, these 24x36-inch drawings– six individual, fact-packed sheets– will prove to be remarkably useful tools. Prepared to meet requirements of the National Plumbing Code, they show pipe schedules, fittings, sump-pump details, water-softener hookups, septic-system details, and many more. Sheets are bound together and color coded for easy reference. Glossary of terms included.

**Only $14.95**

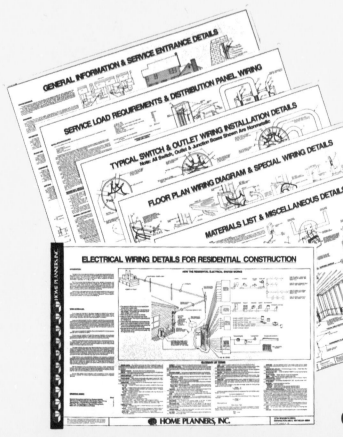

## Complete Electrical Wiring Details for All Types of Residential Construction

Designed to take the mystery out of household electrical systems, these comprehensive 24x36-inch drawings come packed with details. Prepared to meet requirements of the National Electrical Code, the six fact-filled sheets cover a variety of topics, including appliance wattage, wire sizing, switch-installation schematics, cable-routing details, doorbell hookups, and many others. Sheets are bound together and color coded for easy reference. Glossary of terms included.

**Only $14.95**

294

## Plan Your Home with Plan-A-Home™

Plan-A-Home™ is a very useful tool. It's a simple product that will help you design a new home, plan a remodeling project or arrange furniture on an existing plan. Each package contains: more than 700 peel-and-stick *planning symbols* on a self-stick, vinyl sheet, including walls, windows, doors, furniture, kitchen components, bath fixtures, and many more; a reusable, transparent, ¼-inch-scale *planning grid* that can help you create houses up to 140x92 feet; *tracing paper*; and a *felt-tip pen,* with water-soluble ink that wipes away quickly. The transparent planning grid matches the scale of working blueprints, so you can lay it over existing drawings and modify them as necessary.

### Only $24.95

## Residential Construction Details

Home Planners' blueprint package contains everything an experienced builder needs to construct a particular plan. However, it doesn't show the thousands upon thousands of ways building materials come together to form a house. Prepared to meet requirements of the Uniform Building Code, these drawings–eight large, fact-filled sheets–depict the materials and methods used to build foundations, fireplaces, walls, floors, and roofs. What's more, where appropriate, they show acceptable alternatives. Bound together for easy reference.

### Only $14.95

***Get any two of Plumbing, Electrical, and Construction Details for just $22.95 (save $6.95). Get all three for only $29.95 (save $14.90).***

*To order, turn the page . . .*

# The Blueprint Price Schedule

The blueprint package you order will be an invaluable tool for the complete study of the details relating to the construction of your favorite design, as well as the master plan for building your home. Even the smallest of homes require much construction data and architectural detailing. As the house grows in size, so does the need for more data and details. Frequently, a house of only modest size can require an inordinate amount of data and detailing. This may be the result of its irregular shape and/or the complexity of its architectural features. In the pricing of its blueprints, Home Planners, Inc. has taken into account these factors. Before completing the blueprint order form on the opposite page, be sure to refer to the price schedule below for the appropriate blueprint charges for the design of your choice.

Schedule A: Single Sets, $125.00; Four Set Package, $175.00; Eight Set Package, $225.00. Additional Identical Sets in Same Order, $30.00 each. Sepia, $250.00.

Schedule B: Single Sets, $150.00; Four Set Package, $200.00; Eight Set Package, $250.00. Additional Identical Sets in Same Order, $30.00 each. Sepia, $300.00.

Schedule C: Single Sets, $175.00; Four Set Package, $225.00; Eight Set Package, $275.00. Additional Identical Sets in Same Order, $30.00 each. Sepia, $350.00.

Schedule D: Single Sets, $200.00; Four Set Package, $250.00; Eight Set Package, $300.00. Additional Identical Sets in Same Order, $30.00 each. Sepia, $400.00.

| DESIGN NO. | PRICE SCHEDULE | DESIGN NO. | PRICE SCHEDULE | DESIGN NO. | PRICE SCHEDULE | DESIGN NO. | PRICE SCHEDULE | DESIGN NO. | PRICE SCHEDULE |
|---|---|---|---|---|---|---|---|---|---|
| T11075 | A | T11831 | B | T12248 | C | T12570 | A | T12754 | B |
| T11091 | B | T11832 | B | T12251 | D | T12571 | A | T12756 | C |
| T11100 | B | T11833 | B | T12254 | C | T12573 | C | T12757 | C |
| T11130 | B | T11834 | B | T12258 | C | T12579 | D | T12758 | C |
| T11149 | B | T11835 | B | T12264 | C | T12581 | C | T12761 | B |
| T11174 | C | T11850 | B | T12266 | C | T12583 | C | T12763 | C |
| T11191 | A | T11858 | C | T12277 | B | T12585 | B | T12766 | C |
| T11208 | A | T11864 | B | T12283 | C | T12586 | A | T12767 | D |
| T11219 | B | T11865 | B | T12294 | D | T12587 | A | T12768 | D |
| T11220 | B | T11866 | B | T12316 | B | T12589 | C | T12771 | C |
| T11241 | A | T11870 | B | T12317 | D | T12594 | C | T12772 | C |
| T11267 | B | T11887 | B | T12320 | C | T12596 | B | T12774 | B |
| T11295 | C | T11890 | B | T12335 | C | T12597 | B | T12776 | B |
| T11305 | A | T11892 | B | T12349 | B | T12603 | B | T12778 | C |
| T11307 | A | T11896 | B | T12354 | C | T12604 | B | T12779 | D |
| T11308 | A | T11900 | C | T12356 | D | T12605 | B | T12780 | C |
| T11311 | A | T11911 | D | T12360 | B | T12606 | A | T12781 | C |
| T11320 | A | T11920 | B | T12366 | A | T12607 | A | T12782 | C |
| T11321 | A | T11927 | C | T12374 | B | T12608 | A | T12783 | D |
| T11322 | A | T11938 | A | T12377 | A | T12610 | C | T12785 | C |
| T11323 | A | T11945 | B | T12378 | C | T12611 | B | T12786 | B |
| T11325 | B | T11946 | B | T12379 | B | T12612 | B | T12787 | B |
| T11337 | B | T11947 | B | T12386 | B | T12615 | D | T12788 | B |
| T11343 | B | T11948 | B | T12390 | C | T12617 | B | T12789 | C |
| T11346 | B | T11949 | B | T12391 | C | T12618 | B | T12794 | C |
| T11350 | B | T11950 | B | T12392 | D | T12619 | B | T12798 | A |
| T11351 | B | T11956 | A | T12393 | B | T12622 | A | T12800 | B |
| T11352 | B | T11957 | A | T12395 | B | T12624 | B | T12801 | B |
| T11354 | A | T11980 | B | T12396 | B | T12626 | B | T12802 | B |
| T11365 | A | T11981 | B | T12417 | B | T12633 | C | T12803 | B |
| T11366 | A | T11986 | B | T12425 | A | T12638 | C | T12804 | B |
| T11371 | B | T11987 | B | T12426 | A | T12639 | C | T12805 | B |
| T11372 | A | T11989 | C | T12427 | A | T12645 | C | T12806 | B |
| T11375 | B | T11991 | B | T12430 | A | T12646 | B | T12807 | B |
| T11376 | A | T11993 | D | T12431 | A | T12647 | D | T12810 | B |
| T11377 | A | T11997 | D | T12439 | A | T12650 | B | T12811 | B |
| T11378 | B | T12101 | B | T12459 | A | T12655 | A | T12812 | B |
| T11380 | A | T12107 | A | T12464 | A | T12656 | B | T12813 | B |
| T11381 | A | T12124 | B | T12478 | A | T12657 | B | T12814 | B |
| T11382 | A | T12128 | B | T12479 | B | T12658 | A | T12815 | B |
| T11383 | A | T12129 | B | T12480 | A | T12659 | B | T12816 | B |
| T11387 | A | T12131 | B | T12481 | A | T12660 | D | T12817 | B |
| T11388 | A | T12132 | C | T12483 | B | T12661 | A | T12818 | B |
| T11389 | A | T12133 | D | T12484 | A | T12662 | C | T12820 | C |
| T11394 | A | T12134 | C | T12485 | B | T12663 | B | T12821 | A |
| T11406 | A | T12137 | B | T12487 | B | T12664 | B | T12822 | A |
| T11424 | A | T12142 | C | T12488 | A | T12665 | D | T12823 | B |
| T11445 | A | T12144 | C | T12489 | A | T12668 | D | T12824 | B |
| T11449 | A | T12148 | C | T12500 | B | T12670 | D | T12826 | B |
| T11459 | A | T12149 | A | T12501 | B | T12671 | B | T12827 | C |
| T11462 | A | T12150 | A | T12502 | C | T12682 | A | T12828 | B |
| T11477 | A | T12151 | A | T12504 | C | T12683 | D | T12830 | C |
| T11483 | A | T12162 | A | T12505 | A | T12687 | C | T12831 | C |
| T11484 | A | T12170 | B | T12508 | C | T12688 | B | T12832 | C |
| T11485 | A | T12171 | B | T12510 | A | T12701 | C | T12833 | C |
| T11486 | A | T12173 | D | T12511 | B | T12703 | A | T12834 | D |
| T11488 | A | T12174 | B | T12512 | C | T12704 | B | T12835 | C |
| T11499 | B | T12175 | B | T12513 | C | T12705 | B | T12838 | C |
| T11522 | A | T12181 | C | T12515 | C | T12706 | B | T12839 | C |
| T11531 | A | T12183 | D | T12517 | C | T12707 | A | T12840 | C |
| T11701 | B | T12184 | C | T12518 | C | T12708 | C | T12842 | B |
| T11715 | B | T12191 | C | T12519 | C | T12711 | C | T12843 | C |
| T11718 | B | T12192 | D | T12520 | B | T12716 | C | T12844 | C |
| T11719 | A | T12200 | B | T12522 | C | T12718 | C | T12846 | C |
| T11723 | A | T12204 | B | T12525 | A | T12728 | B | T12847 | C |
| T11726 | B | T12206 | B | T12527 | C | T12729 | B | T12850 | C |
| T11736 | B | T12209 | C | T12530 | D | T12731 | B | T12854 | B |
| T11748 | B | T12211 | B | T12534 | D | T12733 | B | T12855 | B |
| T11754 | B | T12212 | D | T12535 | B | T12737 | B | T12858 | C |
| T11761 | C | T12214 | D | T12536 | C | T12738 | B | T12861 | C |
| T11766 | B | T12220 | B | T12538 | B | T12739 | D | T12864 | A |
| T11768 | B | T12221 | C | T12539 | B | T12741 | B | T12869 | B |
| T11773 | B | T12225 | D | T12540 | B | T12742 | B | T12878 | B |
| T11786 | C | T12229 | C | T12542 | B | T12743 | B | T12883 | C |
| T11787 | C | T12230 | D | T12543 | D | T12744 | A | T12884 | B |
| T11788 | C | T12231 | C | T12544 | C | T12746 | C | T12889 | D |
| T11790 | C | T12232 | B | T12558 | A | T12747 | D | T12905 | B |
| T11791 | B | T12236 | C | T12559 | B | T12748 | A | T12915 | C |
| T11793 | C | T12241 | C | T12562 | D | T12750 | B | T12920 | D |
| T11794 | C | T12242 | B | T12563 | B | T12751 | B | T12921 | D |
| T11802 | A | T12243 | C | T12565 | B | T12752 | B | T13126 | A |
| T11829 | B | T12245 | D | T12569 | A | T12753 | B | T13189 | A |

# Before You Order

**1.** STUDY THE DESIGNS . . . found in Home Planners and Heritage Homes plan books. As you review these delightful custom homes, you should keep in mind the total living requirements of your family — both indoors and outdoors. Although we do not make changes in plans, many minor changes can be made prior to construction. If major changes are involved to satisfy your personal requirements, you should consider ordering one set of sepias and having them modified. Consultation with your architect is strongly advised when contemplating major changes.

**2.** HOW TO ORDER BLUEPRINTS . . . After you have chosen the design that satisfies your requirements, or if you have selected one that you wish to study in more detail, simply clip the accompanying order blank and mail with your remittance. However, if it is not convenient for you to send a check or money order, you can use your credit card, or merely indicate C.O.D. shipment. Postman will collect all charges, including postage and C.O.D. fee. C.O.D. shipments are not permitted to Canada or foreign countries. Should time be of essence, as it sometimes is with many of our customers, your telephone order usually can be processed and shipped in the next day's mail. Simply call toll free 1-800-521-6797, (Michigan residents call collect 0-313-477-1850).

**3.** OUR SERVICE . . . Home Planners makes every effort to process and ship each order for blueprints and books within 48 hours. Because of this, we have deemed it unnecessary to acknowledge receipt

## How Many Blueprints Do You Need?

Because additional sets of the same design in each order are only $30.00 each, you save considerably by ordering your total requirements now. To help you determine the exact number of sets, please refer to the handy checklist below.

## Blueprint Checklist

___ **OWNER'S SET(S)**

___ **BUILDER** (Usually requires at least three sets: one as legal document; one for inspection; and at least one for tradesmen — usually more.)

___ **BUILDING PERMIT** (Sometimes two sets are required.)

___ **MORTGAGE SOURCE** (Usually one set for a conventional mortgage; three sets for F.H.A. or V.A. type mortgages.)

___ **SUBDIVISION COMMITTEE** (If any.)

___ **TOTAL NUMBER SETS REQUIRED**

## BLUEPRINT HOTLINE

**PHONE TOLL FREE: 1-800-521-6797.** Orders received by 3 p.m. (Eastern time) will be processed the same day and shipped to you the following day. Use of this line is restricted to blueprint and book ordering only. Michigan residents simply call collect 0-313-477-1850.

**KINDLY NOTE:** When ordering by phone, please state Order Form Key Number located in box at lower left corner of the blueprint order form.

**IN CANADA:** Add 20% to prices listed on this order form and mail in Canadian funds to:
HOME PLANNERS, INC.
20 Cedar St. North
Kitchener, Ontario N2H 2W8
Phone: (519) 743-4169

---

of our customers orders. See order coupon for the postage and handling charges for surface mail, air mail or foreign mail.

**4.** MODIFYING OUR PLANS . . . Slight revisions are easy to do before you start building. (We don't alter plans, by the way.) If you're thinking about major changes, consider ordering a set of sepias. After changes have been made on the sepia, additional sets of plans may be reproduced from the sepia master. Should you decide to revise the plan significantly, we strongly suggest that you consult an experienced architect or designer.

**5.** A NOTE REGARDING REVERSE BLUE-PRINTS . . . As a special service to those wishing to build in reverse of the plan as shown, we do include

an extra set of reversed blueprints for only $30.00 additional with each order. Even though the lettering and dimensions appear backward on reversed blueprints, they make a handy reference because they show the house just as it's being built in reverse from the standard blueprints — thereby helping you visualize the home better.

**6.** OUR EXCHANGE POLICY . . . Since blueprints are printed in response to your order, we cannot honor requests for refunds. However, we will exchange your entire first order for an equal number of blueprints at a price of $20.00 for the first set and $10.00 for each additional set. All sets from the previous order must be returned before the exchange can take place. Please add $3.00 for postage and handling via surface mail; $4.00 via air mail.

---

**TO:** HOME PLANNERS, INC., 23761 RESEARCH DRIVE FARMINGTON HILLS, MICHIGAN 48024

Please rush me the following:

____ SET(S) BLUEPRINTS FOR DESIGN NO(S). . . . . . . . . . . . . . . . . . . . . . . . . . . . . . . . . . . . . . $_____
Kindly refer to Blueprint Price Schedule on opposite page.

____ SEPIA FOR DESIGN NO(S). . . . . . . . . . . . . . . . . . . . . . . . . . . . . . . . . . . . . . . . . . . . . . . . . . $_____

____ MATERIALS LIST just $25.00 for Entire Order (1 List per Set). . . . . . . . . . . . . . . . . . . . . . $_____

____ ADDITIONAL SPECIFICATION OUTLINES @ $5.00 each . . . . . . . . . . . . . . . . . . . . . . . . . . . $_____

____ DETAIL SETS @ $14.95 ea.; any two for $22.95; all three for $29.95 . . . . . . . . . . . . . . . . . . $_____
☐ PLUMBING ☐ ELECTRICAL ☐ CONSTRUCTION

____ PLAN-A-HOME™ Design Kit @ $24.95 ea. (plus $3.00 postage) . . . . . . . . . . . . . . . . . . . . . $_____

Michigan Residents add 4% sales tax $_____

| FOR POSTAGE AND HANDLING PLEASE CHECK ✔ & REMIT | ☐ | $3.00 Added to Order for Surface Mail (UPS) – Any Mdse. |
| | ☐ | $5.00 Added for Priority Mail of One-Three Sets of Blueprints. |
| | ☐ | $8.00 Added for Priority Mail of Four or more Sets of Blueprints. |
| | ☐ | For Canadian orders add $2.00 to above applicable rates. |

$_____

☐ C.O.D. PAY POSTMAN (U.S. ONLY)          TOTAL in U.S. funds $_____

PLEASE PRINT
Name _____
Street _____
City _____ State _____ Zip _____

**CREDIT CARD ORDERS ONLY:** Fill in the boxes below          Prices subject to change without notice
Credit Card No. _____          Expiration Date Month/Year _____

CHECK ONE: ☐ **VISA** ☐ **MasterCard**
Order Form Key TB5          Your Signature _____

## BLUEPRINT ORDERS SHIPPED WITHIN 48 HOURS OF RECEIPT!

**TO:** HOME PLANNERS, INC., 23761 RESEARCH DRIVE FARMINGTON HILLS, MICHIGAN 48024

Please rush me the following:

____ SET(S) BLUEPRINTS FOR DESIGN NO(S). . . . . . . . . . . . . . . . . . . . . . . . . . . . . . . . . . . . . . $_____
Kindly refer to Blueprint Price Schedule on opposite page.

____ SEPIA FOR DESIGN NO(S). . . . . . . . . . . . . . . . . . . . . . . . . . . . . . . . . . . . . . . . . . . . . . . . . . $_____

____ MATERIALS LIST just $25.00 for Entire Order (1 List per Set). . . . . . . . . . . . . . . . . . . . . . $_____

____ ADDITIONAL SPECIFICATION OUTLINES @ $5.00 each . . . . . . . . . . . . . . . . . . . . . . . . . . . $_____

____ DETAIL SETS @ $14.95 ea.; any two for $22.95; all three for $29.95 . . . . . . . . . . . . . . . . . . $_____
☐ PLUMBING ☐ ELECTRICAL ☐ CONSTRUCTION

____ PLAN-A-HOME™ Design Kit @ $24.95 ea. (plus $3.00 postage) . . . . . . . . . . . . . . . . . . . . . $_____

Michigan Residents add 4% sales tax $_____

| FOR POSTAGE AND HANDLING PLEASE CHECK ✔ & REMIT | ☐ | $3.00 Added to Order for Surface Mail (UPS) – Any Mdse. |
| | ☐ | $5.00 Added for Priority Mail of One-Three Sets of Blueprints. |
| | ☐ | $8.00 Added for Priority Mail of Four or more Sets of Blueprints |
| | ☐ | For Canadian orders add $2.00 to above applicable rates. |

$_____

☐ C.O.D. PAY POSTMAN (U.S. ONLY)          TOTAL in U.S. funds $_____

PLEASE PRINT
Name _____
Street _____
City _____ State _____ Zip _____

**CREDIT CARD ORDERS ONLY:** Fill in the boxes below          Prices subject to change without notice
Credit Card No. _____          Expiration Date Month/Year _____

CHECK ONE: ☐ **VISA** ☐ **MasterCard**
Order Form Key TB5          Your Signature

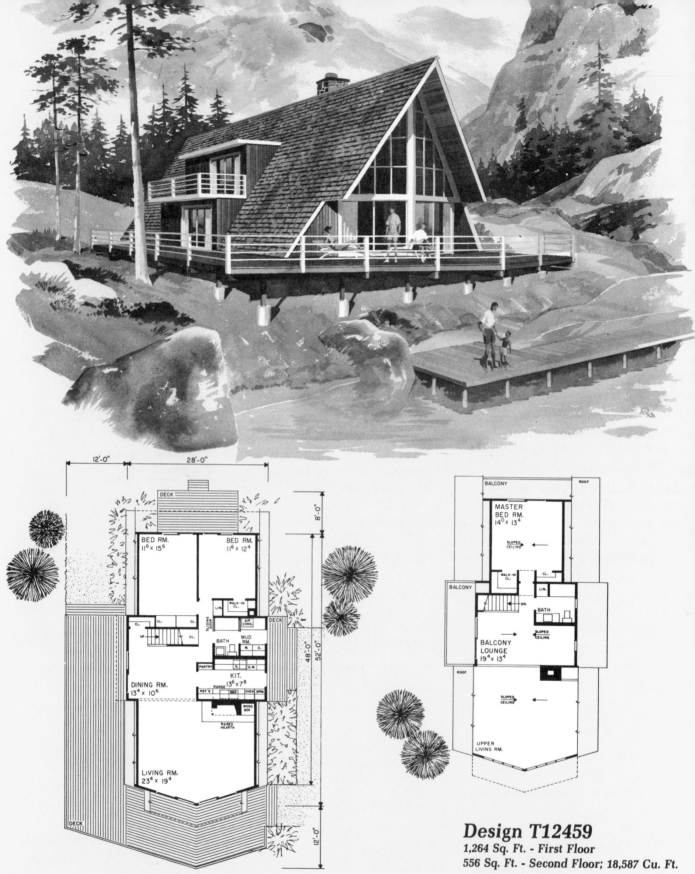

### Design T12459
**1,264 Sq. Ft. - First Floor**
**556 Sq. Ft. - Second Floor; 18,587 Cu. Ft.**

● Dramatic, indeed! The soaring roof projects and heightens the appeal of the slanted glass gable end. The expanse of the roof is broken to provide access to the side deck from the dining room. Above is the balcony of the second floor lounge. This room with its high sloping ceiling looks down into the spacious first floor living room. The master bedroom also has an outdoor balcony. Back downstairs there are loads of features. They include two large bedrooms, a big dining room and a huge living room. Particularly note-worthy is the direct accessibility of the kitchen and mud room/bath from the outdoors. These are truly convenient traffic patterns for the active family. The raised hearth fireplace commands its full share of attention as it rises toward the sloping ceiling.

# VACATION HOMES

*Recent years have seen the vacation home referred to as the second home, or leisure-time home. Many such homes are built with their use as retirement homes in mind. And little wonder, for they can offer an exciting departure from the conventional structures we call home during so much of our lives. Here are designs that are as much fun to look at as they are to live in. They represent a refreshing departure from everyday living patterns. Regardless of size, they will assure a break in the workday routine. If easily accessible for frequent use, each visit, however short, becomes a vacation.*

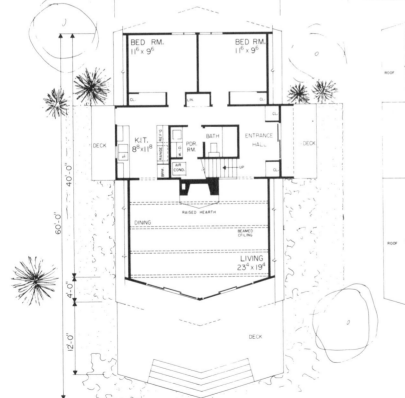

## Design T12431
1,057 Sq. Ft. - First Floor
406 Sq. Ft. - Second Floor; 15,230 Cu. Ft.

● A favorite everywhere – the A-frame vacation home. Its popularity is easily discernible at first glance. The stately appearance is enhanced by the soaring roof lines and the dramatic glass areas. Inside, the breathtaking beauty of outstanding architectural detailing also is apparent. The high ceiling of the living room slopes and has exposed beams. The second floor master suite is a great feature. Observe the raised hearth fireplace and the outdoor balcony. This outdoor spot certainly will be a quiet perch for sunbathing on a warm afternoon.

## Design T12430 1,238 Sq. Ft. - First Floor; 648 Sq. Ft. - Second Floor; 18,743 Cu. Ft.

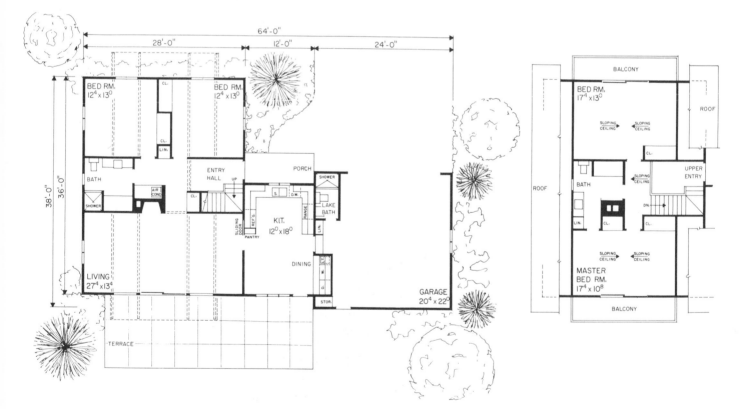

● Another Swiss chalet adaptation which will serve its occupants admirably during the four seasons of the year. The sun-drenched balcony and the terrace will be enjoyed as much by the skiers in the winter as by the swimmers in the summer. All the various areas are equally outstanding. For sleeping, there are four big bedrooms. They are supported by two full baths – one has both tub and stall shower. For relaxation, there is the big living room. It has a fireplace and a large glass area to preserve the view. For eating, there is the U-shaped kitchen and its adjacent dining area. Don't miss beamed ceilings of first floor, nor sloping ceilings of second floor. Note the positioning of the lake bath adjacent to the kitchen entrance. Truly a strategic and convenient location.

# Design T11499
*896 Sq. Ft. - Main Level; 298 Sq. Ft. - Upper Level; 896 Sq. Ft. - Lower Level; 18,784 Cu. Ft.*

● Three level living results in family living patterns which will foster a delightful feeling of informality. Upon arrival at this charming second home, each family member will enthusiastically welcome the change in environment – both indoors and out. Whether looking down into the living room from the dormitory balcony, or walking through the sliding doors onto the huge deck, or participating in some family activity in the game room, everyone will count the hours spent here as relaxing ones. Study the plan carefully.

Note the sleeping facilities on each of the three levels. Two bedrooms and a dormitory in all to sleep the family and friends comfortably. There are two full baths, a separate laundry room and plenty of storage. Don't miss the efficient U-shaped kitchen.

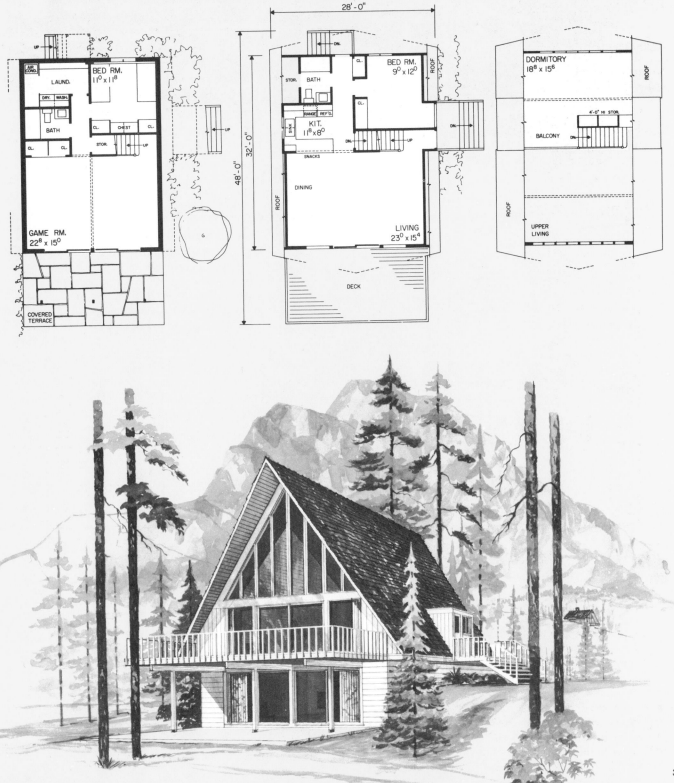

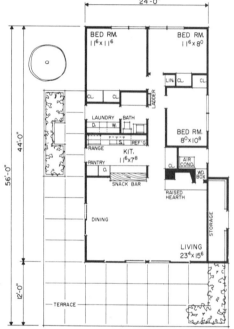

BED RM.
11⁶ x 11⁶

BED RM.
11⁶ x 8⁰

BED RM.
8⁰ x 10⁸

LADDER

LIN. CL. CL.

CL. CL.

LAUNDRY  BATH

D.  W.

RANGE   REF'G

KIT.
11⁶ x 7⁸

PANTRY

SNACK BAR

RAISED HEARTH

AIR COND.

WD. BOX

STORAGE

DINING

LIVING
23⁴ x 15⁶

TERRACE

24'-0"

44'-0"

56'-0"

12'-0"

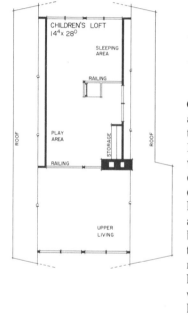

CHILDREN'S LOFT
14⁴ x 28⁰

SLEEPING AREA

RAILING

ROOF

PLAY AREA

STORAGE

RAILING

ROOF

UPPER LIVING

## Design T11459
**1,056 Sq. Ft. - First Floor**
**400 Sq. Ft. - Second Floor**
**17,504 Cu. Ft.**

● There is a heap of vacation living awaiting the gang that descends upon this smart looking chalet adaptation. If you have a narrow site, this design will be of extra interest to you. Should one of your requirements be an abundance of sleeping facilities, you'd hardly do better in such an economically built design. There are three bedrooms downstairs. A ladder leads to the second floor loft. The children will love the idea of sleeping here. In addition, there is a play area which looks down into the first floor living room. A great vacation home.

## Design T12427
**784 Sq. Ft. - First Floor**
**504 Sq. Ft. - Second Floor**
**13,485 Cu. Ft.**

● If ever a design had "vacation home" written all over it, this one has! Perhaps the most carefree characteristic of all is the second floor balcony which looks down into the wood deck. This balcony provides the outdoor living facility for the big master bedroom. Also occupying the second floor is the three-bunk dormitory. The use of bunks would be a fine utilization of this space. Panels through the knee walls give access to an abundant storage area. Downstairs there is yet another bedroom, a full bath and a 27 foot living room.

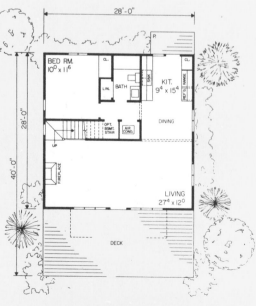

BED RM.
10⁰ x 11⁶

CL.

LIN.

BATH

KIT.
9⁴ x 15⁴

REF'G  RANGE

DINING

OPT. BSMT. STAIR

AIR COND.

UP

FIREPLACE

LIVING
27⁴ x 12⁰

DECK

28'-0"

28'-0"

40'-0"

DORMITORY
17⁴ x 9⁴

STOR.

ROOF

CL.

DN.

BATH

STOR.

STOR.

CL.

MASTER BED RM.
15⁰ x 12⁰

ROOF

STORAGE

BALCONY

## Design T11424

*672 Sq. Ft. - First Floor*
*256 Sq. Ft. - Second Floor*
*8,736 Cu. Ft.*

● This chalet-type vacation home with its steep, overhanging roof, will catch the eye of even the most casual onlooker. It is designed to be completely livable whether the season be for swimming or skiing. The dormitory of the upper level will sleep many vacationers, while the two bedrooms of the first floor provide the more convenient and conventional sleeping facilities. The upper level overlooks the living and dining area with its beamed ceiling. The lower level provides everything that one would want for vacation living.

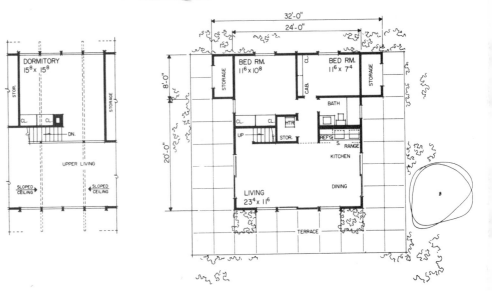

303

## Design T12439 1,312 Sq. Ft.; 17,673 Cu. Ft.

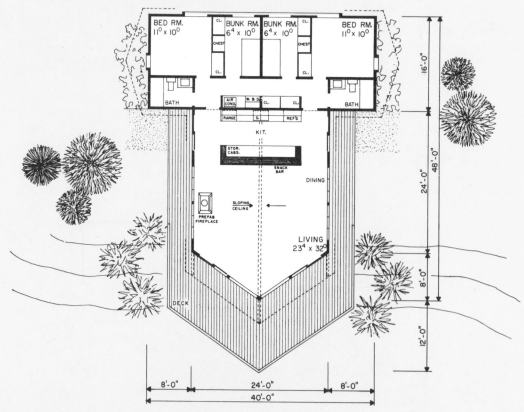

Floor plan labels:

BED RM. 11⁰ x 10⁰ · BUNK RM. 6⁴ x 10⁰ · BUNK RM. 6⁴ x 10⁰ · BED RM. 11⁰ x 10⁰
CL. · CHEST · CHEST · CL. · CL. · CL.
BATH · BATH
AIR COND. · W. & D. · CL.
RANGE · S. · REF'G.
KIT.
STOR. CABS.
SNACK BAR
DINING
SLOPING CEILING
PREFAB FIREPLACE
LIVING 23⁴ x 32⁰
DECK

Dimensions: 16'-0" · 48'-0" · 24'-0" · 8'-0" · 12'-0" · 8'-0" · 24'-0" · 8'-0" · 40'-0"

● A wonderfully organized plan with an exterior that will surely command the attention of each and every passer-by. And what will catch the eye? Certainly the roof lines and the pointed glass gable end wall will be noticed immediately. The delightful deck will be quickly noticed, too. Inside a visitor will be thrilled by the spaciousness of the huge living room. The ceilings slope upward to the exposed ridge beam. A free-standing fireplace will make its contribution to a cheerful atmosphere. The kitchen is separated from the living area by a three foot high snack bar with cupboards below servicing the kitchen. What could improve upon the sleeping zone when it has two bedrooms, two bunk rooms, two full baths, two built-in chests and fine closet space?

## Design T12417 1,520 Sq. Ft.; 19,952 Cu. Ft.

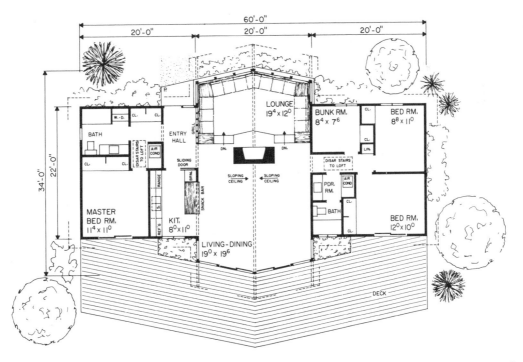

● Have you ever seen a vacation home design that is anything quite like this one? Probably not. The picturesque exterior is dominated by a projecting gable with its wide overhanging roof acting as a dramatic sun visor for the wonderfully large glass area below.

Effectively balancing this 20 foot center section are two 20 foot wings. Inside, and below the high, sloping, beamed ceiling is the huge living area. In addition to the living-dining area, there is the spacious sunken lounge. This pleasant area has a built-in seat-

ing arrangement and a cozy fireplace. The kitchen is efficient and handy to the snack bar and dining area. The parents' and children's sleeping areas are separated and each has a full bath. The large deck is accessible from sliding glass doors.

## Design T12478

**1,137 Sq. Ft. - First Floor**
**257 Sq. Ft. - Second Floor**
**16,218 Cu. Ft.**

● An appealing geometric exterior with a fine floor plan for informal family living. Note the three decks, the big family room, the spacious kitchen, the two fireplaces and the upstairs dormitory.

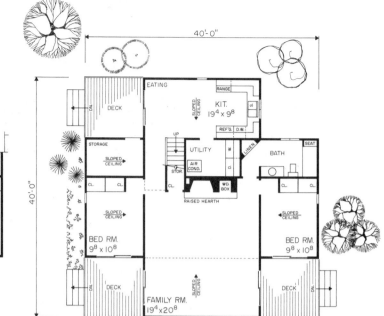

## Design T12480

**826 Sq. Ft. - First Floor**
**533 Sq. Ft. - Second Floor**
**14,650 Cu. Ft.**

● This distinctive contemporary two-story leisure-time home provides excellent living patterns for all. Observe the efficient kitchen, separate laundry, sloped ceilinged living room, two baths and three bedrooms.

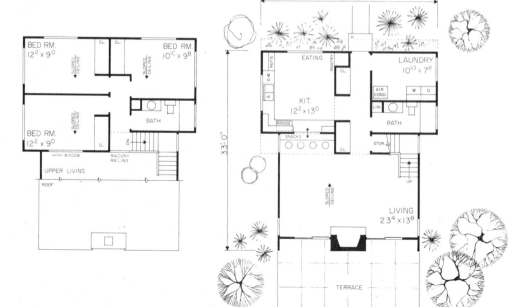

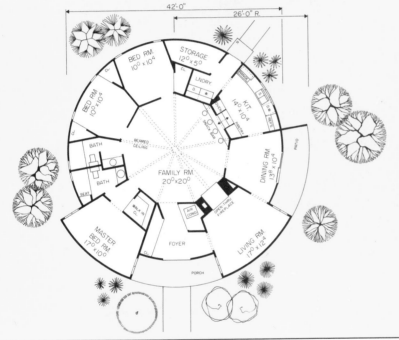

## Design T12479
**1,547 Sq. Ft.; 14,878 Cu. Ft.**

● Here is a unique round house with an equally unique floor plan. The centrally located family room is the focal point around which the various family functions and activities revolve. There is much to study and admire in this plan. For instance, the use of space is most efficient. Notice the strategic location of the kitchen. Don't miss the storage room and laundry. Observe the snack bar, the two-way fireplace, the separate dining room and the two full baths. Fixed glass windows at the beamed ceiling provide natural light from above for the family room.

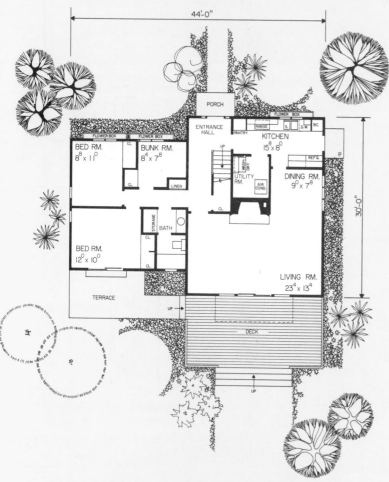

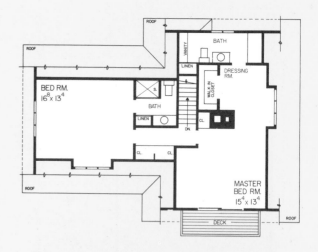

## Design T12481

**1,160 Sq. Ft. - First Floor**
**828 Sq. Ft. - Second Floor; 18,018 Cu. Ft.**

● Five rooms for sleeping! A complete mastersuite plus three bedrooms and a bunk room. Three full baths, one on the first floor and two upstairs. The living room will enjoy easy access to a large deck plus a fireplace. The dining room is conveniently located between the living area and the efficient kitchen which has a pantry and nearby laundry/utility room. Surely a great planned work center for a vacation home.

## Design T12488 1,113 Sq. Ft. - First Floor; 543 Sq. Ft. - Second Floor; 36,055 Cu. Ft.

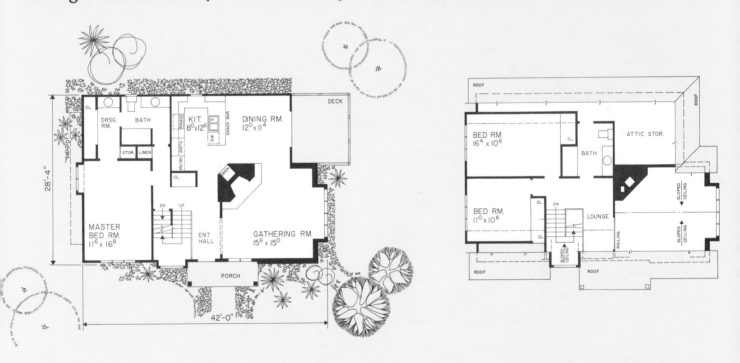

● A cozy cottage for the young at heart! Whether called upon to serve the young active family as a leisure-time retreat at the lake, or the retired couple as a quiet haven in later years, this charming design will perform well. As a year round second home, the up-stairs with its two sizable bedrooms, full bath and lounge area looking down into the gathering room below, will ideally accommodate the younger generation. When called upon to function as a retirement home, the second floor will cater to the visiting family members and friends. Also, it will be available for use as a home office, study, sewing room, music area, the pursuit of hobbies, etc. Of course, as an efficient, economical home for the young, growing family, this design will function well.

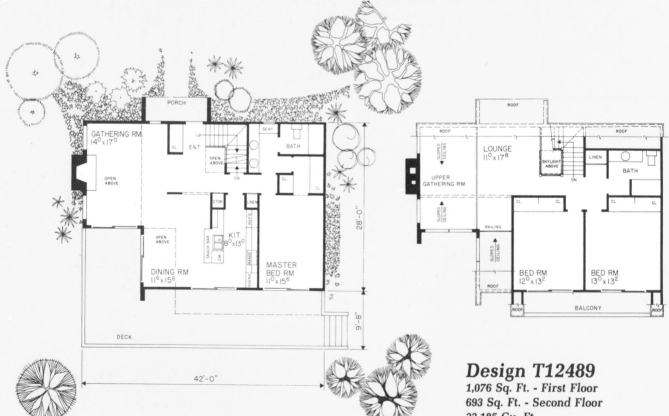

## Design T12489

**1,076 Sq. Ft. - First Floor**
**693 Sq. Ft. - Second Floor**
**33,185 Cu. Ft.**

● Outdoors-oriented families will appreciate the dramatic sliding glass doors and the sweeping decks that make this contemporary perfect. The plan of the first floor features a spacious two-story gathering room with sloping ceiling, a large fireplace and access to the large deck which runs the full length of the house. Also having direct access to the deck is the dining room which is half-open to the second floor above. A snack bar divides the dining room from the compact kitchen. The master bedroom is outstanding with its private bath, walk-in closet and sliding glass door. The second floor is brightened by a skylight and houses two bedrooms, lounge and full bath.

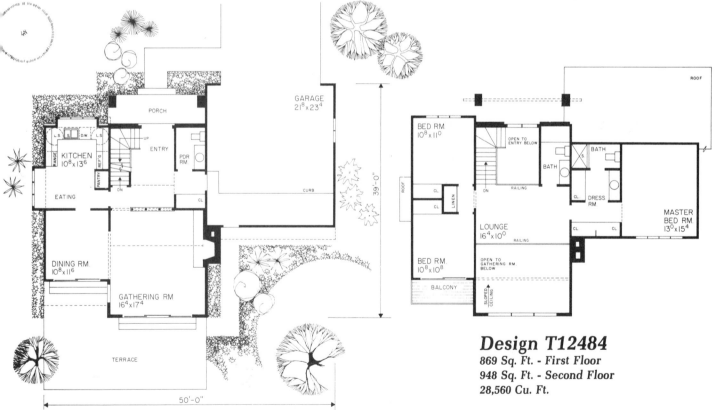

## Design T12484
**869 Sq. Ft. - First Floor**
**948 Sq. Ft. - Second Floor**
**28,560 Cu. Ft.**

● A two-story leisure-time house with all the comforts of home and maybe even a few more. Yet, the enviroment, the atmosphere and the living patterns will be entirely different. Imagine the fun everybody will have during their visits to this delightfully contemporary retreat. The large glass areas preserve the view from the rear. The upstairs lounge looks down into the gathering room. There are two eating areas adjacent to the U-shaped kitchen which could hardly be more efficient. There are 2½ baths, a fireplace, an attached garage and a basement. If you wish to forego the basement, locate the heating equipment where the basement stairs and pantry are located.

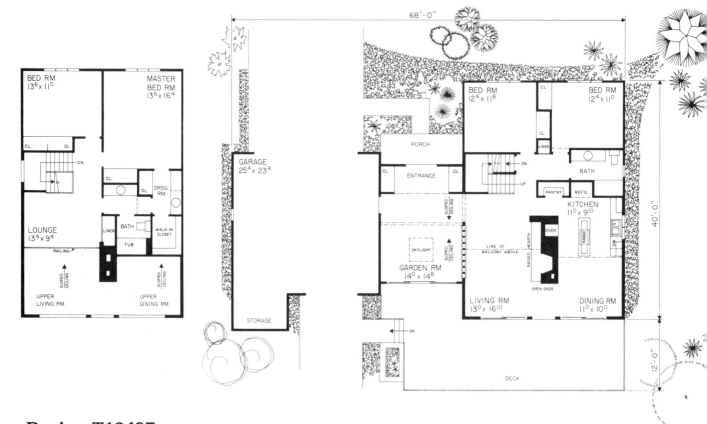

# Design T12487 1,407 Sq. Ft. - First Floor; 833 Sq. Ft. - Second Floor; 35,555 Cu. Ft.

● This contemporary vacation home will be distinctive at any location. The exterior is highlighted by angled roofs and sweeping expanses of wood and glass. Entrance to the home is through a skylight garden room with sloped ceiling. The living area is adjacent including a living room, dining room and kitchen. A massive raised hearth fireplace attractively divides the living area from the work center. Access to the large deck will be achieved through sliding glass doors in the garden, living and dining rooms. Two bedrooms and a bath are in the rear of the plan. The second floor master bedroom, an additional bedroom and lounge, which overlooks the living areas below, create the final finishing touch to this design. Make this your holiday or everyday home.

## Design T12485 1,108 Sq. Ft. - Main Level
### 983 Sq. Ft. - Lower Level; 21,530 Cu. Ft.

● This hillside vacation home gives the appearance of being a one-story from the road. However, since it is built off the edge of a slope, the rear exterior is a full two-story structure. Notice the projecting deck and how it shelters the terrace. Each of the generous glass areas is protected from the summer sun by the overhangs and the extended walls. The clerestory windows of the front exterior provide natural light to the center of the plan.

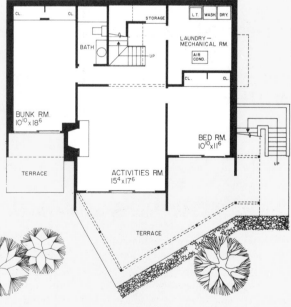

## Design T11486
### 480 Sq. Ft.; 4,118 Cu. Ft.

● You'll be anxious to start building this delightful little vacation home. Whether you do-it-yourself, or engage professional help, you will not have to wait long for its completion.

## Design T12425
### 1,106 Sq. Ft.; 14,599 Cu. Ft.

● You'll adjust to living in this vacation cottage with the greatest of ease. And forevermore the by-word will be, "fun". Imagine, a thirty-one foot living room with access to a large deck!

## Design T11449
### 1,024 Sq. Ft.; 11,264 Cu. Ft.

● If yours is a preference for a vacation home with a distinctive flair, then you need not look any fur-ther. Here is a simple and economically built 32 foot rectangle to meet your needs.

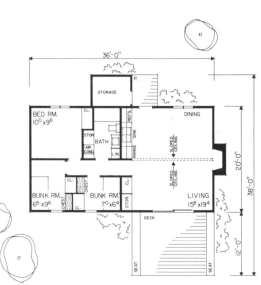

## Design T11488
### 720 Sq. Ft.; 8,518 Cu. Ft.

● The kids won't be able to move into this vacation retreat soon enough. Two bunk rooms plus another bedroom for Mom and Dad. Open-planned living area. A real leisure-time home.

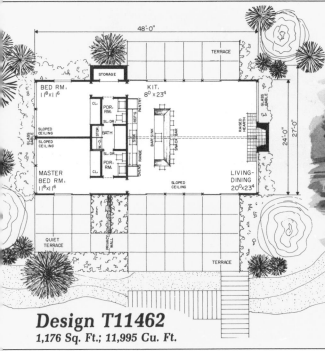

## Design T11462
### 1,176 Sq. Ft.; 11,995 Cu. Ft.

● A second home with the informal living message readily apparent both inside and out. The zoning of this home is indeed most interesting – and practical, too. Study the plan carefully.

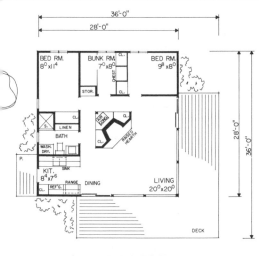

## Design T11485
### 784 Sq. Ft.; 10,192 Cu. Ft.

● Here's a perfect 28 foot square that will surely open up new dimensions in living for its occupants. A fine, lower budget version of T11449 on the opposing page yet retaining many of the fine qualities.

## Design T12464

**960 Sq. Ft. - First Floor**
**448 Sq. Ft. - Second Floor; 16,217 Cu. Ft.**

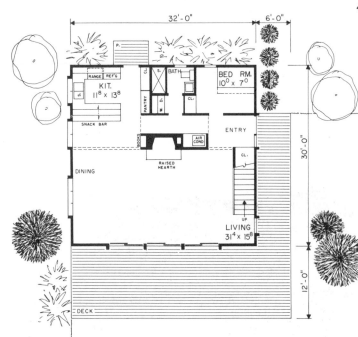

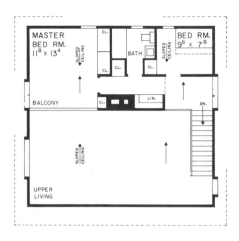

● Almost a perfect square (32 x 30 feet), this economically built leisure home has a wealth of features. The list is a long one and well might begin with that wood deck just outside the sliding glass doors of the 31 foot living area. And what an area it really is – 31 feet in length and with a sloped ceiling! The list of features continues with the U-shaped kitchen, the snack bar, the pantry and closet storage wall, the two full baths (one with stall shower), three bedrooms and raised hearth fireplace. Perhaps the favorite highlight will be the manner in which the second floor overlooks the first floor. The second floor balcony adds even a greater dimension of spaciousness and interior appeal. Don't miss side and rear entries. Observe coat closets placed nearby.

# Design T11445 960 Sq. Ft. - Upper Level; 628 Sq. Ft. - Lower Level; 15,304 Cu. Ft.

● Why not give two-level living a try and make your leisure-time home something delightfully different? If there is plenty of countryside or water around, you'll love viewing it from the upper level. And the best seat in the house will not be inside at all, but one on the balcony or deck. While the upper level is a complete living unit with its two bedrooms, bath, kitchen and spacious living area; the lower level with its one bedroom, bath, utility room (make it a kitchen) and family room could be a complete living unit itself. However called upon to function, this design has plenty of flexible space. Don't miss the fireplace on the upper level.

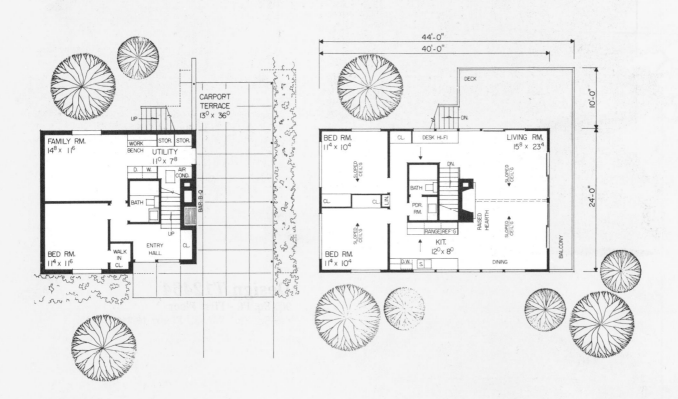

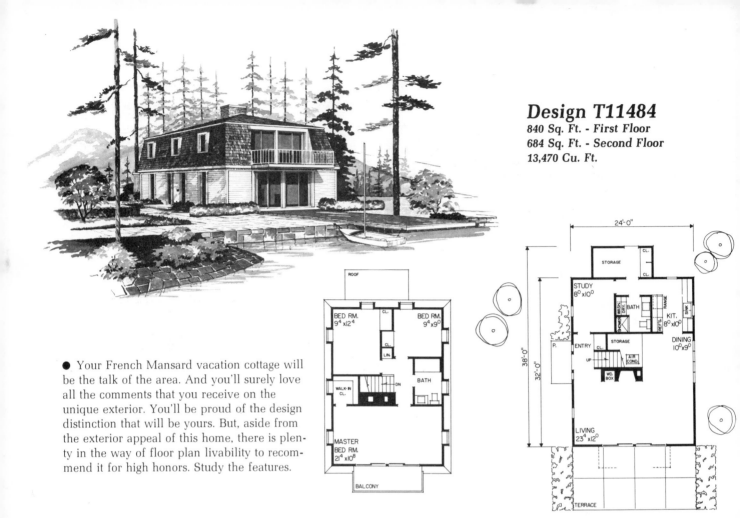

## Design T11484
840 Sq. Ft. - First Floor
684 Sq. Ft. - Second Floor
13,470 Cu. Ft.

● Your French Mansard vacation cottage will be the talk of the area. And you'll surely love all the comments that you receive on the unique exterior. You'll be proud of the design distinction that will be yours. But, aside from the exterior appeal of this home, there is plenty in the way of floor plan livability to recommend it for high honors. Study the features.

## Design T11477
1,446 Sq. Ft.; 14,928 Cu. Ft.

● Who said you can't have a vacation home with French Provincial flair? The intriguing thought of having your own villa is certainly within the realm of distinct possibility. Call it what you like, this hip-roofed, brick veneer summer house has an inviting warmth you will love. Inside, there is space galore. List the outstanding highlights.

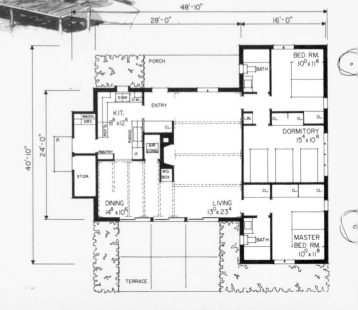

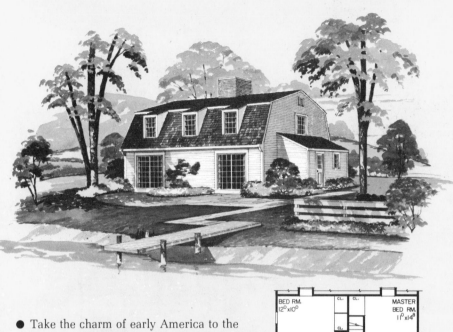

## Design T11483

**816 Sq. Ft. - First Floor**
**642 Sq. Ft. - Second Floor**
**13,513 Cu. Ft.**

● Take the charm of early America to the lakeshore with you. The graciousness of this little gambrel-roofed vacation home will be with you always. In fact, it will improve with age. The narrow, horizontal siding, the wide corner boards, the projecting dormers, the muntined windows and the center chimney create an aura of authenticity. Observe the outstanding livability.

## Design T12426

**1,152 Sq. Ft.; 14,515 Cu. Ft.**

● A touch of traditional pervades the environment around this L-shaped, frame leisure-time home. The narrow horizontal siding, the delicate window treatment and the prudent use of fieldstone, all help set the character. Inside, the floor plan offers wonderful livability. The huge living and dining areas are separated by an appealing thru fireplace. Don't miss the efficient kitchen.

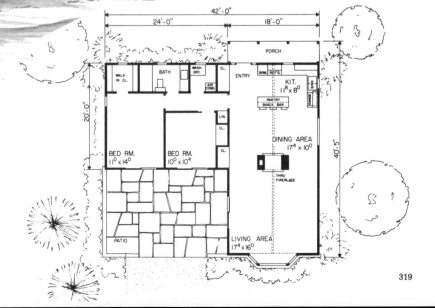

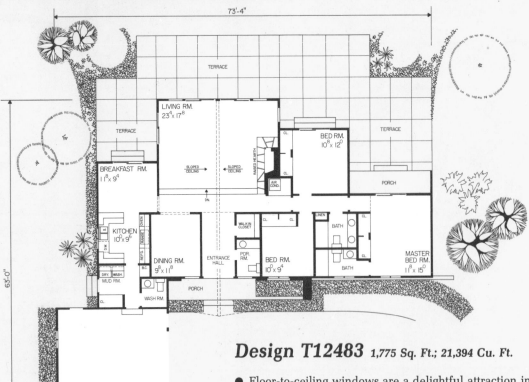

## Design T12483 1,775 Sq. Ft.; 21,394 Cu. Ft.

● Floor-to-ceiling windows are a delightful attraction in the living room. Good looking and a way to take advantage of the beautiful outdoor scenery. For more good looks, sloped ceilings and a raised hearth fireplace plus a terrace that runs the length of the house. A formal dining room is convenient to the efficient U-shaped kitchen with a separate breakfast nook. The laundry/mud room will allow immediate clean-up after a day spent fishing or on the beach. Three bedrooms! Including one with a private bath.